GW00362909

Other Books by Rosemary Daniell

CONFESSIONS OF A (FEMALE) CHAUVINIST

THE WOMAN WHO SPILLED WORDS ALL OVER HERSELF

THE HURRICANE SEASON

FORT BRAGG & OTHER POINTS SOUTH

SLEEPING WITH SOLDIERS:
IN SEARCH OF THE MACHO MAN

FATAL FLOWERS: ON SIN, SEX, AND SUICIDE
IN THE DEEP SOUTH

A SEXUAL TOUR OF THE DEEP SOUTH

SECRETS OF THE
ZONA ROSA

For Iris —

SECRETS OF THE
ZONA ROSA

How Writing (and Sisterhood)
Can Change Women's Lives

*I am so pleased with
what you are doing*

ROSEMARY DANIELL

*with your book —
I see a great success in
your future!*

Rosemary Daniell

2006

OWL BOOKS
Henry Holt and Company
New York

Owl Books
Henry Holt and Company, LLC
Publishers since 1866
175 Fifth Avenue
New York, New York 10010
www.henryholt.com

An Owl Book® and ® are registered trademarks of Henry Holt and Company, LLC.

Distributed in Canada by H. B. Fenn and Company Ltd.

Library of Congress Cataloging-in-Publication Data

Daniell, Rosemary.
    Secrets of the Zona Rosa : how writing (and sisterhood) can change women's lives /
Rosemary Daniell.—1st Owl Books ed.
        p. cm.
        "Owl Books."
        Includes bibliographical references.
        ISBN-13: 978-0-8050-7780-3
        ISBN-10: 0-8050-7780-4
        1. Authorship—Psychological aspects.   2. Women authors.   I. Title.

PN171.P83D36 2006
808'.02019—dc22   2005055000

Henry Holt books are available for special promotions and premiums.
For details contact: Director, Special Markets.

First Edition 2006

Designed by Meryl Sussman Levavi

Printed in the United States of America

10 9 8 7 6 5 4 3 2 1

For the glorious women (and men) of Zona Rosa,

and for those to come

Tell me, what is it you plan to do with

your one wild and precious life?

—Mary Oliver, poet

THE ZONA ROSA PROMISES

To support our sisters in every way

To love their creativity whatever form it may take

To listen without judgment however difficult their stories

To help one another become
the women and writers we were meant to be

To laugh, laugh, laugh along the way

CONTENTS

YOU ARE NOW ENTERING THE ZONA ROSA

What is the Zona Rosa? And what does it mean? These are the questions people ask me more often than any others. Since we in Zona Rosa were originally four women, getting together to talk about writing and life, on the surface it simply means the "feminine zone." Our name came from a quarter in Mexico City, reminding me when I first heard it of a name for a female rock group. But if you think for a minute, you realize that it indicates more, that the *rosa* has been a part of us from our beginnings. And if you look inside yourself, at your inner lips or even more intimate parts—as many women did during the '70s—you see that all women are created pink, with a special relationship to that color. "Always wear shades that occur naturally in the body," a makeup artist once advised, and pink is one of those shades, most notably in that organ Eve Ensler enshrined in *The Vagina Monologues,* and, even in the most repressive of times, through the sensuousness of a pair of full rosy lips, whether assisted or not by Tangee or Revlon. "I was shown around Tutankhamen's tomb in the 1920s. I saw this wonderful pink on the walls and the artifacts. I was so impressed that I vowed to wear it for the rest of my life,"

wrote mega-romance writer, Barbara Cartland. "Pink is the navy blue of India," declared Diana Vreeland, the famous editor of *Vogue,* who, when she became blind
shortly before her death in 1989, said it was the result of looking at too many beautiful things. I, too, have had a lifelong romance with the *terra rosa,* just as I have had
with experience, knowledge, and the letter *Z.* Each spring, the city of Savannah,
where I live, and which I always describe in my writing as a woman, is blanketed in
luscious pink azaleas—and then there are their counterpoints, the pale crape myr-
tle, the aptly named fuchsia, the roses that live up to their name, the hydrangea
turned roseate by a nail judiciously embedded in the soil beneath. In France, cher-
ries are termed *cerises,* surely a prettier, pinker word. The Zona Rosa is six beautiful midlife women wearing pink ruffled bathing caps, swimming nude in a
synchronized flower design in the south of that country. At Codolle, Paris's and
perhaps the world's poshest lingerie atelier, proprietor Poupie Codolle has created *petale de rose,* "the most heavenly pink in the world," according to freelance
writer Daisy Garnett, who willingly shelled out over 555 euros (or $629) for a bra
made for her in that luxe tint. And isn't the soft pink cheek the part of a baby we
want most to touch? Intuitionist Julia Griffin describes the heart chakra as a pink
light, exuding beauty and love. Wouldn't Eve—being smart and a woman—have
eaten the apple anyway, rosy globe that it was, hanging within easy reach, no matter
the price, and even without the snake to egg her on? Pink is the opposite of funda-
mentalism of any kind, which would outlaw it if it could, and which finds that all the
veils in the world can't subdue its charms. Yet there are still those, even among the
enlightened, who would keep us naive, fear-bound, innocent of our strength, of our
radiance within. "She writes about the labia-pink South," a well-known writer said,
quoting a phrase from my work in the *Washington Post,* forgetting that it was in the
rosa that his own book had been nurtured—not to speak of the fact that he, like
each of us, slid into this life out from between the slick pink walls of a woman gra-
cious enough to give him birth. For while men may land on the moon, plot new and
better ways to destroy one another, and generally strut their stuff, Norman
Mailer-style—not admitting for a moment that it is from their feminine side, their
anima, that their better books and paintings evolve—it is still up to women to give

comfort and life. "Nothing can soothe the soul but the senses," wrote Oscar Wilde, who surely knew, and while other words also denote the salves with which we ease our way—bath, bed, chocolate, silk, scent, fur—it falls to this shade, this vibrant inner passage, to define the ultimate, the primary, in richness, fecundity, pleasure. So what is the Zona Rosa? It is the pièce de résistance, the zone where all things female are not only allowed but prevail; where women tell their truths, truths men beg entry to hear, or at times, simply beg to enter. Or it is as easy, as accessible, as my five-year-old great-niece, Faye, twirling in a pink feather boa, already in possession of her considerable powers. So what does it mean that you are now entering the Zona Rosa? It means *Beware,* for whether you are man or woman, you are about to be immersed in that region where you will be in danger of seeing in new ways, of looking through rose-colored glasses, even of creating art.

SECRETS OF THE
ZONA ROSA

CHAPTER ONE

THE STORY OF MY WRITING (AND OTHER) LIFE

Why Where You Are Now Is Good Enough

1.

Map out your future, but do it in pencil.

—JON BON JOVI

"What am I doing here?" I asked myself for the umpteenth time, sitting on the deck of my friend and sister Zona Rosan Lynn's borrowed beach house at the end of a long road on the coast of South Carolina.

Of course, I knew the ostensible reasons I had left my house in Savannah, loaded with suitcases filled with notes, quotations, and student manuscripts collected over the past two decades; file folder after file folder that had come to fill my bedroom and study, stacked atop an armoire, a cedar chest, on shelves, dresser tops, and every available surface. I had come to this remote place that ends at the ocean, to write the successor to the first book I wrote about Zona Rosa, the creative writing workshops I have been leading for twenty-four years.

For this book, I planned to draw on what I've learned during that time—how to encourage beginning writers to dig deep, work through past and present traumas, take magnificent risks, and become their wonderful, inimitable selves on the page as well as in life. In addition, I planned to outline the kind of practical writing advice we use every day in Zona Rosa—plus throw in a lot of the fun and laughter that is our hallmark.

When I wrote the first book, I thought of it as a one-shot account of what was still a small, if growing and wonderful, band of women. Telling their stories—and running the workshop—was my own hands-on labor of love, after which I would get on with my real work, which I considered to be writing and promoting my own literary poetry, fiction, and creative nonfiction.

But after *The Woman Who Spilled Words All Over Herself* was published, Zona Rosa began to swell until it reached the proportions of a gorgeous monster. What had started with four women meeting in the living room of my tiny Victorian apartment in Savannah had become a series of regular groups in Savannah, Charleston, and Atlanta, and then one-, two-, and five-day workshops in other cities, towns, and even other countries. For the past five years, we have enjoyed one- and two-week delicious retreats in France and Italy in addition to our annual beach and mountain retreats closer to home—we call them "Pajama Parties for Grown-up Girls with Smarts"—with others in the works for other points as yet undetermined.

Like literary Mary Kay or Tupperware parties, these workshops are planned via flyer, e-mail, and word of mouth by women who want to host a Zona Rosa workshop. All we need is a living room, a community or women's center, an inn or a rented house, and a group of women (and sometimes men) who have a burning story to tell, who feel they have put their creativity on hold for too long, or who, if they are already skilled writers, want to jump-start their work and heal themselves along the way.

Today, thousands of people—some of whom shine in my mind like distant stars, others of whom rush to the surface like flashing meteors—have participated in these workshops. In addition, satellite Zona Rosa, or Sub Rosa, groups are beginning to form, based on guidelines I created for those who wish to use them. ("We call it our 'Sort-of Zona Rosa,'" said Beverly, accomplished poet and a shaker and mover in her own right, of her sisters in New Orleans, where I've led two intensive workshops.)

Along the way I have been helped by many generous, intelligent, and talented women. Indeed, it often seems that whoever and whatever is needed for Zona Rosa to fatten and grow is immediately provided by the universe, as though I had put out the request without even knowing it. As psychologist Wayne Dyer wrote, quoting a Buddhist proverb, "When the teacher is ready, the students will come."

It was not exactly what I had had in mind those years ago when, as a nine-year-old, I sat in the green stuffed chair in the children's room at Atlanta's Carnegie Library, dreaming of having my own story on the shelves. Or when I read the poem "We frogs / love bogs," in the poetry section of one of Mother's *Ladies' Home Journals*, and thought, yes, I can do that.

Yet even as I wondered how I could have come to devote myself to Zona Rosa, and other people's lives and writing, I knew the answer.

2.

There are years that are questions and years that are answers.

—ZORA NEALE HURSTON

I Was a Door My Mother in Her Madness Opened. In 1975, I stood with my sister Anne beside our mother Melissa's bed in intensive care where she lay in a coma after taking the overdose of pills that was to end her life. This was not an unexpected event, as Mother had been telling Anne and me that she was planning to kill herself for at least twenty years; that she wouldn't live past sixty, the birthday that had taken place nine days before.

Anne and I, both young mothers with husbands, had often been put out by Mother, feeling hopeless, then frustrated by our attempts to talk her out of the melancholia that reached back to her childhood. But after her death, our awareness of her largely unrealized gift for language, of the centered, beautiful southern woman she could have been, overwhelmed both of us; especially when we discovered that before her death, she had destroyed her best and most personal pieces of writing.

Just before Mother's overdose, I had been leading a writing workshop in Georgia's state prison for women in Milledgeville. It was the same antebellum town where Mother—attending Georgia State College for Women (now Georgia State College and University), growing plump on the starchy school food, wearing the de rigueur white shirtwaist and navy pleated skirt, and unable to see even one of her many beaus without written permission from her parents in Atlanta—had felt like a prisoner herself. Each day, driving beneath the live oaks to the prison, I would think about her, the limitations she had placed on her life, and those that had been placed there by others.

At the prison I was learning that the women in the writing group, supposed outlaws on the lowest rung of society, were not that different from Mother, and indeed, most of the women I had known. They shared our struggles with low self-esteem, other-directedness, and an inability to put ourselves and our talents first—though for them, these problems were magnified to the highest degree. I was also learning that their desires and ideals were not that different from ours, as evidenced by their girl talk, their ever-changing hairdos, and their interest in the latest issues of *Glamour* and *Cosmopolitan*.

Practically every woman in the group was there because of something to do with a man—killing a man who had abused her for years, shooting a rival for a man's affections, or helping a man with an armed robbery. And in a way, though I had been more fortunate in my escapes, I knew what it was like to be them: like many of them, I, too, was a high school dropout who had run away, first from an abusive father, then from the violent young man I had married at sixteen.

At our prison-wide poetry reading, white burly males stood guard around the perimeter of the auditorium. As the women read from their poems—their honest accounts of their real experiences, penned during our six weeks together—the tough-looking women in the audience hooted and hollered in identification, and my own heart stretched with pride.

A week later, standing beside Mother's bed as she lay dying, her round face finally smoothed of the lines of a lifelong tension, I felt once more how little she—like the women in the prison—had been able to tell of her own truths. How little permission she had been given—whether by herself or others—to express them.

Although I didn't know it yet, Zona Rosa was born in that

moment; an unrealized passion that would lead me to spend much of the rest of my life seeking to help women like Mother and women in prisons of all kinds to achieve their dreams.

3.

We are most deeply asleep at the switch when we fancy we control any switches at all.

—Annie Dillard

Had anyone told me that I would spend the next two and a half decades helping other women find themselves as writers, I would have shaken my head in protest. If I had imagined that I would spend hour upon untold hour obsessing over how to cajole, stimulate, shock, and tickle them into recognizing their own gifts, reading and marking up their manuscripts with purple ink, often in the middle of the night, and thinking not about my life and writing, but about theirs—I would have run in the other direction.

Like many young writers, I was narcissistic, primarily concerned with my own writing and getting it into print. I knew where I was going, and the next place was to write *Fatal Flowers*, a memoir inspired by Mother's death and our lives as southern women.

Three years later, I walked out of my little furnished flat in Savannah, where I lived without a television set or stereo (or, for a while, a phone), carrying the finished manuscript in a typewriter-paper box. As I tripped down the cobbled street toward the post office, I felt as if I was holding a newborn baby. When I saw crowds lining the sidewalks, I asked someone what was happening. "It's St. Patrick's Day—the parade," a man answered, as though wondering what planet I was from; and in truth, I had been so obsessed with the book that the world outside it had shrunk into the distance.

But I felt the celebration was in perfect accord with my mood, my new lightness and buoyancy. The heaviness I had felt at Mother's death had totally left me, as though the pain in which the book had been conceived had moved from my body into my words. Though I didn't know it then, I was experiencing for the first time the healing powers of creative writing.

Yet while I would go on to write more books, my life as I knew it was about to end; indeed, it was soon to be neatly dissected into what I would come to think of as "before and after." One of these changes would be more glorious, another more nightmarish, than I could ever have imagined.

First, I was about to start the tiny as-yet-unnamed group that would later become the miracle known as Zona Rosa—the miracle that would ultimately, over the years, help me resolve the pain of my next discovery. For I was about to learn that two of my three beloved adult children were suffering from chronic mental illnesses that, unattended, could possibly lead to their homelessness, even their deaths.

Still reeling from that news, I would become involved with the sexy man who would become my fourth husband; a blond replica of my charming boozy dad who, though fifteen years younger than I, would be hospitalized after the first Gulf War with post-traumatic stress syndrome, alcoholism, and near-fatal heart attacks, leading me to fear for his life, too.

And while this book is not about those traumas, but about the story of Zona Rosa and its healing powers, it shows, in a perfect example of the synchronicity of the universe, that the convergence of these events was no accident.

What I had created to facilitate women like Mother—to help others heal themselves through creative writing—would end up healing me as well.

4.

As far as we can discern, the sole purpose of existence is to kindle a light in the darkness of being.

—CARL JUNG

Queens of Denial Need Not Apply. Even as I dealt with these difficulties (later, I would learn to use the word *challenges*), Zona Rosa began to take over, squeezing out any possible pain and despair. My better qualities of curiosity and an avid interest in the lives of others were emerging, as the Zona Rosans' stories became my stories, their concerns, my concerns. As a writer, I had always found myself more drawn to truth than to fiction. And now, my whole life was a kaleidoscope of such truths, as one woman after another entered the group and shared her story.

I had read somewhere that whether you're a man or woman, if you're depressed it's best to spend time with women, as we are more nurturing. Invariably, the estrogen-rich environment of Zona Rosa was a jolt of exactly what I needed to get on with my life. When I was being tested, the Zona Rosans were right there along with me, my own personal support group during what was fast becoming the best and worst of years. It was something the others told me happened to them, too, sending them home so energized that they went straight to their desks to explore that most exciting territory: themselves.

I was also discovering that teaching is a process that flows both ways. It was like passing along my own recipes, and receiving theirs in return. And while I planned a direction for each workshop in advance—should we focus on writing blocks, revision, the use of dreams?—I never knew quite what would happen. As Julie Atlas Muz, a performance burlesque artist, told the *New York Times,* "It's like bank robbery theater. You know you're going to rob the bank, but you don't really know how until you do it, and that's exciting."

Even now, I learn something new at every meeting—and more important, I experience an intimacy that is far headier than any of the words we write and speak, however much we might revere them. More often than not, there is a near-mystical synchronicity; in one month many of the women may write about, say, cows, and in another their menstrual periods (or lack of them). And more times than I can remember, tears have come to my eyes as I read aloud from their manuscripts. That we have no taboos on either feelings or content encourages honesty, and allows us to enjoy the shock of intimacy over and over again.

"We don't come to Zona Rosa wearing our little white gloves, tell our stories, then go home," said June, a longtime member who started out as a secretary and single mother and is now a college professor, inspiring others. "We come to be changed."

Our bonds run deeper than our surface similarities and differences: through the years we have shared infidelities, divorces, addictions, life-threatening illnesses, and even deaths, some so shocking as to be off the charts.

But not all of the Zona Rosans' trials are so extreme. In fact, many fall into the realm of what society calls ordinary (though "ordinary," like a hangnail or a paper cut, can be excruciating), such as divorce; or even something as simple as a midlife crisis, during which someone realizes that the creativity and enthusiasm she felt as a girl is fast-waning, maybe even gone altogether.

At forty-four, Ronnie was going through with the divorce her writer-husband had initiated after she had helped support and raise his two sons by a previous marriage. During that period, Ronnie—who has worked since high school and cleans houses for a living—often found herself bursting into tears; but then, before long, coming up with highly original ideas for her own writing, especially while ironing her clients' shirts. When I suggested that perhaps she was more talented than her long-blocked husband, she began writing about the even harder things in her life, such as her mother's suicide when she was six, and how she had found her mother's body after coming in from school one day.

Indeed, writing can be better than Valium for relieving psychological pain, whatever its source. An emergency room psych nurse, Vivian, had seen too much tragedy caused by alcohol and drugs to use them to relieve her own stress. But when she discovered the uses of denial (or "fiction," as it's called in literature), she found relief from the gunshot wounds and cardiac arrests of her everyday life through writing a flowery thriller set in 1940s Hawaii.

Then there are those events that fall into the realm of the unexpected, such as when Sherri's use of a onetime over-the-counter treatment for a yeast infection turned the inside of her vagina into a raging fireplace, sending her to specialists in Texas while ruining her sex life, and almost her marriage (so vivid were her descriptions that I still veer in the other direction whenever I pass a display of these products). Or when Ora's operation to staple her stomach left her skinnier but barely able to eat; or when Caressa's husband up and left her for a woman he'd met on the Internet.

Sometimes the stories are so shocking that in any other setting, they might cause eye-rolling and flickers of disbelief. But in Zona Rosa, we listen, whatever the content. I was pleased when Nancy, a newcomer, described being a psychic who had worked with the FBI, citing regular full-fledged conversations with Osama bin Laden and Al Qaeda long before September 11. Though Nancy could have been the model for the anti-heroine in Helen Fielding's comic novel *Olivia Joules and the Overactive Imagination,* everyone looked at her seriously, some even asking questions.

Furthermore, some of us let our pain hang out so clearly that questioning it would have been tantamount to cruelty. At fifty, Marianne still couldn't talk about her experiences growing up in a satanic cult, and the only way she could write about them was to juxtapose passages of the torture she had experienced with others in which she described scenes of her true love, gardening.

"Why, I've never heard of such a thing!" one of the newer, more rigid members of the group will inevitably gasp at such revelations, which is when I quickly step in to assert the teller's right to share her truths. Flinching, like negative language, isn't allowed. Zona Rosa is a place where women can and do write and say anything.

Not that there aren't conflicts: Allison, a chiropractor and self-proclaimed lesbian and medical intuitive, was a boyish blonde whose charisma fairly vibrated across the room as she entered. She sometimes put her arm around the other women's shoulders as they spoke, and made remarks, whenever manuscripts about heterosexual angst were read, about how terrible it was for us that we had to live with men. She was also given to making comments like "Yeah, I fuck a guy every couple of years just to see what I'm not missing." Thereafter my e-mail would be flooded with complaints; one woman, a professed Christian, wrote that she didn't like Allison to be there because homosexuality was a sin.

But I found Allison's warmth and outspokenness refreshing, even an abrasive antidote for what, in a group of women, can too easily turn into a sticky sweetness. Knowing I was risking alienating some of them—as I often had to do to maintain our standards of acceptance—I explained to each woman why I thought it was important for Allison to be with us. After all, we were grown women, weren't we, used to fending for ourselves sexually and otherwise?

Maria, a devout Catholic and one of the four original Zona Rosans, held her lips in a rigid line whenever anything about sex was read ("Maria, how's your blood pressure?" someone would inevitably ask), although she was honest in her answer after I read a graphic poem by Joyce Maynard on the ineffectiveness of some men and their pricks. "I don't hate it because it's not true—I hate it because it *is*!" she exclaimed in her thick Italian accent before realigning her lips to their original horizontal position. (It was good, I would think later, that Maria hadn't been there the night Deborah and Eden described finding each other's G-spots.)

Whatever the situation, we become one another's mentors, therapists, girlfriends, cheerleaders, and support group. "I want to be in the foxhole with writers like me," said Tracy, who had experienced a devastating childhood with an alcoholic father and a long-suffering mother. (Yet Tracy believes that the Tourette's and depression that led her to hear and speak to voices are the reason for the great wit and dialogue in her writing; a classic example of how pain and trauma can inform creativity.)

Many of us are southerners brought up to believe that blood kin are the only ones who will, in the crunch, support us. But in Zona Rosa, we quickly learn otherwise. "I came to Zona Rosa tonight because this is where I need to be," is the phrase most often used by the recently traumatized.

Cleo's husband unexpectedly died outside a karaoke bar where they had gone with friends. A couple of months later, her mother passed away, equally unexpectedly. But when we flew to Italy for our six-day Zona Rosa retreat two days after her mother's funeral, a determined Cleo was with us.

5.

Once you become real, you can't become unreal again. It lasts for always.

—MARGERY WILLIAMS, *THE VELVETEEN RABBIT*

In her book *Icebound,* Jerri Nielson describes how she depended on the support of the "Polies," the coworkers she lived with as she went through diagnosing and biopsying her own breast cancer while isolated at the South Pole. When I read Jerri's description of the extreme physical and emotional intimacy of living with the group at a place where leaving was not an option, I knew what she meant. I too had come to depend on the women of Zona Rosa, even though at times they didn't know that what they were giving me was the strength to go on—to tackle my own challenges as I watched them struggle with theirs.

That we were all women in Zona Rosa was a choice I had made from the beginning to avoid the alpha-male syndrome in which a man comes into the room and all the women change, becoming less free, more guarded. (After a while, as I became more sure of myself as leader, dominant males—more about them later—would become less of a problem for me and for the group.)

My goals for Zona Rosa were simple: that we would support one another in our creative and life goals, and that wherever we might be in our lives, we would always adhere to standards of excellence in both writing and telling our truths. I learned that often when I was talking to the Zona Rosans, I was also talking to myself, telling myself what I too needed to hear. When I asked them to time-line their writing and personal goals, to show me on paper how they would find the time to write, I was really talking about my own problems with time, which now—with Zona Rosa and two adult kids in need of care—were as acute as theirs. Time, and how to find it, steal it, and best use it, seemed to be a common denominator for all of us except the most privileged (and they had their own demons, be they too many houses, too much traveling, or too many houseguests).

Yet available time didn't always equal more and better writing; it was often the mothers with full-time jobs who were the most productive. (Later, you will meet Pamella, Marsha, and others who ingeniously managed to defeat the limitations of that temporal medium that we all swim in.) It was no accident that "How I remain creative in the midst of the chaos that is my life" has been among our more popular "exorcises," as we call exercises in Zona Rosa (we also call them Pilates on Paper—because they're sometimes hard to do but also good for us).

I also knew that because the creative holds the spark of the divine, we often mystify it, thinking we have to be special people—gifted in some way beyond the ordinary—to even dare tap into our creative reserve. We often wrongly imagine that our favorite authors' works were born full-blown, never having gone through the messiness, the chaos that is the creative process. "Perfection is terrible, it cannot have children," wrote the poet Sylvia Plath, describing the impossibility of virgin birth, whether of a life or a work of literature. (Considering Plath, I wonder if she could have saved herself if she'd had Zona Rosa in her life.) Mary O'Hara, most famous for *My Friend Flicka*, wrote an entire book, *Novel-in-the-Making*, about what she went through in writing another one.

I believed that the process could be broken down, made simple—that a writer is simply a person who writes, that the way to write a book is by writing one word, then another. Toward that end, I created credos and acronyms, made charts, searched out quotes, and talked, endlessly talked, about what might be holding us back, and how we can break that process down into doable increments. As if from a constantly bubbling well (or was it like mother's milk, with the Zona Rosans as my multiple infants?) I made notes in my Zona Rosa notebooks; in my personal journals, I marked further ideas with a purple *ZR* in the margin, another part of my search for ways to simplify what, in truth, is a highly complex activity.

For my part, I found that, because of my involvement with the Zona Rosans and their lives, I could be happy, no matter what else was happening—whether one of my kids was on the phone with yet another life-threatening crisis or the house needed a new heating and air-conditioning system yesterday or my husband, Zane, and I were once more in the throes of our conflicts.

Indeed, over the years, I have only canceled three Zona Rosa groups, so loath am I to miss their company. I have led them with a kidney infection, an ankle broken in three places, and a bad cold that seemed to go away during the hours of the group, only to come on full-fledged when I collapsed afterward. When I read that the actress Fanny Kemble performed with a cancer in her breast, I understood perfectly. I have left my home after dealing with family crises so devastating that had I not had Zona Rosa, I could easily have taken to my bed, and no one would have complained of my self-indulgence. As therapist and life coach Martha Beck writes, "Whatever you are a genius of isn't difficult for you," and obviously leading Zona Rosa was as natural to me as breathing.

6.

I don't have time to put on makeup. I need that time to clean my rifle.

—HENRIETTE MANTEL

Zona Rosa was not only delicious and healing but addictive. And as the years went by, I would periodically wonder whether I should give it up, just as I would sometimes wonder whether I should give up chocolate or booze. Was the time I gave it interfering with my own writing? Yes. Was reading manuscripts by people who didn't yet write well hurting my own writing? No.

And should I go ahead with one of my more literary projects—324 pages of a memoir of my life with my children languished in my backpack beside my bed—rather than beginning another book on Zona Rosa? Sometimes, as I plowed through yet another stack of Zona Rosa manuscripts, I could feel my iBook, with its small green pulsing light, calling out to me, as though in not going to it, I was denying some living thing.

And at moments I was stabbed with envy, that bête noire of the writer's life, when my writer friends produced yet another book, often to acclaim. "As a writer, what does it feel like to have another writer in your city come out with a bestseller?" a *New York Post* reporter called to ask after my friend John Berendt's *Midnight in the Garden of Good and Evil* had hit the list for countless weeks.

I knew that the caller was a hot young New York journalist—I would soon see his byline in *Vanity Fair* and other venues—and I suspected, given the competitive milieu in which he worked, that he might be asking the question as much for himself as of me. Hearing my own words ringing in my ears, I told him what I often told the Zona Rosans, that envy is the gift that helps us know what we want for ourselves. "I've never heard anyone put it that way before," he said, sounding surprised, even delighted. Even as I spoke, I realized afresh how true my words were—that we were not living in a world of scarcity; that there was room for excellence; and that the truths I shared with the Zona Rosans worked for me, the reporter, and all of us.

I knew that John had worked long and hard on his book, seven years to be exact, never suspecting the success to come his way. ("What? I couldn't afford that!" he answered when someone asked whether he planned to buy a house in Savannah when his book came out.) I also knew that he had made his living during that time by doing annual reports for businesses from the little apartment he had rented for the duration. And that when he had come to Zona Rosa to read from his finely honed passages before his book was published, we were among the few in town who knew that he was serious about what he was doing, and not just another local eccentric passing himself off as a writer.

Now I was missing that kind of commitment myself. Or was it that my priorities had changed? I couldn't help thinking about how the manila folders of poems in progress I had once taken everywhere with me, from doctors' offices to the auto tag line, had now been replaced by folders of manuscripts by the Zona Rosans. The book reviews I had once written for the *New York Times,* the *Philadelphia Inquirer,* and *Newsday,* as well as the features for major magazines such as *Self*, *New York Woman*, *Mademoiselle*, and *Harper's Bazaar*, had long since fallen by the wayside.

I was leading not only a double but a triple life, my suitcase always packed, going off to lead groups, then coming home to kiss or fight with Zane, and to check in with my two adult kids, both of whom I had moved to Savannah to be near me. Long car trips alone, once anathema to me, were now my times to relax (they also gave me a chance to listen to books I would never have time to read in print; the pages seemed to scroll before me as did the actual highway, and I found myself marking them in my mind with an imaginary purple felt tip.)

Days when I had time to take a cup of coffee out to the back steps, where I would sit talking to my cat, Amber, to put up my summer or winter clothes, or to scrub the blue Italian tiles I'd had laid on the kitchen and laundry room floors (not knowing the white grout would also mean gallons of Clorox, directly applied) felt almost like a vacation.

Once, feeling my old life slipping away, and wanting to reassure myself, I scrawled a double-sided list, titling it "My Writing (and Other) Life" to see how much of my time I had spent on writing, writing-related activities, and Zona Rosa, and how much on what had become the increasing complexities of family (see the chart).

As I read it over—especially the right-hand column, in which I had sketched my personal life at the time—I was amazed I had achieved anything at all.

This turned out to be an exorcise that can and has been used by the Zona Rosans over and over to gain perspective on anything and everything—from marriages and careers, to hair and weight, or even the state of our closets. Whatever the subject, I always suggest, out of my belief that we need as many positive strokes as possible, that we allow ourselves full credit for what we *have* done, despite the obstacles in our paths.

Yet the book I was thinking about writing did not focus on the women I once imagined I'd write about—women who were bush pilots or foreign correspondents—but rather, those who only a short time before had been struggling in the sorghum syrup of middle-class expectations: women who had freed themselves through creative writing, overcoming obstacles that were at least as frightening as any posed by, say, skydiving.

THE STORY OF MY WRITING (AND OTHER) LIFE

Begin journal, questioning
everything I had been taught.
Discover poetry.
Write book reviews.

Write poetry.
Write book reviews.
Write *A Sexual Tour of
the Deep South.*

Direct Georgia Poetry
in the Schools program.
Work in poetry in the schools.
Receive NEA grant in poetry.

Write *Fatal Flowers.*

Book tour.
(My picture in *Time!*)

Start Zona Rosa.
Write *Sleeping with Soldiers.*
Book tour, TV appearances.

Zona Rosa expands to two groups.

Write *Fort Bragg & Other
Points South.*
Write magazine pieces.

Second NEA grant,
this time in fiction.

Write *The Hurricane Season*
(my best book so far, I think,
but it falls through the cracks).

Housewife in the suburbs,
unhappy in second marriage.
Post-partum depression.
Affair with Famous Southern Poet.
Visit New York, meet artists.
Divorce. Remarry.
Go to New York with third husband,
meet writers & actors.

Insanity of Open Marriage.
Mother commits suicide.
Father dies of cancer.
Divorce again.
Living alone in Savannah.
Lovers, lovers & more lovers.
Work on offshore oil rig.

Meet Zane, live with him,
break up while discovering, facing,
and dealing with son Dwayne's
and daughter Lily's illnesses:
stress as a way of life.

Marry Zane.
Chaos & crises re kids.

Chaos & crises redux.
Treatment centers, treatment
centers & more treatment centers
& figuring out how to pay for them.
Twelve-step groups as a way of life.
Anxiety attacks while driving
but I keep traveling anyway.

Zane in Germany with military.
Travel to Hamburg, Berlin,
Amsterdam, London, and Paris.

Zona Rosa keeps growing.

Crises with one or both kids
every time I go abroad.

More chaos & crisis re kids.
Zane in the first Gulf War, then
to alcohol rehab in Heidelberg.

Visiting Writer, Bradford
College, Massachusetts;
University of Wyoming, Laramie.
Go home on holidays to
lead Zona Rosa.

I break my leg in three places:
three surgeries & time off!

Write *The Woman Who
Spilled Words All Over
Herself: Writing and Living
the Zona Rosa Way*.

Writers' colonies:
Ucross, Yaddo; Ucross
visiting writer, Lynchburg College,
Virginia.

More chaos, crisis, & pain
re kids. One grandson adopted,
another, Daniel, dies of crib death.
Send Lily to Mexico for
two years in a *santatorio*.

Writing *The Murderous Sky*,
also *My Anarchist's Heart*.
Lecturer in poetry,
Emory University.

I bring Lily to live with us
in Savannah. I'm traveling
to Atlanta three days a week.

Zona Rosa takes off:
groups in Savannah, Atlanta,
Charleston, and other cities.
Our first weeklong retreat
in Lexington, Kentucky.
A review in *People*.
Southern Living writes us up.

I move Dwayne to Savannah.
Now both kids live near me.
Lily becomes more stable;
Dwayne's illness is acute.

More weeklong retreats,
and our first retreat in France.

Fatal Flowers wins first
Palimpsest Prize and is
reprinted. Satisfaction,
recognition.

Zona Rosa becomes a tour
stop for visiting authors.

Zane now out of the military
and an over-the-road truck driver,
has a heart attack,
quadruple bypass, staph
infection, and almost dies.

Write and organize essays
for *Confessions of a (Female)
Chauvinist*. Write foreword
in I.C.U. waiting room.

Zane recovers but
begins drinking again.
Alcohol rehab again.
Hospitalization for post-traumatic
stress disorder from first Gulf War.
Dwayne stabilizes. Lily has a relapse.

I lead Zona Rosa,
no matter what.

The Writers' Colony at Dairy
Hollow for three Augusts
(our annual sabbatical from Zona Rosa).
Zona Rosa groups all over
the place—and our second
European retreat, this time
in Italy!

Crisis with Lily while I'm
in Tuscany, Venice. Zona Rosan
Janet helps get me through with
hypnotherapy. The other women
gather round. Support from my
other daughter Lulu, who is now
a psychiatrist and healer.

Zane drinking, son fine,
daughter undone again.

Weeklong Zona Rosa
retreats now a tradition.
Getting ready for our
third annual retreat in Europe,
this time for two weeks
in the south of France!

More crises at home:
rent an apartment for daughter
across the street from me. Seek

Write treatment for Zona Rosa sitcom. Begin *Secrets of the Zona Rosa*.	new treatment methods, which work this time. Zane begins writing his story.
	Lily's art & life take off.
Notes for Zona Rosa workbook, Zona Rosa cookbook, et al.	
I AM NOW ZONA ROSA THROUGH & THROUGH!	Whatever happens I will be fine!

Sometimes more so: "I was more scared of getting sober than I was of standing on the strut of a plane, ready to jump," a writer friend said to me of an article she was writing for *Cosmopolitan* during the period when she was also dealing with her alcoholism.

And sometimes people lived with both kinds of fear. Alice, who lives at the edge of a natural forest in North Carolina, sometimes hears a jaguar scream outside her window, and alone in the house in the middle of the night, she has seen bears press their noses to the glass, smearing it with the snot she has to clean up the next day. But for a long time, it seemed that pushing her writing to the light of day was what frightened her most—until the well-known writer Paul Auster accepted one of her stories for a prestigious anthology, an acceptance that was followed a couple of years later by another.

Still, I could still remember being where Alice had been, poised, but scared to jump, and I found I could easily help people who were at the precipice.

7.

This is happiness; to be dissolved into something great.
— WILLA CATHER

"That's the most commercial thing you've ever written!" my friend Bruce Feiler said of my poem "Gigi." We were at a literary conference, and Bruce had just read from *Abraham*, the book that had catapulted him to the bestseller lists; then I had read my poem about a cat who improves her station in life by being open to everything, or "whoring herself to the end." It was a poem I often used in Zona Rosa to discuss the benefits of risk taking.

"Writing isn't just about commerce," I teased Bruce after the audience left the room.

I was especially delighted to be on the program with Bruce, as I had known him before he had finished his first book. A Savannah native, he was in Japan teaching English after graduating from Yale when his dad began bringing his pieces by, asking me to read them. Thinking he was just a kid, I had promptly given them to my seventeen-year-old assistant, Caitlin, who came back to say, "You've got to read these!" And that had been the beginning of a literary friendship in which our difference in age had no meaning—and during which I had had the pleasure of watching him go from a talented twenty-something to, by his late thirties, the author of seven books, two of them bestsellers. In the process, he had become an inspiration to me as well as to the Zona Rosans.

Indeed, Zona Rosa was a constant reminder of the truth of my remark to Bruce. "This is not just about writing; it's about community!" exclaimed my friend Carol Polsgrove.

"It's about what I dreamed being a writer would be like!" I knew that as a longtime social activist, as well as the daughter of missionaries to Africa, *community* was Carol's favorite word—and that this was high praise indeed. As she continued, comparing Zona Rosa to the Highlander School, where civil rights workers gathered to learn certain principles, I remembered my own dream of sitting at my typewriter all day, then cooking up huge pots of soup to serve to any artist friends who might drop by. I too saw the writer's life as one of shared experiences.

Since writing the first Zona Rosa book, I have learned more—*much* more—about how to help people achieve their dreams, whether as published authors or as people simply seeking to express themselves. Most important, via the marvelous serendipity of the universe, I have been given a crash course on the healing powers of creative writing. In 1995, while serving as visiting writer at the state university in Wyoming, I walked past the senior citizens center in Laramie and saw a sign that read, "Journal Writing Workshop: Reduce Your Blood Pressure." It said what I suspected; in fact, I was already writing about my belief that creative writing helps reframe and heal trauma.

It was a belief that had begun that day I walked out of my little apartment in Savannah, carrying the finished manuscript for *Fatal Flowers,* feeling light and free, as though my grief at Mother's life and death had been transferred to the squiggly black symbols on those pages. And I had found it was an experience I could count on, even—and especially—when I wrote about a subject that started with pit-of-the-stomach anxiety, or when the censor inside me told me this was something I couldn't possibly write about. In fact, I had even come to welcome such fear as a sign that its cause was something I needed to explore in language.

What I didn't know was that there would soon be actual data to support my beliefs. And after *Fatal Flowers* came out, I read the research showing that writing—writing about real things, not merely diary-keeping—has positive effects on blood pressure and arthritis, and protects against Alzheimer's (novelist Iris Murdoch's case to the contrary). Counselors and therapists often prescribe a heavy dose of journal writing to young women hospitalized for severe anxiety. "My friends and I all keep journals," said one young woman, "just so we can lead our lives."

When our lives are split by crisis, our creativity rises to the surface, often in dramatic ways. Sometimes a crisis is as subtle as a sense of increasing urgency that we can no longer deny. But whatever its degree, many of us are inherently drawn to sharing our stories as a way to salve our emotional wounds.

This kind of healing has been demonstrated to me over and over by the Zona Rosans in stories of all kinds. These women share, more than anything else, stories of courage, perseverance, and healing. And the obstacles these Zona Rosans faced in telling them have been far more profound than the usual stumbling blocks of syntax, grammar, and form. They were often people for whom writing has been a life or death matter, and through the years I have seen miracles.

Yes, these are the stories, the endless stories, that need to be told, I think, as I watch the setting sun—a perfect Zona Rosa fuchsia—descend over the marsh from Lynn's deck. Indeed, they dart into my brain like small silver fish, while others swirl by like whole schools—so many of them that I can barely keep count. And I wonder how I could have ever, even for a moment, considered giving up this gorgeous monster, this sprawling creation so endlessly surprising, serendipitous, even awe-inspiring, that has added so much to my life, at the same time supporting me and everything I believe in.

And after all, isn't this why I am here—to tell the Zona Rosans' stories, as well as describe what has possibly been the greatest privilege of my life, that of being with them as they healed their lives?

After each chapter in this book, you will find a "Knee-jerk Reaction" that might be holding you back in your writing and in life. Following the reaction will be one or more exorcises, or "Pilates on Paper," that will help counteract it, as well as other exorcises sprinkled throughout each chapter. You may want to begin a journal specifically for these exorcises. At the end of most of the chapters, you will also find a Book Therapy section describing books to further inspire you.

Knee-jerk Reaction #1: Thinking that where we are now in our lives and writing is not good enough—that we can't get where we want to go from here. Not realizing this may be the very place we need to be to jump-start our future growth.

PILATES ON PAPER

Write The Story of Your Life So Far, with you as heroine. Start by listing all the good stuff you've done, then address all the personal matters that could have held you back but didn't. If you wish, use my format in "The Story of My

Writing (and Other) Life," listing your achievements on the left side of the page, what you could have allowed to become impediments on the right. Leave out the stuff that you usually tell yourself, like "It's no wonder I've never done anything—I never even finished high school!" Well, I didn't either. And even if you don't yet know what you want to do with the rest of your life, list the things you *have* done, from "became office manager" and "got the kids off to school every day," to "daydreamed about living on sardines and ouzo on an island off the coast of Greece" and "scoured the library and read at least a book a week, no matter how busy I was" (one of my first clues that I was destined to become a writer), no matter how mundane they seem to you. As in those magazine pieces in which celebs tell about their early jobs bagging groceries or serving cappuccino at Starbucks, we've all been there—and we've learned from our experiences, even if it was what we didn't want!

The Gift of Envy: Think back to the kids you went to high school with—are there any whose lives you now envy? When you peruse a magazine, what kind of woman, what kind of lifestyle, captures your attention? Envy is a gift that tells us what we want more of for ourselves. In the past, we may have brushed such feelings aside as unpleasant, but now look back at them, and use them as signposts. Statistics show that many women feel depressed after looking through fashion magazines and comparing themselves to the models, and what they imagine to be the models' lives. Instead, use the images for your own purposes; go through them and clip photos that compose a present-tense picture of your dream self and paste them into your journal or create a collage, adding any description you feel like making: e.g., "She's on her way to have a relaxing massage. And though she knows there are other things she could be doing, she feels like she deserves it!" Create affirmations for the front of your journal to go along with the pictures—e.g., "I pamper myself whenever possible"—and read them and look at your dream photos frequently. *Remember, you're the star of your own life!* Twenty years ago I pasted pictures of my ideal self in a loose-leaf notebook, and it's amazing how many of the images have come true. My favorite is of an elegant woman carrying a fur coat and a spiffy briefcase in the aisle of a plane, that, were I as flawless as the model, could be a picture of me today as I take off for yet another Zona Rosa workshop. When I recently bought my treasure, a vintage mink, the picture of how and where I would wear it flashed to mind, illustrating how our unconscious is constantly leading us toward the goals we may have set long before.

And Can You Think of Why Some Might Envy You? As far as you know, that single, thrice-married-and-divorced comedienne with a drug problem and her own network show may yearn for your stable marriage and suburban existence. Sometimes what people envy in us comes as a surprise. I remember my amazement when, as my writing career was beginning, a New York writer from one of the richest families in America (translation: she'll never have to work for a living) told me she envied me my freedom—my little Savannah flat and my dates with foreign sailors—not to speak of the way the words poured onto the page when I sat down at my manual typewriter! That I might be up in the middle of the night, agonizing over my checkbook, wondering how I could afford to write my next book, probably never occurred to her—nor did the fact that I might envy her the time that money can buy. (By the way, despite our different lifestyles, we've both gone on to achieve our writing dreams.)

BOOK THERAPY ONE:
HOW BOOKS HEAL OUR LIVES

I gave my daughter Lily a collection of postcards of international paintings *by* women *of* women reading. Every one of them makes me want to recline immediately with a good book, as does my favorite photo by world-famous Cartier-Bresson, in which we only see a woman's crossed (and beautiful) legs and her elegant, fine-boned hands, holding the book in her lap. The only way this picture could be made more seductive would be to add a box of chocolates by her side, or a tray of cocktails and a plate of caviar (or Fritos and bean dip, if that's more your speed).

In Zona Rosa we are avid readers, indeed, literary gourmets, and at every meeting we pass around the "review book," a notebook in which we write short informal reviews of books we've recently read and liked or disliked or both (and why, which is good for sensitizing our literary taste buds). Some of us also list mini-reviews of books read in a book-length tome we share at the end of the year. It always gives the rest of us great ideas about books we may have missed. (And, as usual, those who have the least time seem to get the most reading done; some, like Anne, read as many as seventy books a year.)

Through the years, we've found that the perfect cure for anything is to be found in a book. Thus, I'm suggesting throughout this one that you embark, if you haven't already, on various forms of book therapy, reading books that might not be among your usual slew of novels and other reading for entertainment (though these, too, can be delicious sources of healing and inspiration). Now is the time to read some books written by women who started out in one place, and, through their own efforts, ended up in another, far better one.

Among the books that inspired me are Jill Ker Conway's *The Road from Coorain,* which begins on a sheep farm in Australia's outback where Jill leads a lonely existence with a demanding, alcoholic mother. Later she travels three thousand miles to put space between them, eventually becoming president of Smith College.

In *Madam Secretary: A Memoir,* Madeleine Albright describes how she went from being a suburban housewife, content to write for a local paper—her husband, the temperamental "star" of the family, told her he wouldn't divorce her if he won a Pulitzer; he didn't win it, but he divorced her anyway—to serving as secretary of state during the Clinton administration. She found that her experiences as a wife and mother had prepared her well for dealing with the men of Washington. Nothing they said or did was any surprise to her, she says; after stressful moments, she would go home and knit caps for her grandchildren.

When I taught at the University of Wyoming, Laramie, I heard stories of ranch women, isolated by the weather for six months of the year with only a shortwave radio, and their subsequent breakdowns. In *Breaking Clean,* Judy Blunt describes being brought up on such a ranch in Montana, where the chores she and her mother were destined to do without ceasing had been laid out for generations. As is expected of her, she marries a nearby rancher much like her father at eighteen, moving into a duplicate life of motherhood and hard work without a breather. (Her empathy with the ranch animals in her care—heightened by her own plight?—is the most beautiful part of the book.) But over the years, something bends inside her, leading her to question, then to act. By the end of the book, she is leading a different life, as a candidate for an M.F.A. in creative writing at the University of Montana, the ranch far behind her.

In Susan Vreeland's *The Passion of Artemisia,* a novel based on the life of Artemisia Gentileschi, a passionate seventeenth-century Italian painter, we suffer along with her as, at age eighteen, she is tried in papal court for having been raped by her famous father's friend, her mentor (her fingers are squeezed so tightly between cloths that they are injured; she is examined vaginally behind a thin scrim in front of a courtroom full of men to determine whether she's telling the truth). An unhappy marriage is arranged by her father because she is now sexually "ruined." Then we thrill to her ascent—through her own efforts, and in a time of many great artists—as she becomes one of Florence's most renowned and controversial painters, as well as mother to a beloved daughter and friend to such famous men as Galileo. Along the way, she expresses her anger at her treatment as a woman in her paintings, through radical depictions of the women of the Bible, who, instead of passively enduring their fates, as was traditional in the works of many male painters of the time, are fiery-eyed, strong—and capable of retribution.

Alas, Oprah has abandoned her memoir, saying the time wasn't right (as a writer I understand). But we can still gather from her talk-show truth-telling that her rise wasn't easy, nor did she start out in a place that would lead her to have great expectations for her life. Or, as a journalist put it, "That a poor, abused black woman from Mississippi would become one of the wealthiest, most influential women in America is nothing short of a miracle."

But then, I see miracles in Zona Rosa every day!

CHAPTER TWO

WE ARE ALL DOORS UNTIL SOMEONE SLAMS US

How We Can Empower Ourselves No Matter What

1.

Until Wordsworth, daffodils were called weeds.

—REBECCA WEST

"Back When I Was Still Me" is one of the many open-ended exorcises we do in Zona Rosa. It's a device every woman needs in her mental jewelry box, the perfect piece to pull out when we begin to lose sight of who we really are.

All of us have had moments, I believe, when we suddenly know what makes us special, and what we're here for; when, if we look back at the movie of our lives, we see the glitter-sprinkled path of our true destiny clearly marked, opening up before us. These may be moments of discovery or success—when in a flash, we realize our particular genius—or an awareness of the sheer wonder of our existence on earth, suddenly shining down on us like a ray of sunlight. At these times, which usually come during periods of noninterference, we are truly happy, and not because someone told us we should be.

For many of us, these moments come before puberty, or Before the Shit Hit the Fan—before someone told us we had to make a living, get married, and/or have kids, not to speak of fulfilling our parents' dreams for us. But there are other such moments, and we can learn to recognize and treasure them.

It's an exorcise I use myself when stress gets the better of me, varying it to suit my needs. When my adult children's crises feel overwhelming, I may reflect back to a time when, eleven years old, only innocently aware of boys and bathed in a golden glow, I walked alone in the city dump behind my grandmother's house, amid discarded truck tires, Old Crow bottles, and broken couches, imagining myself doing great things, though what they would be was still veiled, a mystery.

If Zane and I are in conflict, I may start with the phrase, "When I was still single . . ." to go back to that time in which life consisted of writing—and going out dancing, getting ready to go out (with plenty of time to paint my toenails), having great sex, and, incidentally, eating and sleeping. At other times, I may think of more recent, and usually solitary pleasures—of stepping into a bar in New Orleans' French Quarter to listen to a Zydeco band, or a train trip alone to Florence when I fell in love with the Italian countryside, the beautiful people on horseback galloping parallel to my window.

I have a whole cache of these memories, and by looking back at a time when I felt in touch with the *real* me—even if favorably airbrushed by memory—I am reminded afresh that that self is still there, a possibility for the future, even if she is submerged for the time being beneath the layers of wife, mother, and teacher.

But the important thing is to uncover, build upon, and treasure these memories—to revisit them and tend to them, as though we were our grandmothers, polishing silver with a soft cloth.

But when our memories are painful, it can be difficult to open them up and use them in our writing.

"I was a door until my parents slammed me," a second-grader wrote in my class (later, I amended his line to "We are all doors until someone slams us"). Most of us have felt like that kid, though it wasn't necessarily our parents who held us back. Sometimes it's as simple as a fourth-grade teacher who frowned and said nothing more than "You need a comma there" when, excited and beaming, we turned in our first effort at a poem or story.

And even if that same teacher went on to compliment us on our plot or originality, we would still remember that first comment more vividly, because of our human tendency to recall what wounds us and points out our imperfections, rather than the positive strokes that emphasize our specialness.

But more often, those who slam us have been closer to home; indeed, they're intimate terrorists—those who know how to cut us to the quick, because they know where the quick is.

Some of us find it hard to remember what we were like Before and After a traumatic event that we've allowed to define us. In fact, we may not even know what our story is yet, and our first task may be uncovering it beneath the detritus of "monkey mind," or what Natalie Goldberg calls the distractions that clutter our brains.

But some come to Zona Rosa with their stories tripping off

the tips of their tongues, so intense is their desire not only to tell it, but to tell it in full-color detail. The women you will meet next had such a burning desire to heal themselves that they were willing to relive the pain of the past and, in Isabel's case, go through the hard work of transforming it into a book.

2.

In the middle of my life, I found myself in a dark wood where the straight way was lost.

—DANTE

In Defense of (Certain) Southern Women. Some women seem so privileged that it's hard to imagine that they've been slammed. Isabel's intimate terrorist, her husband, Henry, was a well-off community member. Indeed, when they finally divorced, their Episcopal church was split in loyalties, her female minister refusing to counsel Isabel regarding her post-divorce trauma because Henry was also a member—and, Isabel said, because of his considerable financial contributions.

Though she now describes herself as a nomad, living in one friend's borrowed house, then another's, Isabel is still—in demeanor, dress, and Peachtree Road diction—the perfect picture of a southern belle turned Buckhead matron. She grew up in Druid Hills, another oak-lined Atlanta enclave, and she had a mother who like many southern mothers led her to believe that propriety, and not what one really felt, was the important thing. As our mother and grandmothers had taught my sister Anne and me, a stiff upper lip was everything.

After a brief marriage during which she had a daughter and became a fourth-grade teacher, Isabel met Henry, the powerful attorney and Coca-Cola heir she saw as the man of her dreams. Soon their lives were an airbrushed video, a movie that seemed it would go on forever: they were beautiful people living in a beautiful house, enjoying their beautiful friends at the country club and the Episcopal church, most of whom were rich like them, and along the way having great sex. This honeymoon period went on for years—it took that long for the monsters beneath to surface.

Henry had two adult children by a previous marriage, a son and daughter. When his son, Henry Junior, began to act strangely, Isabel approached Henry about his son's mental health. She even began to seek treatment for her stepson when she saw that Henry wasn't about to do it.

Along the way, Henry Senior began showing similar symptoms. Bipolar disorder, it appeared, ran in the family. Instead of the dream life she had been enjoying, Isabel soon found herself living with a man with severe mood swings who was a compulsive liar, liked to dress in women's clothes, and was, during those mood swings, given to other strange sexual proclivities. He was also having an affair with his secretary, which Isabel learned was an oft-repeated pattern. Nor would he hear of any wrongs of his family members—the narcissistic, spoiled daughter, the wealthy, imperious mother-in-law, who controlled them all by doling out her money, or even the obviously ill son.

It was Isabel who ended up instigating therapy and staying with it as she struggled to deal with the craziness with which she was surrounded. One of the therapists she and Henry saw together, whom Henry paid $50,000 for double and triple sessions over the period of a year, pronounced *her* crazy; another, more sympathetic doctor said that the reason for her TMJ, or pain from the way she clinched her jaw, was the stress in her life. Still, like many women, she hung in there, trying to make things right, whatever the cost to herself.

But then Henry took her fate into his own hands, asking for a divorce. And this was only the beginning of what pundit Dorothy Parker would have referred to as "What fresh hell is this?" Because Henry was an attorney with many friends in the legal community it was hard for Isabel to find an unbiased lawyer to work on her behalf. Henry, she knew, was determined to leave her with little or nothing. During a fifteen-hour deposition, she was asked about her sex life, and Henry's attorneys read aloud from her personal diaries ("Did you write that you wanted to kill Henry's secretary [and his lover]?" "Yes.").

In the end, Isabel was forced to leave her Buckhead home, which he had been awarded, with nothing but her clothes and personal items; the check for $500,000 that Henry had given her as an initial payment on the settlement she had reluctantly agreed to bounced, leaving her with three dollars in her purse.

Throughout, the Zona Rosans, her daughter, Margaret, and her remaining friends—some of whom asked her to house-sit while they traveled, or otherwise gave her a home—were her mainstay. Isabel was not a natural writer, and it was a pleasure to watch her work with the difficult material of her story until she had forced beauty from it, a beauty that came from her determination to tell the truth, whatever the cost.

Problems in writing are usually problems in life, and Isabel's seemed to be that she didn't easily identify with women unlike herself. "Think about a woman sitting at a bus stop, waiting to go to her job at McDonald's, who has a husband just as crazy, but who doesn't have the resources you have," I would say, warning her against distancing the other women in the group—and her reader—with what might come across as elitism. I knew that though her divorce settlement hadn't been fair in comparison to Henry's wealth, it was unlikely that the single or even married women in the group who worked all day to go home to kids and chaos, and who struggled to find time for their writing, would be empathetic.

When I said these things, Isabel would look at me blankly. But then she would come back with more pages, and I would see my comments reflected in the changes she had made.

Writing is undoubtedly the most perfect mirror ever created, and, as Isabel got to know herself—and us—better, she also revealed her sense of humor: "I came to Zona Rosa and saw a lot of women with bad haircuts, so I thought that must be what a writer looks like," she wrote, explaining why she was letting her own naturally curly hair go gray and unruly. In one of the funniest passages in her book, she imagines Henry's boxers hanging from a flagpole above their church.

What kept Isabel going was her determination to put her pain outside herself. "[Writing the book] was like my own psychotherapy, chemotherapy, and radiation combined," she wrote, confirming the healing power of an honest account, as well as the way revision revises us. "I no longer have the desire to define myself by my story. I have put down the cross." She also told us that she was in touch again with her long-held dream of moving to a cottage in the English countryside. By sharing her story with the Zona Rosans, Isabel had been able to move beyond it and embrace her future.

3.

If we can't tell the truth about ourselves, how can we tell the truth about others?

—VIRGINIA WOOLF

"Yes, it was bad," Honor, who went to the same Episcopal church, said of Isabel and Henry's divorce. "Everybody was talking about it." It was hard to tell from Honor's comment whether she had been sympathetic to Henry or to Isabel. To make clear where I stood, I said I thought Isabel was gutsy in baring her deepest feelings in a group that included women like Honor, whom she had only known socially before the chaos of her divorce.

A retired private school teacher, Honor was an earth mother in Birkenstocks and no-nonsense, graying bob. She told us she wanted to write imaginative and informative books for children drawing on her travels around the globe; a book in progress was *Ear Flaps,* an account of hats and headdresses worn by kids all over the world.

"What a great idea!" I said as we passed around the composite Honor had made, complete with clever texts and colorful drawings. I was excited at having her in the group, and at the prospect of getting to know yet another fascinating woman.

But Honor, unlike Isabel, seemed somehow stranded. Over the months when the children's story didn't sell right away, she appeared to lose energy. Things weren't happening as fast as she wished with her writing, and I suspected there was something—a truth, a real subject, as opposed to a contrived one—locked inside her.

Then one night she surprised us.

"I stopped my mother from verbally abusing my nephew at a family dinner at our home last Thanksgiving," she burst out after we read Karen's exorcise about her painful relationship with her mother. "I saw her hit her grandson—my nephew—and talk down to her granddaughter—my niece—for no reason. She had my niece in tears. 'You are a child abuser!' I said. It was the first time I had ever confronted her."

Abruptly, she became silent, appearing shocked by what she had said.

"That sounds like something you need to write about," I said gently.

"Oh no, I'm not ready to go *there*," she said in a tone that made me know not to push further.

During the next year, Honor worked on her children's stories, and produced a wonderful—and useful—account of how she had reduced her cholesterol naturally through diet and had avoided the need for medication. The piece was so informative that several of us asked for copies so that we could use her methods ourselves. But still, she seemed static, as though she were running in place.

Honor had been in the group three years when her breakthrough came. That evening, I was amazed to see that she had turned in one of our most difficult exorcises, "Write About the Thing You Most Don't Want to Write About (And If You Can't Do That, Write About Why You Can't)."

As I read from the two-page, single-spaced piece titled "Mother," we were rapt. This was a more vulnerable Honor:

It was easy for me to tell our children I loved them. I never had to beat them with hangers and sticks or kick them in corners or throw plates at them to make them right. I never held my hand over my daughter's mouth and her head under running water, gagging her to make her stop crying because she was terrified. . . .

I never sent her to the hospital bleeding from a head wound I had caused. I never gave her enemas to keep her bowels moving. And never was I tempted with my children to replay the strongest message of my own childhood: "You are spoiled, you are bad." . . . I never understood just what . . . made me so bad. . . . How could I understand? I never had a voice to ask. Even when I tried to kill myself.

I paused for a moment before reading further:

I concluded that my mother suffers from mental illness. Now I think of her as a sick relative. This perception has helped me accept her for who she is and given me peace.

As though a dam had broken, Honor told us about her suicide attempts in college, when she finally thought she had escaped. But it had been a hell, it turned out, that traveled with her.

A couple of months later, I received a note from Honor saying she needed to take a sabbatical from the group. Since she had retired, she needed to cut her expenses. I wasn't surprised. Later, she would tell me that the piece had merely been an exercise in craft—that she had been healed of that pain long before. But I knew that Honor had done what she had come to Zona Rosa to do.

4.

To love oneself is the beginning of a lifelong romance.

—OSCAR WILDE

One night, Karen stood beside my chair at the end of the evening. "I need for you to be gentle with me," she said. She was referring to the purple marks I put on their manuscripts in my attempts to help them with syntax and grammar. For Karen, apparently, this was an issue: she wrote me an e-mail that would have been tear-drenched had it been on paper about how devastated she had been by my critique. My comments are nothing to what an agent or editor might think or say, I wrote back. I didn't want to be like that critical fourth-grade teacher I described earlier in this chapter, and I thought I had followed the rule of praising first, then pointing out how, in my view, the writer might improve her work. As in psychologist Eric Berne's theory of the three parts of the personality (parent, adult, and child), my goal was to play the nurturing mother. I knew that like the little shame flower, we open in sunlight and close in the dark. Over the years only three women, including Karen, had protested my critiques. But had I become their pseudo "critical parent" without knowing it?

With all of the Zona Rosans, I continually kept a "parallel chart"—that is, a chart of my own feelings in relation to them at the same time as I strove for objectivity in my dealings with them. Indeed, it was the "parallel chart" that helped me maintain that detachment. I hadn't known what I was doing, only that I was doing it, until I read "The Writing Cure" by Melanie Thernstrom in the *The New York Times Magazine,* in which the author described new methods in which medical students are taught to use literature and creative writing to facilitate empathy. In a similar way, I had long been jotting notes in my journals about the subtexts I saw in the lives and writing of the Zona Rosans. Without these assessments, I would have, for example, taken Joanne at face value when she declared, "I suck, my life sucks, my writing sucks."

But I was also relatively tough-skinned, something some of the Zona Rosans had not yet achieved, and I needed to take that into consideration, along with the fact that our tendency to put ourselves down means that we really don't need that from anyone else.

※

Janet's self-deprecatory, irreverent humor often kept us in stitches. Emulating Phyllis Diller, she referred to her golf-playing, Republican husband of forty years as "Fang." On the other hand, Janet is a serious liberal activist, as well as a successful hypnotherapist aware of the powers of the unconscious and holistic forms of healing. The BBC recently reported that holding a more prosaic view of your spouse means you are less likely to be disappointed, and Janet's funny asides might be her way of keeping her marriage going.

Indeed, when Janet was around, the mere mention of certain key words could fill the room with laughter. And her ability to tickle our funny bones never abated, no matter how dire her circumstances, which, as we will learn later in this book, were often dire.

Among her many stories is the one about when she was protesting the removal of a tree in her native Wisconsin, and the tree men sent out by the city called her "The Bitch on Walkup Road." "I told them I was going to get a T-shirt printed with the words, *The Bitch on Walkup Road—and Proud of It!*" she said.

Another time, she was taken to a police station after a protest, and when the police officers routinely asked whether she had any identifying marks, she had told them, "Yes, I have a rose tattooed on my left boob—and the stem just keeps getting longer and longer!" Even the cops had not been able to contain themselves, she said.

But one of the rules in Zona Rosa is that we don't say negative things about ourselves, our work, or other Zona Rosans and their work. When I called her to task for what was, as often as not, a self-deprecating style, she came up with a defense that was in itself a work of comic genius, leading me to modify my original suggestion to "Unless you're as funny as Roseanne, and it's an art form for you, don't do it."

I went on to explain that when we write our stories we may use the tool of irony in order to avoid hagiography, or making a myth of our own perfection; indeed, that it is our quirks, our fabulous (and oft-inimitable) flaws, that make us lovable, both in our lives and our writing. But this conscious humor is very different from constantly and unconsciously feeding ourselves— in a knee-jerk manner, as a talisman against the pain of possible failure—negative messages.

And even though the culture, and our mothers, may tell us otherwise, we don't have to be perfect to be loved or to achieve. In fact, Oprah has had her highest ratings when she was overweight.

It's well-known that the flaw in a work of art is often what gives it its special style, its panache. This applies to us as well, as we'll see later in an exorcise that asks us to check out the "Flaws, Fatal Flaws, and Fabulous Flaws" in both our writing and our lives—indeed, the very ones that may make us "fabulous."

※

"Dear God, please help me to see myself as I really am," goes a famous Jewish prayer that concludes, "No matter how beautiful that is!"

But for most of us, seeing the beautiful in ourselves is the last thing on our minds. "When you have those negative thoughts about yourself, e-mail them to me, with a subject line of 'For the Big Trash Can with a Pink Bow Around It,'" I say to those Zona Rosans who tend to crucify themselves with language. "I'll delete them and you can go on about your business, no longer burdened by your negative thoughts."

After this suggestion, I give the next step: "Then write affirmations—messages from 'The Sweetheart inside You'— the nurturing parent, the one who tells you, yes, you *can* do it— and put them where you will see them every day, anywhere from the first page of your journal to the bulletin board over your desk to the door of your refrigerator."

Affirmations and visualizations are the most important accessories a woman can have, and are a useful defense against negative energy from ourselves and others. They aren't new— Shakti Gawain's book *Creative Visualization* was first published in 1987, and the core message of the ever-popular *A Course in Miracles* is affirmative: we are already healed, but we just don't know it, or at least we live as if we don't know it. But I also know that they work as long as we use them. Or as some of us say in 12-step programs, "It works if you work it."

5.

Great spirits have always encountered opposition from mediocre minds.

—ALBERT EINSTEIN

"Be careful who you show your writing to. Even if they love you, they may have a hidden agenda—they may want you to stay the same, even to fail," I advise the Zona Rosans. "Or, not understanding the healing power of creative writing, they may feel you're putting yourself through unnecessary hell."

Or they may be intimate terrorists in disguise. I met Siobhan in the Atlanta airport when she sat down beside me, looking exhausted, her two-year-old son in tow. Noticing that I was reading manuscripts, she asked me what I was doing. She was on her way back from Colorado to her in-laws' house on St. Simon's Island, seventy-five miles from Savannah. As we talked, her story came out: her husband, a jazz musician, had died of an overdose the year before, and she had been reduced to living with the in-laws who she was sure were trying to take her son, their only grandson, from her.

The next month, when she came to Zona Rosa in Savannah, she was reluctant to let me read what she had written. "I read it to my mother-in-law, and she said, 'Why are you even trying? And why are you exposing yourself like that? You can't write!'"

But then we read her piece—the story of Gray Bomb, the cat she had loved as a child who ended up tearing a baby rabbit apart within her hearing after her mother wouldn't let her keep it in the house.

I came to the last line in which she had simply written, in

one heartrending line, her first reference to her dead husband: *I couldn't save the rabbit, and I couldn't save you.*

"Tell your mother-in-law that you can definitely write—indeed, that you've already penned a masterpiece!" I said.

❋

"Having a mother too nice to rebel against may be the worst thing that can happen to a woman's creativity," I often tell the Zona Rosans.

At first we didn't realize that Celeste and Karen were so alike. Celeste was an ex-radical, a serious reader and a librarian for the Atlanta Public Library; Karen worked in a bookstore part-time, was long married to an attorney, and had a college-age daughter. Celeste was tall, blond, and rangy, while Karen was short, plump, and pretty. But both were writing novels set in the rural South about feisty young women in flight from their roots.

Recognizing each other through their novels-in-progress, they began doing the exorcises I threw out each month in tandem. In a gestalt that often happens in Zona Rosa, they became a win-win team.

First they wrote about their fear of success—a common phenomenon for women, especially southern women, no matter how educated. We knew, intellectually, about the Impostor Syndrome, in which we achieve, but don't feel deserving of our successes. Indeed, this is so common that one of our exorcises is to free-associate about our fear of success.

I'm afraid to keep writing my novel, Karen's piece began. *What if it is picked up and loved? What if . . . people visit from all over and . . . my life changes? I would wonder if . . . maybe they messed up—picked me . . . by mistake.*

As I read, the room fell silent with what I had learned was recognition.

I know there is no amount of success that is enough to fill . . . that hole of bottomless bad.

Success can't come . . . to a girl. Girls type. Girls cook. Girls change diapers, wipe shit out of commodes over and over. Girls acquiesce. Girls dumb down. Girls are too sensitive. . . . Girls can't hold a penis to boys. . . .

I was taught to be a Sunday School teacher, choir member, church-attending, praying-to-God robot. Robots don't do success. Religious people don't desire success of money or material things. . . .

Success is a sin. Being a girl is a sin. Having money is a sin. Breathing is a sin. If everything ends up being a sin, no wonder Eve ate the damn apple.

There was silence in the room for a few seconds, then everyone burst into applause. There was not one woman there who didn't know what Karen meant.

※

Through the exorcises Karen and Celeste learned that, despite their educations, their urban lifestyles, they were held in similar thrall to rural southern mothers who believed, like many who've never left the places where they started out, that what they had been taught about life is true for everyone—leading them to have little understanding of daughters who had long since grown beyond the confines of home.

Or as Ronnie put it, "Mothers are the damaged daughters of *their* mothers."

I had seen it time after time—the manicured or not-so-manicured southern mother, seeking to direct the life of her middle-aged daughter, held herself in the thrall of fear, especially the fear of what *they* might think. Because she has remained conventional, she sees her adult daughter's creativity as a threat.

Throughout the world mothers have oppressed their daughters—in extreme cases, submitting them to foot-binding or genital mutilation—wanting above all (and often for good reason) for their daughters to be "safe." In the South, a lot of this had to do with Bible Belt religion, and the taboos it lays out for women, some as stringent as any laid out by the Taliban. "Go upstairs and take a nap (or a bath)," a southern mother might suggest to a daughter who even *looks* as if she's about to say or do something unseemly.

I knew Mother had squirmed with shame at my insistence on writing openly about anger and sexuality, the two subjects forbidden discussion—along with anything else that might make the all-powerful male uncomfortable—to southern women. If I hadn't realized early on that that was her problem, not mine, I might have been intimidated (though I did cringe at finding that not only had she destroyed her own best pieces of writing, but also her copy of my first book, *A Sexual Tour of the Deep South,* before taking the overdose that killed her).

Anne recently found an article Mother had written for the Sunday supplement of the *Atlanta-Journal Constitution* in 1969; in it her originality and wit are evident. But her subject—how her stepfather, Granddaddy Carroll, had controlled the choices of men she and her sisters could date—revealed an underlying darkness, a too-ready submission to patriarchy.

At Tucker High School during the early '50s, where I was a cheerleader with little more on my mind than boys and how

I could copy someone's algebra homework, our tenth-grade home ec textbook had a chapter on "How to Be a Good Wife": "Plan ahead . . . to have a delicious meal on time. . . . Take 15 minutes to touch up your makeup, put a ribbon in your hair. . . . Take a few minutes to wash the children's hands and faces, comb their hair. . . . Don't greet him with problems or complaints. . . . Arrange his pillow and offer to take off his shoes. . . . [Above all] never complain."

Nor was this merely because it was the '50s. In 2004, at the Whitney Biennial in New York, Anne and I were struck by the meticulous paintings in which Amy Cutler depicted women tending tigers, mending their coats; as pack animals, carrying donkeys on their backs; and cooling others with their lower bodies, which had been replaced by electric fans—images that seemed like the idea of *The Stepford Wives* pushed to the extreme.

Is it any wonder that we still have these ideas? Most of us have read the statistics: girls lose 15 IQ points at age sixteen because of cultural pressures; with each child a woman's income over her lifetime is reduced. In the late '70s, at the height of the women's movement, the *Ladies' Home Journal* conducted a survey that found that women who held traditional values had more feelings of sadness and depression, possibly because they felt so little control over their lives.

And in a post-feminist world, we need only look at the immediate popularity of *Desperate Housewives,* a TV show the *New York Times* called "campy and shamelessly sexist," to realize that our collective unconscious is still imprinted with the "traditional" roles that our mothers, aunts, grandmothers, and great-grandmothers probably played, even if they died long before we were born.

Nor does the southern male reverence for women who stay in their place add to our comfort in stepping out of it.

In *All Over but the Shoutin'*, Rick Bragg reverently describes a mother who picked cotton and went without a new dress for thirteen years so he could become the man he is today.

"What that woman needed wasn't a *cake*!" Anne exclaimed when I reported that, upon reading Rick's book, Pat Conroy had jumped into his car in South Carolina to drive to Possum Trot, Alabama, to give Rick's mother a cake—her prize, I assumed, for her years of selfless service to the southern male.

I love Rick and his writing, but when we led a panel on memoir together at a writers' conference in Alabama, I told him that I had spent my whole life trying not to become a woman like his mama. Much less one whose main pleasure in life was praying with the preacher over the kitchen radio.

6.

One knows what one has lost, but not what one might find.

—GEORGE SAND

" 'You'll never get a man to marry you—you ask too many questions,' " Claire told us, quoting what her romance-writer mom had told her, growing up in Charleston.

It was hard to imagine Claire having any difficulty in attracting the opposite sex: she was the mother of two teenage boys, but in her size 2 jeans, with her blond bob, she was a doll. That she had been a Charleston debutante was easy to imagine.

" 'Go to the party and gurgle and chirp and be nice—it's what you do best,' " she continued, telling us what her stepfather had advised.

Janet, who has a wicked wit, wearing a look that meant a *bon mot* was coming, quickly brought me back to the present. "Yeah, that's like telling *them* to go to a party and don't burp, fart, or scratch their balls!"

But Claire wasn't about to give up center stage. Southern princess that she was, she had no compunction about taking up the group's time to talk confidently about, say, her lack of confidence, or whether she should hire an assistant ("Wait till you're actually doing something and *need* the help," I advised). She would think out loud until I asked her to stop. At our annual retreat at the beach, it was hard for her to sit still, even on the blue Pilates ball she had brought with her: she alternately lay on the floor cocooned in bedding she had brought from home, her head on a lace-edged pillowcase—later I would learn she had back problems—or stalked around the beach house living room behind the big stuffed chairs, quoting from her therapist or her voluminous journals ("I will go to Rosemary Daniell's Zona Rosa writing workshop and I will enjoy myself and nobody will laugh at me," she had written over and over before her first meeting) about why she was stuck—why she couldn't start writing. And after several days, we were all wondering, too.

Pamella had commented about how people change overnight in Zona Rosa—"and sometimes even faster." And the next day came one of those Zona Rosa miracles that keeps me leading the group year after year.

"I may go back into Savannah to be with my husband for the rest of the week—he's going out of town on Sunday," Claire said in the kitchen when I went in to get coffee. Her handsome attorney spouse and her two good-looking boys were a part of her self-image. But I recognized the fear behind her desire to flee just as she was edging up on truth; it was as though she was standing, fully rigged out in a parachute, on the strut of an airplane wing, unable to bring herself to jump.

I also wondered if she was in danger of falling—or had already fallen—into what medical intuitive Carolyn Myss calls "woundology" or "victimology"—that is, staying stuck in a wound from the past.

"Why don't you stay just one more day?" I said casually, then added that I wanted her to begin listing in a separate notebook all the people who had slammed her in her life, and to write as much about each one as she could until she ran out.

To jump-start the process, I asked about her high school days, and to my amazement—I had assumed she had been a cheerleader, one of the most popular girls in school—she described a friendless time when she didn't want anyone to get close to her for fear that they would find out about her defects, especially her socially prominent but dysfunctional family. "Boys I dated would say their moms warned them not to get too involved with me because my family was so crazy," she said. "We had money, but Mother was like the front yard— manicured—in front of other people, and like the backyard— a mess—around us."

Every time I walked through the common room that day, I saw a more composed Claire, her notebook in front of her. And the next day, as we began our workshop, I noticed that she sat perched on the couch near me, her energy calmed for once. She had titled her piece "Green and White Polka Dots," she said. But after our amusement at the title, we sat mesmerized by a story so dark that it took our breath away.

In it, her parents, both heavy drinkers who fought every night at the dinner table, became angry when Claire, age eight, couldn't stop crying. Her father, who mocked her when she cried—here, Claire made a face like his—and who had instructed everyone in the household, including the servants, to call her "Miss Crybaby," told her, after whispering with her mother, to go into the attic and bring down the green and white polka-dotted diaper left from her younger sister's babyhood.

Then he made her take off her pants and lie on the floor, and told her mother to hold her legs up and pin the diaper on her with a big diaper pin shaped like an elephant. Next he told her to get into her baby sister's high chair, which he clamped firmly shut, instructing her to eat or else.

As Claire sat in the high chair, trying to eat, her father and mother went into the kitchen. Then she heard a knock at the front door, and a voice much like that of the older boy from down the street whom she had a crush on. "Why, hello, Freddie," she heard someone say, "Claire's back here—why don't you come on back?"

Next she heard the clumping of feet toward the dining room. As she struggled to escape the high chair, she could feel the food she had forced down coming back up.

But it was her father who came into the dining room, looking delighted with his little joke. He had gone out the back door to come back to the front door, where he had pretended to be the object of Claire's crush.

But by then the damage had been done. And there was much more, such as the fact that no one in the house was allowed to close a door—not even a bathroom door—without her father's permission, that he would break it down if Claire couldn't get from the toilet fast enough to open it. That when their baby Easter rabbits lay bloodied and torn apart on the back porch, killed by the family dog, her father had forbidden her and her older brother to cry. That her father had punched her brother repeatedly with his fist, bloodying his nose, when he was only six, and that the family cook, Pearl, would stand in the hot kitchen, on her feet all day with high blood pressure (the one room in the house without air-conditioning), moaning, "You pore chirren. If only I could take you out of this place. But I'm just a pore black woman . . ."

After her brother's stay in a mental hospital in his teens, their father had disowned him, and he had gone to live with Lucille and her family, becoming as culturally black as white. When he killed himself at thirty-one, he surrounded himself with the stuffed animals he loved.

After reading her story, and letting the rest of it pour out, Claire suddenly looked light, like an angel, ready to float to the heavens. As we applauded with tears in our eyes, I felt once again the amazing power of Zona Rosa, of telling our truths.

7.

All art comes from a sense of outrage.

—GLENN CLOSE

A Diva Gets Down, or How a Home Girl Tells Her Truths. Although it's often the intimate terrorists in our lives who slam us, it's sometimes something as impersonal, as large, ugly, and anonymous as a prejudice that, like a dagger, goes straight to the heart. When Barbra brought her piece, "The First Cut Goes the Deepest," to the group, we were shocked.

First, with her dreadlocks and showy jewelry, Barbra was sassy and irreverent, as well as prolific, producing pages of monologue for her book, *Sisters Tell the Story*, in which she was recording true stories of other African-American women. She also said she hated the exorcises and didn't want to do them. But she continued to drive two and a half hours each way to come to Zona Rosa.

"I wrote about 'the thing you most don't want to write about,'" she said one Saturday, surprising us by referring to that most difficult—and rewarding—exorcise.

I began reading her piece on how she had gone on a bus trip with her mother at age nine, excited that they were having an adventure, and looking forward to the fried chicken lunch her mother had packed—until a white man at a café in a bus station said, when she wandered too close, "We don't serve nigras—go to the side door." His casual remark, driving her back to her mother's side, cut her like a knife.

As I read, tears began pouring down Barbra's rouged cheeks, and we all looked on in amazement. Where was the cynical, wisecracking woman we knew, the one who had had her own column in a Miami newspaper before coming "north" to Georgia to change professions and become a dedicated educator? The woman who won a Golden Apple Award for her teaching and had a history of achievement that any woman would be proud of? The woman who, in addition, had cared as a single mom for her schizophrenic son for twenty years?

I remembered how impressed I had been when I first met her at a writers' conference, where she had been one of only two African-American participants; how, during our individual conference, I had been stunned by her talent. And how I had also wondered about the obvious chip on her shoulder. As we flipped through page after page of first her poems, then her columns, then the sisters' stories, I could see that she wasn't absorbing the positive things I was saying.

Now it was as though something inside her had suddenly dissolved, a slammed door finally opening. Barbra didn't resist when Carolyn put an arm around her shoulder, offering a Kleenex.

Within three months, the piece had been published. Barbra had had the courage to not only share her worst moment with the Zona Rosans, but to see it in print; she had also received two major summer fellowships, one from the Journalism Education Association, and another from the National Endowment for the Humanities at Tufts University. She had inscribed *Power to the Pink!* in pink felt-tip pen across the acceptance letter that she shared with the group.

"I feel as if I have been resurrected and someone finally knows what I feel," she wrote in her next e-mail. "This week I have been . . . breaking my back gardening . . . the flowers are beautiful and bring me much joy . . . I have tulips, pansies, daisies, purple verbena, lots of pink everything."

As she concluded, she reverted to the old Barbra: "Tomorrow and Saturday are writing days . . . I've been working on an anti-exorcise exorcise!"

8.

Light Happens.

—BUMPER STICKER, EUREKA SPRINGS, ARKANSAS

As Zane and I drove through the Colorado mountains, we went into a store where campers stopped for supplies. Inside we saw a large poster titled WHAT TO DO IF YOU SEE A GRIZZLY. Beneath the picture of a ferocious-looking bear it read: *1. Stand still. 2. Run in the other direction. 3. Fight it with any and everything you have.* We all hope that we don't encounter a grizzly, and we don't need to go around looking for them. But we do need to know what a bear looks like.

In the same way we need to know how to recognize those who would slam us. Naturally, we don't want to live our lives looking for sources of oppression, whether external or internal. But if we let victimization, or the threat of it, go unacknowledged, not only can it hinder our writing, but it can become the story of our lives.

While writing this chapter, I was reading *Reading Lolita in Tehran.* Like its courageous author, Azar Nafisi, we can choose to live above and around what would slam us—in her case, an oppressive Muslim regime at war with Iraq. At night, lying awake listening to bombs, her children asleep nearby, she read and reread Henry James, F. Scott Fitzgerald, and Dorothy Sayers, underlining passages—a defense I recognized, for I had done the same thing during the worst of times with my adult children's illnesses, only my reading had been the Zona Rosans' manuscripts.

Like the women in Nafisi's reading group, we in Zona Rosa exist outside time and place. Like them, we learn from stories, our own and others'. And once we have shared a woman's story, have been with her as she struggled to get it down on paper, she is as imprinted on our souls as though we are family, no matter how far away she might travel, or how long it has been since we've seen her.

True, no one can slam us unless we let them. But often our hurts happen before we are able to defend ourselves, or are outside our control. In Zona Rosa we learn that whether we've been slammed by others, ourselves, or the culture, we have the tools inside us to heal. We also learn that *problems in writing are usually problems in life*—that once we begin to address the latter, it's much easier to wrestle with the former.

Then, with the help of our writing, and within the healing pink light of Zona Rosa, we can begin to open our slammed hearts.

Knee-jerk Reaction #2: Resisting exploration of the pain of the past and staying stuck there, while continuing to subscribe to negative beliefs about ourselves instilled in us by others. Ignoring the past (especially the painful parts) when looking for inspiration.

PILATES ON PAPER

I Was a Door until_____Slammed Me. Complete as many of these sentences as you wish, until you run out. Don't worry, as did Claire, that you've been slammed too many times and by too many intimate terrorists to enumerate. Like her, you'll come to the end of your list—and to a new lightness and freedom.

When Are You Going to Stop Pretending You Don't Know Who You Are, and What You Were Sent Here to Do? a Jewish rabbi asked. "What do I want?" is often a hard question. But when we change it to "What was I sent here to do?" we may see the answer more clearly. When we complete the statement *"Back when I was still me,"* we receive further clues. What we

want more of is usually what we recall with pleasure and longing, those moments when, for a brief time, we recognized our
own genius. I recently wrote among my affirmations that my
life is "like a strand of pearls, made up of perfect moments"—
because I believe it's possible to live these moments continu-
ously, in present tense. *Also, who would you be if you didn't have
a name?* I learned from listening to Janet's past-life tapes that
there's a deeper self inside me, beyond the me of the transient
present.

**Look at a Snapshot of Yourself from the Past. What Do You
See and Feel?** Photographs have long been used by writers to
introduce us to the emotional lives of their characters. Meryl, a
professional photographer as well as a writer and Zona Rosan,
is photographing women at midlife, holding a photo of themselves as a girl, for a book in which opposing pages will feature
text in which the women talk about their lives. Everyone who's
experienced this so far, she says, reports a heady emotional experience. (When Meryl did this exorcise herself, looking at a
photo of herself in high school, her hair poufed by fat rollers
because it was what her boyfriend liked, she burst into tears.)

When I've Been Truly Happy. Describe the moments when
you've been truly happy—right-this-minute happy, not
thinking-about-fifteen-minutes-from-now or next-year happy.
And not happy because someone told you you should be, like
on your wedding day or in the delivery room, or because you're
at a party and everyone else is celebratory. But really happy, in
your heart. When Celeste did this exorcise, we saw a sunnier,
more sensuous Celeste—one who savors time in a beach chair,
a thermos of iced tea beside her, reading *Bergdoff Blondes* or

Vanity Fair—rather than the serious librarian hunched over her computer at Atlanta's Carnegie Library, ordering books for the rest of us.

Describe the Monster inside You Who Says You Can't Do It. Whose voice does the monster have? Have you heard it before? And how often do you follow her lead in labeling yourself? Write a message to yourself from "The Sweetheart inside You," the nurturing and faithful friend who says that yes, you can do it. Write a list of affirmations against the beliefs created when you were slammed. Sometimes simply visualizing and/or saying the word *STOP!*—like a stop sign inside your brain—is enough. Remember: *Changing the tapes inside your head can change your life!*

What I Admire about Myself. Write a page or more about what you admire about yourself. When Jossie did this, she said she was surprised by all the great things about her, and what she had achieved through the years—and as an added bonus, she felt wonderful! Jossie, who has never married or had children (she made decisions early on not to follow the dictates of her Catholic clan) has no regrets (which, like guilt—which a therapist once described to me as "the useless emotion"—zaps energy without giving back). Before she retired to her dream house in Savannah, a life of adventure travel, and finishing her first novel, she had a decades-long career in Washington with the federal government and the DEA—which led her to become our resident organizing-your-paperwork expert. Jossie even feels gratitude toward all the many men she has dated for helping her know what she likes and dislikes in a man. Today, she lives with an adventurous man she made no special effort to meet, but who came to *her* as she was being herself, sitting in a Starbucks, deep in thought.

Create a Stroke/Gratitude/Pleasure Book for the nice things others say to you, the perfect moments in your life, and everything, no matter how small, for which you're grateful. Or simply make these entries or sections in your regular journal (I label mine in the margin—"Stroke" (a compliment), "Blessing," or "Gratitude"—so it's easy to flip through the pages and read the nice stuff at any time). Reread these entries each morning, before your brain is cluttered with the debris of the day. And *always, always* write them first, before addressing "Problems in Progress" (as I call the infinite and never-ending psychological knots I'm seeking to untie at any moment). I open my journal in a certain sequence: first, I read through the goals and affirmations that fill the first two pages; then, I go to the day's date and write the current good stuff; next, I describe my dreams from the night before in exact detail (more about this later); and last, I address Problems in Progress, which by that time have begun to pale in the light of the rest.

BOOK THERAPY TWO: SOME BOOKS MY SOUL CRIED OUT FOR

Because this chapter is about how we've been slammed, and how we might need not only to heal our wounds but to go on, empowered and with confidence, I suggest that all of us keep beside our bed a slew of books that enrich our lives and embolden us. These are the books in which we underline pages, stick full of Post-its, and reread whenever need be. They are the books my soul cried out for at times of crisis, and they proved to be more healing than chicken soup (or a chocolate martini, if that's more your style).

A few of the books beside my bed are *There's a Spiritual Solution to Every Problem* by psychologist Wayne Dyer; *Finding Your Own North Star* by life coach Martha Beck; *Simple Abundance: A Daybook of Comfort and Joy,* by Sarah Ban Breathnach, which is worth having simply for her list of "Bliss Blockers"; *Exuberance: The Passion for Life,* Kay Redfield Jamison's exploration of that divine emotion; *The Soul's Code,* by scholar James Hillman, in which he interprets Carl Jung for our lives and tells us to grow *down* rather than up—and back to who we were meant to be; *A Course in Miracles,* based on the belief that we're already healed—we just don't know it yet, put together by the Foundation for Inner Peace; and *The Road Less Traveled,* by Dr. M. Scott Peck.

You may notice that none of these books deal with specific problems, though I have also read an abundance of those, from Dr. Susan Forward's *Emotional Blackmail* to, if I'm in the mood for anarchy, *Change Your Life and Everyone in It,* by Michele Weiner Davis. I usually keep a couple around when I'm dealing with a special issue. But I find it better to read from the universal truths, as they inevitably filter down, serving the same purpose with half the angst: when we're feeling good about ourselves and our destiny, specific problems seem to resolve themselves almost effortlessly.

And don't forget the great poets of comfort, such as Hafiz and Rumi. These are not the edgy poems of our times—which I also love!—but the timeless ones that remind us that we're all part of the human condition. And though I suggest we all read at least a poem a day—*The New Yorker* and the annual *Best*

Poetry anthologies are good sources, as well as collections by the poets we discover in literary magazines—Hafiz's and Rumi's are the poems I keep by my bed for the times when I need a more universal view.

Beside our bed is also where we need to keep our personal and writing journals (more about the latter later), our affirmation and stroke books, and a blank book for our favorite quotes (where do you think I got all the quotes for this book?), preferably all between pretty, flowered, or otherwise pleasing covers!

With these books—and all this wisdom—at hand, I think you'll find it impossible to stay slammed for long—all you have to do is open them!

CHAPTER THREE

IF I WAS REALLY WILD

Why Courage and Daring Are Not Just for Other Women

1.

Do what you fear most and the death of fear is certain.

—MARK TWAIN

"I woke up in a tattoo parlor in Tijuana. You can imagine my surprise," a primly coifed woman says to her three women companions as they sit playing bridge, in a *New Yorker* cartoon.

We can only guess how she got there, and where her tattoo was, not to speak of how her bridge partners responded.

As you probably noticed in the previous chapter, we didn't discuss the kind of slamming for which women are famous. Because in Zona Rosa, we *don't*—we don't backbite, gossip, put down, or make fun, except in the most loving way. Indeed, instead of corralling each other into ever more conventional (and soul-killing) behavior, we are cowgirls, a girl gang, full of

Brenda Starrs and Sigourney Weavers, egging each other on toward ever more rewarding, if oft challenging, thinking and behavior.

"Women don't perspire, they glow," many of our mothers drove home to us. But in Zona Rosa, we encourage one another not only to perspire, but to sweat, both literally and figuratively. "Say yes to stress," we say, counteracting such messages with a Zona Rosa credo. For whether that stress is negative or positive, it's usually what we need to keep our creative juices flowing.

And a good place to start is with "If I Was Really Wild," an exorcise in which we imagine what we would do were fear not an obstacle. Or start with the phrase, "Imagine My Surprise When . . ." Think, say, of unlikely romance writer Kathleen Turner in *Romancing the Stone,* caught up in the jungle with only a delicious Michael Douglas to save her. Or of your favorite action heroine—Batgirl, Catwoman, Xena the Warrior Princess, Buffy the Vampire Slayer, or Wonder Woman—who collectively advise us in an article in *Fitness* magazine to, among other things, "Fight for What You Believe In," "Be Resourceful," "Don't Be Afraid of Your Own Strength," And "Tap Into Your Inner Vixen."

So go ahead—shock yourself! You might find your vixen, and that she's someone you want to keep around.

❀

This chapter is about Zona Rosans who took risks in their lives, and about how risk taking heals and strengthens us. It's about how failing to take those leaps keeps us hovering, like a hot-air balloon going nowhere. Indeed, what most of us have learned along the way is that the only risk may be not taking one. And since writing itself is a risk, we need to stay in practice.

At the Peggy Guggenheim Museum in Venice, I bought geometrically-fractured glasses that break vision up into fragments; whenever I hold them before my eyes, I immediately see the world afresh. And it's that way with risks. Sometimes we need them simply to get a new perspective.

Often our leaps are in the realm of the physical, liberating us to the more difficult task of writing (and sharing) our truths. At our Zona Rosa retreat in Italy, Lynn told us about the time she bungee-jumped, and Pamella described a high-altitude ropes course—risks they took not because they *weren't* afraid, but because they *were*. At our retreat in Aix-en-Provence, Deborah and Lynn, both petite, lugged major baggage up the four stone flights of our residence hotel to their aeries above, while the rest of us marveled.

It was no accident that soon all three would also stun us with their emotional feistiness, their ability to take risks in more than the physical. Lynn would defy negative messages given to her by her father so deep that had they been holes, they would have reached China—by writing about things she had barely been able to tell a therapist only months before. She also sued the insurance company where she worked for discrimination (receiving a settlement in her favor), and, after a period of "transition"—read fear and depression—landed a job in which she is treated with the respect she deserves. (Despite her claim of low self-esteem, Lynn had also shown her stuff pre-Zona Rosa, taking the bar exam over and over, until she had finally succeeded.)

Within a year, Deborah, nearing fifty—inspired by her experiences in Zona Rosa—would go through what I would come to think of as Deborah's Extreme Makeover (not that she needed one otherwise; with her sheer, flippy skirts and her spaghetti-strap tops, she personifies a sexy kind of glamour). She would make a 180-degree change, leaving behind her job as CEO to a failing company and its toxic male execs to go through the pain of bankruptcy, giving up a huge house and a wardrobe that could have stocked a posh atelier ("How many people *really* need fifty garter belts?!"). Along the way, she would become, *sans* lingerie, the Madonna of the Atlanta poetry circuit.

To let go of her fears and celebrate her forty-ninth birthday, Becky fulfilled her lifelong dream of skydiving, despite her mother's terminal illness, her own multiple sclerosis, and a newly discovered lump in her breast. She liked it so much she did it again the following week. It was this spirit that was helping her write the story of how she, a good Catholic girl from a conservative family, had gotten pregnant out of wedlock at age fifteen, and had gone on to raise her son.

"Motherhood: 24/7. Are you man enough to try it?" said Maria Shriver, describing an inscription to be placed at the Sacramento Museum dedicated to women's contributions to California history. And anyone who thinks women aren't natural risk-takers need only note her words. The mere fact that we give birth makes us the species' gutsiest creatures.

But the most meaningful risks may be the ones we've chosen—ones that we fear, even if ever so slightly. For some women, that might simply mean having dinner alone in a posh restaurant (and better yet, demanding a good table when the maître d' tries to seat you by the kitchen door). Or, to up the ante, having dinner alone in a posh restaurant in a foreign country. Or going into a bar alone anywhere, an act men take for granted, but one that has long frightened women, whether because of cultural taboos or worst-case scenarios like *Looking for Mr. Goodbar*.

Or it may be going on Match.com to meet men for the first time at age sixty-nine, as Cleo did. Though this wouldn't have felt like a risk for Deborah, who had been married five times, and who met men by the droves via the same method, it was a high-charge one for Cleo, who, before being suddenly and shockingly widowed two years before, had expected her happy marriage to go on forever.

Your risk might even change your life, as did Ora's one phone call to a ship docked in New Orleans to request Mardi Gras dates—down to hair color and height—for her and a girlfriend. At the time Ora was a twice-divorced single mom, working for the local phone company—but her bold move led to her marriage to a handsome naval commander. And, in a perfect example of the Zona Rosa credo, "No guts, no story," it became the basis for her hilarious novel, *Dial-a-Sailor*.

Sometimes a risk is simply standing by your guns, your gut-level response, despite advice from the "experts." When Ora attended a romance writers' workshop and heard the leader describe how a romance novel should be like the movie *Jaws*, in which the reader encounters first a big shark, then a bigger one, then the biggest, she felt a moment's uncertainty—then knew intuitively that her book, while about a romance, was destined to be more multidimensional than that.

And sometimes the risk is as simple as finally insisting that your domineering husband go to marriage counseling, as Helen did five years into the group (with glowing results in both her poetry and her life). Or it might be telling your significant other that you're going away to spend time alone. "Why can't you write at home?" Anne's husband asked as she packed for three weeks at a writers' colony, a question almost every woman who takes such a trip hears echoing behind her as she closes the door—a question that, were she honest, she might answer, "Because of you—and questions like this!"

In fact, if we're still fearful, we can even road-test such desires. When Rhonda did the exorcise "If I Was Really Wild," she wrote a poem that began, "If I was really wild / I would sell my house / buy a camper and live on the beach."

Soon, she wrote to say that "I realized my house was the only thing holding me back"—that she was buying an RV in order to travel around the country as part of a growing group of single women living on the road, writing along the way, in what she planned to call Rhonda's Big Adventure.

But a few months later she wrote to report the results of the trial run she now called Rhonda's Little Adventure: "I loved the RV, but not the noisy campgrounds. And I missed my friends and my cat!" She also found that she could make enough money to keep her house by working part-time, and still write: she was seventy-three pages into her first novel. Sometimes taking a risk can show us what we *don't* want to do—which can be just as valuable.

Indeed, one of the biggest leaps we may take as women is that of insisting on our solitude. "What everyone really wants is just to be left alone," many say, but they always seem to mean men. In his book *Dark Star Safari,* travel writer Paul Theroux writes of his desire to revisit Africa "without a cell phone, and with no way [anyone in London] can reach me." We tend to think of even having this desire as unfriendly, unfeminine, and a male prerogative—especially of the likes of Paul Theroux. (Later, we'll observe how Henry Miller and other male writers have had no problem at all insisting on their solitude, and whatever else it took to nurture their creativity.)

Times when we are alone may be the only moments when we're truly free of what I call Knee-jerk Nurturing, or the Bondage of the Pink (the downside of our female acculturation). We may even be loath to admit that our most deeply happy moments often come when we are alone and no one else's happiness depends on us—when we are free to be ourselves.

It's also good to imagine things we might never do, or even want to do. When I read supermodel and makeup mogul Lauren Hutton's life plan in *AARP* magazine (yes, she's over fifty), I was revved. But not because I wanted, as she had done, to crash a motorcycle, spend a year recovering, then get right back on one; or eat live termites in Africa while visiting tribes known for their cannibalistic tendencies. Instead I felt strengthened by her guts, her ability to follow her plan (two months in New York for work, then two months somewhere else, preferably dangerous), which meant that the next day, I might be able to take some extra step toward achieving my own goals, even if that just meant changing my own tire for the first time.

2.

I travel a lot; I hate having my life disrupted by routine.
—CASKIE STINNET, FREE SPIRIT

Travel, especially travel alone, sets many women free. Susan F., a world traveler who was with us for our first retreat in France, thrilled me with her tale of striding into a bar in Marseilles to recruit a guide from among the men there. (Susan has since died of cancer, and hearing that she was terminally ill in a hospice in a distant city, I imagined the memories from her well-filled life and the many books she had read giving her comfort at the end). As Debra Klein wrote in the *New York Times* travel section, "When geography dictates that I can't complete my journey without a boat, pickup truck or even a machete to cut a path . . . I must hire a local guide. . . . [And] I have to believe [that his] main concern is earning a living rather than in harming me."

When Carol O. did the exorcise "When I Have Felt Empowered," she found that after moving for her husband's job, she loved the dislocation of being in a new and different place: "It is a Saint Louis winter kind of day," she wrote about moving with her husband and kids from the Deep South to a completely unknown city, "and no one knows me. No one but my lone husband tucked away in some building. . . . It is my car and me and these three little girls of mine on this frigid winter morning. . . . [But] I have something in me that knows how to create a new life. . . . I know how to drive, bum around, get lost, ask questions, start up a conversation. . . . I am a portable creature. . . . empowered. . . . [by] what I carry around in this skin." Being in a new and unfamiliar territory helped Carol assess herself in strong and vivid language.

Temple, an elegant Charlestonian who lives on a romantic island, had a breakdown/breakthrough (as we call them in Zona Rosa) in her late thirties, when her children were in their teens. She followed hospitalization with a trip alone to Europe, and "I was scared every minute. I had never been alone like that."

But back at home she was able to make the changes she needed to become her real self: she told her surgeon husband that she wanted to live part of each year away from home, in their other house in Highlands, North Carolina. "I go there to write. And when he visits, we have a grand time!"

Along the way, Temple got an M.F.A. in creative writing and collaborated with her analyst of eight years on a book about how Jungian dream analysis changed her life. Her analysis also left her honest in the way only a person who has gone down to the dark cellar of self and come back up can be. "Shivers went down my spine when she said that when her abusive mother was dying, she thought to herself, 'Die, bitch, die,'" a Zona Rosan still struggling with her own issues with her own mother commented, then marveled, "Especially since she said it in that elegant accent of hers."

As Temple spoke, I thought of Janet Frame, the New Zealand writer portrayed in Jane Campion's true-life film, *An Angel at My Table*. Frame, in a mental hospital after an excruciating young adulthood, and on the eve of a lobotomy, gets the news that she's just received a big literary prize. Virtually leaping from her bed, she travels alone to Italy and Greece, where she begins life anew and has her first love affair.

I also remembered my own travel fears. When I first began driving around the country, staying in motels alone, what I was doing seemed strange and scary, as did the people (often burly truck drivers and tough waitresses) I met along the way, until I learned to love it. Now I can't pass a Best Western or Comfort Inn without being suffused with the image of the pleasure I might feel, checking in to lie between the cool white sheets with take-out food and a good book.

Later, when my adult children became ill, I went through a period of years during which I suffered driving phobia— extreme panic attacks while going over bridges and driving on expressways. Even though I knew these were caused by my displaced fears for my kids (with a little rage thrown in—I would deliberately hustle up a few cuss words as I approached the huge Savannah bridge), I still felt the terror. But because I was determined not to miss any Zona Rosa groups, I sought out alternate routes, until the panic finally receded of its own accord, and I was free to speed down the highways along with the rest.

Ten years later, when things were even worse on the home front, I determined to travel in Europe alone for the first time. I would go to Paris before our retreat, and after it, I would board a train for Nice, then Florence, where I would stay for a time, then take another train on to Rome for a week there. I planned to do this even though I had been admitted to the ER three times during the past six months from the effects of stress, which caused symptoms that mimicked heart attack or stroke (this happened twice while I was on the road; I'd become an expert at looking for hospitals along the way).

As I made my plans, I used that old trick of thinking of the worst thing that could happen, say, if I fell into a faint on the streets of Rome. Some kindly person would pick me up, I imagined, and call an ambulance. Or what if I was caught during a train strike in Tuscany, with bad directions and nary a word of Italian, as really happened? As also really happened, a cute English- and Italian-speaking guy with dreadlocks might become my protector, lugging my baggage across the Pisa town square until we found the right bus for Florence, then delight me during our trip with tales of growing up African, and flag a taxi for me when we arrived.

Over the years, I've learned to "trust in the kindness of strangers," as Blanche DuBois says in *A Streetcar Named Desire*. I discovered that those burly truck drivers were often the best guys to ask for help if I had trouble on the road, and that those tough-talking waitresses were the same folks one might turn to for information, advice, or even comfort.

The first time I drove cross-country and back alone (*sans* cell phone—such extravagances weren't even on my radar then), Zane complimented me on my time (though I was only a little faster than the Pony Express, whose progress I had been following via plaques at rest stops across Nebraska). I arrived in Cheyenne just in time for my book signing.

As I began my trip back east a month later, I suddenly saw a flash of myself, as if in a movie, having a flat tire in Kansas. And lo and behold, the moment I crossed the Colorado line into that state, a tire popped beneath me. As I rummaged through the massive amounts of luggage filling every available space in my Camaro, searching out the spare and that little book that told how to do it, I prayed for help.

And at that moment, a huge semi whizzed to a stop behind me. A Sam Shepard look-alike jumped out of the cab, changed the tire within seconds, and—being a man of few words—all my Prince Charming said before whizzing off again was, "Heard it on the CB. S'prised nobody stopped before now." Little did he know that he had become part of my growing repertoire of travel stories, and thus fodder for my writing.

3.

Each friend represents a world in us, a world possibly not born until they arrive, and it is only by this meeting that a new world is
born.

—ANAÏS NIN

How Our Favorite Femme Manifests Her Destiny. For some, risk is a
way of life; they keep their lives in a tropical storm state, the
search for truths more important than comfort. In Zona Rosa,
we're ready to be shaken by them, and willing to learn from
their examples.

Pamella likes to pretend she's an ordinary woman—"a
wife, mother, and grandmother." But anyone who knows her
knows that's not the whole story. Whenever I think I have a fix
on her, she shakes the champagne bottle that is her life again,
the bubbles fly, and before we know it, she's in a whole new
configuration.

Wherever we are, Pamella seeks out available risks, however
small—from ocean kayaking at the beach to plunging into the
pool outside our château, despite the early fall weather, during
our retreat in the South of France. She swears by them like
some of us swear by our favorite face cream. "Always pack a
corkscrew and a bathing suit," she advised me during a period
when I was all work and no play.

Over the years Pamella's skirts have gotten shorter, her tops
more revealing, her figure better. She gets up at five A.M. to do
Pilates or swim, and some mornings, write. She's one of the
few women who truly look good with hair shorn to pixie
length—she even manages to make those blond spikes look

sexy, enviable. Nor does she care about what the magazines say about sunscreen.

"Are you Sharon Stone?" an entranced cabbie asked her in Aix-en-Provence, when she and her sister Kathy were en route to providing Foods of the Goddesses for our retreat, a box of smuggled-in powdered buttermilk spilled amid the black clothes in her Air France luggage.

Pamella has learned over the years the truth of our credo that the only real risk in life is not taking one. "I was at a writers' conference on the coast of North Carolina," she said, "and Fanny Flagg"—the famous actress and author of *Fried Green Tomatoes at the Whistle Stop Café*—"was there. One morning, I saw her standing outside her cottage as I walked toward the water, where I intended to go out in one of the little boats tied there. As I passed her, I almost asked if she'd like to go, too—but then thought that I didn't want to disturb her privacy. That night, at the conference, she came up to me and said, 'I saw you earlier today, walking toward the lake.' And I wondered if she would have liked to have gone out in the boat with me." Her story was also a perfect illustration of the way that we often use "good manners" to mask our own fear.

When she wrote "Potential Has a Shelf Life," a piece honoring her father, it embodied her belief that life is too short to spend in fear—or humorlessness. Pamella's deceased dad apparently knew it, too; he was a charmer who carved "I Love You" into the lawn in front of their house as a surprise for her prim-lipped mother.

But Pamella wasn't always this way, we learned when she first came to Zona Rosa. In one of her first exorcises, she wrote that, until her forties, she had done just about everything her mother had told her to do—she got married (to her high school sweetheart, Mike), got a college degree, had children (two sons), and worked as a teacher of classical piano. For thirty years, her life was made up of leading little hands across the keyboard, traveling to Japan to study with a master teacher, and getting her students ready for their recitals.

Then, during a massage, something broke inside her: in what felt like a near-death experience, she had the breakdown that she would later see as a breakthrough. She went home, where, worrying friends and family, she sat in her house for six weeks staring into space, barely speaking or sleeping. After a while, she began therapy and everything that she had stuffed down began surfacing. She told her students she wouldn't be available for a while, and she divorced Mike, though they continued to live in the same house, even when she started going out at night with other men. By the time she came to Zona Rosa, they had remarried in a romantic church wedding, she was teaching piano again, though on a more limited basis, and she had penned her first book.

What we didn't yet know was that she was a woman of constant change, a harem dancer constantly shedding her veils. That she wasn't afraid to listen to her gut, to do what it told her, made her life an adventure, and we all watched, breath held, wondering what she might do next, whether it be reconciling with her mother, confronting Mike yet again, or starting a new business.

"All I really have is my word," she said after a forum in which participants were encouraged to look honestly at their lives. Pamella was bombarded with epiphanies, and within minutes, she was on the phone in the hallway, calling first Mike, then her mother, confessing to the times when she hadn't been honest with them. "I always blamed Mother, thinking she didn't love me, but suddenly I realized *I* had rejected *her* all those years. And that it was time for me to make amends."

As for her relationship with Mike, she had just rung the bell that would send them into the next round of the kind of ongoing intimacy that can make a long-lasting relationship exciting. Rather than avoiding confrontation about unresolved issues, she brought them to the foreground, unafraid of the turmoil that doing so might bring. "I don't settle," she wrote for the exorcise "What I Admire about Myself," and she didn't mean for men or diamond rings, but that she doesn't settle for any less than the best from herself.

"What is this?" I asked, pointing at a weekly block of time as we went over her six-month time line, the writing-and-life plan I ask each Zona Rosan to make on a regular basis. "Oh, that's when I work at the church soup kitchen," she said, surprising me yet again. It wasn't as though her life wasn't already complicated, but she still found time to give of herself.

What I was learning from Pamella and women like her is that their lives move fast—they're manifesting their destinies at a pace that would make even Wayne Dyer dizzy. They act on the messages they get from the universe, and if they aren't coming fast enough, they do whatever it takes to stir up the atmosphere.

4.

Friends who love your creative life are the best suns in the world.

—UNKNOWN

I knew from experience about the kind of risk that comes from the sense that we'd better do something differently—or else.

Sometimes it's as though we're standing on a ledge, a fire behind us, with no choice but to jump.

At first, all I knew about Linda was that she worked at MIT in Boston. And from her serious, intelligent demeanor, I assumed she was a physicist, working at a high level on projects that would be beyond my comprehension. She had flown down to Charleston for a one-day Zona Rosa workshop at the Center for Women, and I assumed, too, that she must have big bucks to spend so much for such a short journey. But when her story tumbled out—she was actually a secretary—we realized what a risk she had taken to be with us.

"I'd lost my mind in 1994. . . . I knew enough to look like I was doing okay, until you looked in my eyes and saw . . . a loose entity needing a safe place to hide," she wrote me a couple of years later, describing why she had come. "I was penniless in the travel budget department. But I was also in danger of never regaining my soul. . . . Once again as I had so many times before in my life, I was engaging [by coming to Zona Rosa] in a high-risk venture I call 'jumping the river.'"

Next, Linda revealed her gift for metaphor:

> It's a . . . river that I fashion after a view of the Colorado River that I'd once seen while visiting a Mexican church almost directly on the riverbank in a small town in New Mexico. I'd never seen the Colorado at all, let alone up close—it was terrifying and compelling all at once. That day it was raging the way a hurricane does—carrying along whole trees, a refrigerator, all kinds of debris at the pace of a runaway train. It represented to me the way life is: if you are already living in compromised circumstances and don't take a risk and jump . . . to the other side, you'll never leave where you are.

You can't worry about falling in, drowning, or even whether you can swim; you can [only] stay or go. . . .

I live and work in one of the country's intellectually elite strongholds. Too often that eliteness is synonymous with arrogance and hubris—characteristics that are the kiss of death for floundering creativity. . . . [And] I needed to create . . . because, although a pianist as a child, indeed, a prodigy, I'd given up my music decades earlier rather than risk death at my own hands. Playing and wounding [cutting] myself were inexplicably intermingled. . . . Learning would only take place if I could trust the teacher and feel safe. . . . [And] yes, it's worth the process. It's also awful. . . . Awful and Grand and sometimes both at once. . . . At Zona Rosa, you can bleed and smile . . . at the same time and not be thought a fool. Or, if thought a fool, accepted nevertheless.

Needless to say, none of us thought Linda a fool, and when she came back for yet another workshop, then another, then for our annual five-day retreat at the beach, we all hugged her with the love that comes from having shared our truths.

5.

If you don't risk anything, you risk even more.

—ERICA JONG

Some Really Tough Femmes. "If I told you I don't live in fear, I'd be lying," Salima Tlemcanti, investigative reporter for *El Walan*, one of Algeria's daily newspapers, told a reporter for *O*, after describing repeated threats to her family's life and hers. And in many parts of the world, just being a woman is enough to put us in harm's way. "Where I wander, the shape of my body and the timbre of my voice define me far more than any nationality or race," world traveler and adventurer Elinor Burkett wrote in *More*.

Christina, an attractive redhead, and the mother of two, told us in her charming Eastern European accent that eighteen years before, at age twenty, she had walked out of Communist Romania on a bright, moonlit night, past guards who, if they saw her, would gang-rape her, then let their dogs tear her apart, or at best, merely shoot her. She and a friend walked for two weeks, ending up in a refugee camp that was more like a prison than a retreat. After years of struggle, she ended up in London, with a good job, married to a German national who had recently been transferred by Mercedes-Benz to Charleston, South Carolina, where she now sat in our Zona Rosa group.

As she told her story, we sat mesmerized before what we already saw as a *Lifetime* movie. But when I commented on her courage, Christina balked, denying that she had been courageous at all. "I just had to go. It was worse than in East Germany behind the wall. I just couldn't stay there and lead the same life as my mother."

"But didn't other women stay behind?" I asked. When she conceded that they had, that she was in fact sending money home to them, I persisted, "Well, you *were* courageous—whether you know it or not!"

❊

When I sat down beside a stranger in the dining hall at Skidmore College, where I was taking part in the International Women's Writing Guild, I didn't know that I was about to meet a woman whose intuitiveness and ability to follow her gut would knock me out. Daniela had been stabbed and left unconscious in Central Park a decade before, she told me. During her coma, she had many visions, including a recurrent one in which she saw an island. When she came out of the coma months later, "my whole way of thinking and looking at the world had changed."

An artist and a world traveler, Daniela resumed her peripatetic lifestyle after she recovered, traveling abroad to complete commissions. "One day in London, I walked a different route, and as I passed a small travel agency, I did a double take: there in the window was a picture of the very island I had seen over and over in my dream state," she said.

"When I went inside and asked where the island was, the agent explained that it was a sparsely inhabited Greek island off the city of Naples. I immediately flew to Italy, took the ferry to the island, and knew the moment I disembarked that I was meant to be there. I ended up staying ten years." As Daniela spoke, I felt that I was meant to visit her island, too, and we parted with the promise of visiting it together after our next Zona Rosa retreat in Tuscany.

❋

The two women we will meet next share Daniela's stunning certainty. Risk-takers extraordinaire, their trust in synchronicity is so woven into their psyches that they accept it without thought, like having blue or brown eyes.

They also know deep inside what it means to follow a hunch that others might think is crazy. When Nikki Hardin, a single mom and freelance writer, moved to Charleston, South Carolina, she was barely making ends meet, but she decided to start a publication for women that would feature the kind of writing she liked to read. With a few bucks—a *very* few bucks—and the help of a girlfriend, *skirt!* was born, and soon they were giving their tabloid-style publication away around town.

At first, not being natives to a city known as a closed society, they found selling advertising next to impossible. But soon Barbara Hagerty, a bona fide Charleston blue blood and well-known local writer, offered to write columns for them—providing, in effect, an entree to the business community.

A few years later, *skirt!* was still a shoestring operation, but Nikki and friends plopped down five hundred dollars for an office on Charleston's famous King Street. "I was really scared; that was a *lot* of money to me then," she said.

Not long after, when the adjacent building was torn down, they looked at the exposed wall on their old-new building to see the words *Skirt Factory*.

"It was then that I knew we were meant to be!" Nikki told the Zona Rosans.

Ten years later, Morris Newspapers bought the rights, with plans to publish *skirt!* in a half-dozen plus cities—a deal that left Nikki with total editorial control of the magazine that she had loved into life, and enough money to provide for her and her children, well, *forever*.

Now Nikki had the resources to take a trip to Mexico, something she had long dreamed of. And dreaded. Despite starting a magazine from scratch, Nikki still had her own fears, which she was facing one by one: to celebrate her fiftieth birthday, she'd had a spiral design, a spiritual symbol, tattooed on her wrist—"It hurt like hell, but once you start, you can't stop"—and now she was about to take her first trip alone to a foreign country.

I met Charlotte at a Zona Rosa group in Eureka Springs, Arkansas, which is known as the Key West of the Ozarks, and is one of those funky places where people who are "different" congregate, drawn by the healing waters and who knows what in the air (probably marijuana, the legalization of which the local weekly, *The Lovely County Citizen*, regularly champions). With her long dark braid, her vintage garb, and her Scarlett O'Hara waistline, Charlotte, at fifty-one, had acted, or as some would say, acted out, throughout her life, and I sensed a sister. For one thing, we both had on our favorite thrift-shop cowboy boots, mine embossed with red roses.

At fifteen, Charlotte had eloped to Mexico with the Red Alley Cat (the only name she calls him) to escape a dad destroyed by his part in World War II—"When he came home, his luggage was filled with empty liquor bottles"—a beautiful mom made sad and rigid by her experiences, and her Texas hometown, where she was one of the few Jewish kids in her high school. (Amazingly, she graduated, even though her husband, barely older than she, had to sign her report cards.)

After she managed to escape the Red Alley Cat—it wasn't easy; he had turned out to be a stalker—she moved to Moscow, Idaho, where she started her first shop, named *GlamOrama*, and inadvertently became an events planner, a job that she seemed born to do. When she noticed a man celebrating Mardi Gras alone in his shop on Main Street, she planned a full-fledged Mardi Gras for Moscow. Cameramen came from New Orleans to film the event, and she used the proceeds to bring real Russian musicians to the town: "I thought since they lived in Moscow, they should know what real Russians looked like!"

Later, she moved to Seattle, where she started her second *GlamOrama* (in which she, by then a certified minister, married people by satellite under a white canopy). "Then I knew it was time to sell." (Like Nikki, Charlotte knows a hunch when she feels one.) She ended up in Eureka Springs—"I researched it and felt this was the place where I could spend the rest of my life"—paying cash for a house with the proceeds from her shop.

With her, she brought the memoir she had written during the past few years. It was littered with grammatical errors she was happy to fix, as per my Zona Rosa crash-course suggestions.

The book expresses her wisdom about relationships—"I'm only good for two and a half years, which is why Carlos, the man in the story, is a composite lover"—and reconciling with one's roots. Two weeks after her mother's last visit to Eureka Springs, where Charlotte encouraged her to read *The Stranger* by Albert Camus and *The Women's Room* by Marilyn French, her mother died. Soon Charlotte found herself flying back to the Texas town she had escaped to be sure her mom was buried in her favorite snake bracelet, and to make things right with her several remaining aunts.

To my delight, Charlotte used a language uniquely her own (as had her sister Texan, Mary Karr, in her book, *The Liars' Club*). "I'm detwinged," she would say of the Carloses, meaning she no longer got hurt by men. Her metaphor for her life, and the sad lives of her mother and father, was the road trip, as per her book's title, *Road Trip of Love: Tales of a Texas Jew Girl*. " 'Do you *have* to talk in poetry?' " she said a boyfriend asked her once.

And was it hard for a single woman her age to meet men in Eureka Springs? "Half the men here don't have any teeth, and the other half are playing on *my* team," she said. Because of her bent toward theater, Charlotte was drawn to gay men and they to her. A part of her book was about caring for a friend dying of AIDS—and he was only one of the dying friends she had nurtured. "I just have a talent for it, I guess," she conceded when I asked.

But did Charlotte consider herself the risk-taker, the fount of wisdom, the wise woman we all saw her as? No—like many of us, she saw herself as only having done what she had to do along the way.

In the meantime, the main thing on her mind was getting the town of Eureka Springs off its ass—"town wrangling," as she called it. She had already started a Sunday-night movie series, with movies projected onto the side of a downtown building, though not without a fight from the members of the town council, one of whom complained that the theater curtains—*painted* on the side of the building—might get moldy.

The next time I received a manuscript from her, it was wrapped in a wrinkled Bette Davis scarf, held together by a pink button that read *There are no rules.* She also enclosed a copy of *The Lovely County Citizen* with the headline, BAD CHARLOTTE, above a piece that described how she was shaking up the town.

6.

One can never consent to creep when one feels the impulse to soar.

—HELEN KELLER

Rebel Girl, or Undercover in Academe. "You write like you're following yourself around," Courtney commented to me once, and it's true that I might have been one of the first volunteers for a reality show on a writer at her desk.

Yet letting yourself be seen as you truly are may still be the biggest risk of all. And it's one we take all the time in Zona Rosa.

Some of my acquaintances—but none of the Zona Rosans—were amazed when I let Connie take years' worth of my personal journals—cartons and cartons of them—home with her to use as source material for her Ph.D. dissertation on women writers and journal-keeping.

Connie, a gorgeous blonde with alabaster skin, was no stranger to risk herself. She had grown up hard and emotionally fatherless, with a beloved mother who worked as a waitress until her death. After that, Connie did whatever it took to get the education she knew would make the difference, from being a phone sex worker ("Boring!") to being a teaching assistant, while living with the Malaysian banker boyfriend who was the subject of her chick-lit novels. Indeed, I constantly marveled at her ability to switch from humorist to academic, thrilling to her achievements in both.

Connie wanted to write about women writers and journal-keeping, using Anaïs Nin's diaries, for which, along with her affair with Henry Miller, she is famous, and my unpublished journals as sources. As we sat at my dining room table, some of the journals laid out before us, and Connie's boy-toy assistant searching my attic for more boxes of the tomes I had kept for thirty-five years, I felt the twinge I feel before any unknown endeavor. After all, I had already refused the journals to a university that wanted them for their library, using the excuse that I needed them as source material.

But as I explored my feelings aloud with Connie, I realized

that it was primarily the newer—the rawer and less resolved—journals that I felt reluctant to share. As she and her assistant hurried off with a hunk spanning ten years, I didn't know that (as often happens with what at first feels risky) I would soon be so comfortable with her process that I would be giving her the more recent journals as well.

Over the months, as the trust between us grew, our collaboration became a source of joy: knowing more about each other only deepened our friendship. As I avidly read the chapters she sent each month to get my approval on the quotes she had taken from my journals, I had a new view of myself, as seen through her eyes. "Do you realize how much you identify with animals in your dreams?" she asked, pointing out what I had never realized, despite my interest in totem animals. And she paid me the ultimate compliment, telling me that yes, I had achieved my major life goal, despite all the messiness along the way: "You are by far more liberated, more resistant to patriarchy, than Anaïs ever was!" True, I could barely believe the powerful quotes she'd managed to extract from my daily accounts, from the craziness that was my life—as I read them, *I* was even impressed by me!

Along the way Connie made our project more fun by sending the chunks of her manuscript in shocking pink envelopes, inscribed with purple felt-tip pen, sealed with heart-shaped pussycat stickers. By the time her dissertation was pronounced brilliant by her academic advisors, we in Zona Rosa felt as if we were getting our own Ph.D.'s.

But even more exciting were the credos on life, work, and men Connie shared with us at our retreat in the South of France. As she lay back on the couch in her usual Botticelli pose, wearing what she calls one of her "floaty things," the aquamarine tattoo of a seal—her totem animal—showing on a white breast, she read from a series of knee-jerk reactions, followed by her own personal truths:

1. Nice girls get approval. *I would rather have respect.*
2. Women shouldn't take up too much room, or laugh too loudly. *Personal space and guffaws are good for you.*
3. Don't shine too brightly—you might make others jealous. *Stars don't question themselves.*
4. Line your nest only with unassuming feathers. *Vibrant colors and shiny objects help your wings grow bigger.*
5. Don't feel comfortable in your own skin until you've dieted yourself into nonexistence. *Sumptuous figures are more interesting.*
6. The tits in porno movies are the only perfect ones; make yours match by any means necessary. *I'm grateful for my healthy, voluptuous breasts!*
7. Marriage is better than living together. *Better for **him.***
8. The man should have an orgasm at all times; yours are optional. *I like to come first—and I let him know it.*
9. Men are more entitled to achieve their goals than women. *Men are no more—and no less—entitled to achieve their goals than us.*
10. It's okay to be struggling in a net as long as you look cute in all that mesh. *Do I look like a fish to you?*
11. Wear the collar of your class; bow to the moneyed. *This attitude compromises your potential.*
12. And if you get a Ph.D. in the humanities, you should make a career out of teaching because it's respectable and provides a regular income. *I would rather make a career out of my talent for creative writing—academies are called institutions for a reason!*

7.

The best way to make your dreams come true is to wake up.

—PAUL VALÉRY

We Need to Be More Like Cats, Tails High in the Air, Pursuing Our Own Truths, the Need to Be Ladylike Be Damned. It's true that people are sometimes in awe of writers, because writers are people who think. And like psychologists, they also observe. Though the women in Zona Rosa love it when other women are bright, it's not generally popular for women to have sharp edges, or even too much ambition (think Hillary Clinton). Most women prefer to be perceived as either nurturing and approachable or beautiful and mysterious (think Jackie Kennedy, her grace under pressure), images that pay off in the patriarchal world.

Indeed, many of us would be hesitant to remark, as Zona Rosan Marianne L. did to a car salesman while road-testing a new Nissan Maxima, "It's very nice. But where would I put my chain saw?"

And yes, it sometimes serves our purposes to keep those around us comfortable. When I was single, I often told men I had just met that I was a schoolteacher rather than a writer, which I knew might intimidate them. Indeed, my ability to look feminine while remaining strong inside felt like money in the bank. As a friend observed, "They think you'll be malleable because you look so girly. Then they find out that you've got a core of steel."

Zane endeared himself to me by *not* being intimidated— and by reading *Fatal Flowers* within days of our first night together, then calling to discuss it with me. "I want to have some kind of relationship with you," he said, despite my having an evident—and even contrary—brain.

Sometimes our unwillingness to tell our truths comes from our fear of rocking the boat, *our* boat, the one we've voluntarily set sail in. We're like one of those fluffy little dogs, carried along in someone's purse, and reluctant to give up our perch.

But if we had to deny our powers of experience and observation, novels like *The Nanny Diaries,* not to speak of those of Edith Wharton or Jane Austen, wouldn't exist. Nor would *Nickel and Dimed,* Barbara Ehrenreich's edgy account of trying to live for a year off blue-collar jobs in which she often yearned for knee pads while scrubbing marble foyers as her well-off women employers stood over her.

Yet isn't this one of the things we're taught as women? Not to be too sharp, too critical, too smart? Always to be "sweet and nice," not to offend, or make anyone uncomfortable at any cost—in other words, not to take verbal and intellectual risks? But as Dr. Phil says of marriage, "The moment you have to stop being yourself in a relationship, the cost is too high." And the same can be said of our intellectual lives, our relationship to the world.

After all, we don't live in a country where we're likely to be jailed or tortured for speaking out. Unlike Taslima Nasrin, the Bangladeshi poet who questioned Islam and its effects on women, we won't have a fatwa put on our heads and have to flee to a faraway country. Unlike women in some Latin American countries, we are unlikely to be "disappeared" for our political incorrectness.

True, some women have been—temporarily—silenced when others politely but pointedly (the worst way!) turned away from what they have to say. Nancy Venable Raine describes sitting beside a well-dressed woman at a luncheon who turned to her to remark, "I read your article in *The New York Times Magazine* about your rape. It was well written. But do you think people really want to read about things like that?" Nancy was in the middle of a book, and it was months before she could write again. But write she did, finally publishing her moving *After Silence: Rape and My Journey Back* to rave reviews.

Too often we remain paralyzed by niceness, because we fear what Naomi Wolf described in a commencement address to women students: "What's the worst thing that will happen? So you might get called a bitch, or aggressive, or a slut, or the hostess will change the subject. . . . Then, once you are not immobilized by niceness . . . people *will* yell at you. They *will* interrupt you, put you down, try to make you feel small, and suggest it's a personal problem. And the world won't end. . . . And you will lose some friends and some lovers, and find you don't miss them, and new ones will find you."

But, as she said in conclusion, "You will still go dancing all night, still flirt and dress up and party. . . . And as time goes on you will know with surpassing certainty that there is only one thing more dangerous and frightening and harmful to your well-being than speaking your truth. And that is the certain psychic death of not speaking."

8.

Chief of all dangers attending this new development of feminine freedom is the intoxication which comes with unfettered liberty.

—UNKNOWN, CA. 1914

Women Who Think Too Much:
A Cautionary Tale of the Wrong Sort

"Honey," I confessed, "I've been thinking . . ."

"I know you've been thinking," my husband said, "and I want a divorce!"

"But honey, surely it's not that serious."

"It is serious," [he] said, lower lip aquiver. "You think as much as college professors, and college professors don't make any money!"

"That's a faulty syllogism," I said impatiently. . . . "I'm going to the library," I snarled as I stomped out the door.

I headed for the library, in the mood for some Nietzsche, with NPR on the radio. I roared into the parking lot and ran up to the big glass doors—they didn't open. . . .

As I sank to the ground clawing at the unfeeling glass, whimpering for Zarathustra, a poster caught my eye. "Friend, is heavy thinking ruining your life?" it asked.

You probably recognize the line. It comes from the standard Thinker's Anonymous poster. Which is why I am what I am today: a recovering thinker.

Though our heroine saves her job, and her marriage, by giving up thinking, Martha Baker, the book reviewer, journalist, and former Zona Rosan who forwarded this message from St. Louis, is personally addicted to thinking and proud of it.

But like a lot of patriarchal humor, the story cut a bit too close to the quick for many of us because one of the risks we're often most reluctant to take is to let ourselves be as smart as we are. Eve's big sin was her willingness to risk death in order to eat from the tree of knowledge. She wanted, above all, to know things—and doing so is still a big boo-boo for women. But not letting ourselves know them can be dangerous for us as writers—especially since art itself is an act of aggression, even anarchy.

9.

> All good fortune is a gift of the gods, and ... you don't win the favor of the ancient gods by being good, but by being bold.
>
> —ANITA BROOKNER

Chutzpah Chicks, or Unleashing Your Inner Bitch. "Don't you know those are the tool of the oppressor?" Maggie, eighty-six, leaned over to say as I perused the note cards decorated with red stilettos that Jenny, knowing my passion for shoes, had just given me. Some women can't be squashed, and Maggie is one of those.

At the International Women's Writing Guild conference at Skidmore College, 2004, I noticed that the women who were former nuns (some were also lesbians) didn't appear to suffer the same lack of confidence with which we heteros, long infected with the need to please, are engraved. "Angry women who know what they want are dangerous women!" one commented with approval from the podium. "Those babies"—your creative projects— "are going to start tumbling out of your vulva—yes, your *vulva!*" she shouted to the group to hoots and fingers raised in a V for Vulva—or was it Victory?

But not every convent is a Smith College in nun's clothing. In her memoir, *The Spiral Staircase: My Climb out of Darkness,*

theologian Karen Armstrong writes about how life as a novi-
tiate led her to become the scholar, author, and renowned theologian she is today—but only after her body and psyche
rebelled over and over against the rigidity to which she struggled to submit, berating herself every step of the way.

The research regarding what our repressed rage costs us is
well established: women are four times more likely to experience depression than men, who often act theirs out through
drinking, anger, and violence. (Though there's less depression
among working women: upper middle-class women are more
likely to suffer under patriarchy than blue-collar women because of social expectations, historian Gerda Lerner writes in
Why History Matters.)

In *The Road Less Traveled,* Dr. M. Scott Peck describes two
kinds of people: those who project outward, blaming everyone
but themselves for everything that happens in their lives, and
those who turn inward, thinking they're responsible for everything, no matter how clearly they've been wronged. I don't
know of research on this phenomenon, but I suspect women
make up a larger percentage of the latter category, as evidenced
by the multitude of women's magazines we consume each
month, telling us how to perfect ourselves inside and out, while
the guys in our lives are still looking up sports scores.

Ronnie always looked inward to see how she could have
behaved differently when confronted with oppression. Even
when she had good reason for anger—a husband who rejected
her out of the blue after she helped raise his teenage sons, or an
on-site landlord who sexually harassed her into giving up her
apartment (she dutifully continued paying the rent until the
lease was up)—she still looked for ways to change herself. And

while this is a good first step, it can leave us feeling that our real feelings aren't legitimate.

When I suggested that she unleash her Inner Bitch by doing the exorcise "If the Ball of My Rage Unraveled," I could feel her resistance. Like a lot of us, Donna feared being even more overwhelmed and out of control if she poured her "irrational" feelings out on paper. I recognized her need for a stiff upper lip, to be in control, as I had often shared it.

But I also knew that taking that risk works: that once our rage (or whatever feeling is nagging at us) is outside us in words, we can put it up on a shelf, so to speak, where we can take it down, turn it around, and look at it when we wish. As Pamella put it, "If I don't want to pull the thread on that ball of yarn yet, I don't have to. But I still know it's there."

When my daughter Lulu sent me a Web page, "My Cat Hates You," I suddenly got it as I looked at the photos of snarling felines. Cats are in touch with their feelings, feel free to express displeasure, even anger, while dogs are people pleasers—the very thing we women are expected to be. Yet the true feminine may lie in the feistiness required to be truly ourselves—think of a tigress protecting her territory, her young—rather than in conceding to cultural imperatives.

Or as Sandy declared in a Zona Rosa workshop in Eureka Springs, speaking of how she had put herself on hold, "It's my fucking turn now!" After the group's spontaneous applause, I said, "And that's what will be written on our first Zona Rosa T-shirt!"

10.

You were once wild. Don't let them tame you.

—ISADORA DUNCAN

Have you ever seen a cat lying in the grass at three A.M. on a moonlit night? Sometimes, if I wake to go to the bathroom, I see my pet, Amber, reclining amid the weeds, surveying her kingdom as confidently as though it were the middle of the day. If there are dangers in the tall grasses around her, she doesn't acknowledge them. She is at home in the world in a way few humans are. And being female, it seems, never impedes her adventuring instincts.

"The two things people—especially women—think they need and don't are security and defenses," a therapist friend once said to me. And when we begin to take risks in writing and in life, our fears fall like dominoes. Each incidence of putting ourselves in peril, however slight, extends itself to our writing hands, our ability to let our ideas flow, no matter how wild and crazy those ideas may be. Soon, we too are less afraid of both of the world and the blank page.

Knee-jerk Reaction #3: Mistaking the excitement of a possible challenge for a fear to which we should succumb. Thinking that we are more fragile than we are. Imagining that certain risks are only for other people.

PILATES ON PAPER

If I Was Really Wild I Would . . . what would I do? You might ask for a marriage sabbatical (or, better yet, tactfully tell your significant other of your plans) . . . not make homemade pumpkin pie for Thanksgiving dinner, or the Goddess forbid, make it at all . . . buy yourself a fur coat, or a little yellow convertible, instead of getting the kitchen repainted . . . wear a beret, or a flower in your hair . . . paint your front door pink (as I did recently, despite Zane's protests) . . . take that trip around the world—*alone.* Then ask yourself, *What's holding me back?* Now choose three of your "wild" dreams, and make a plan for making each of them come true, starting with something you can do today toward your goal (shop for the perfect fake flower, go to Home Depot for that wild paint color, call a travel agent to check out ticket prices), no matter how small. In addition, list the obstacles, both internal and external, that you see in your path, and write out the actions and affirmations you'll use to counter them.

What Would Lauren Hutton Do? Or Scarlett O'Hara (though not that mealy-mouthed Melanie), or even the heroine of the Victoria Holt romance you read last week? Who is your favorite risk-taking movie heroine? Uma Thurman in *Kill Bill II*? Linda Hamilton in the *Terminator* movies? Or Demi Moore in *G. I. Jane*?—now there was a girl who could kick ass! (Thelma and Louise don't qualify. I don't think women have to kill themselves in order to be free!) Whose boldness, chutzpah, takes your breath away? Pick your own role model, and every time you feel a fear, ask yourself what *she* would do.

The Wild Boy—or Girl—Inside You. When I dreamed of a Johnny Depp look-alike, a brown-eyed boy I wanted to run away to Mexico with, I knew immediately who he was: that Wild Boy Inside Me, and the person I really wanted to run away with was my real self! When you receive messages from the universe, in the form of dreams or Freudian slips—those words that pop out when we think we meant something else—about your wildest, deepest self, the one who says yes, I *can* move to the South of France, get a divorce, make it on my own, or just have other plans the next time my mother-in-law invites herself to visit—pay attention!

Or, have you had, like Temple and Pamella, **a Breakdown That Turned Out to Be a Breakthrough?** When your body and brain have shut down, then gone into overdrive, giving you messages as to your truths, your need for change? When I have a pain anywhere, I ask my body what it's telling me, and it always answers. A pain in the neck is, often as not, a someone who is a literal pain in the neck; hunched shoulders mean I'm shoulder-ing too much, like the women in Amy Cutler's paintings (see chapter 2), who are depicted as literal pack animals. As Dr. Phil told his television audience, "Not writing it down is like looking at your face without a mirror," so make sure to commit your "breakdown" to paper. Then, describe the times when you've gone inside for answers, and followed through on them.

What Part Does Synchronicity Play in Your Life? Synchronic-ity, like love, requires recognition to bring it to life. Nikki Hardin realized hers when she saw the words *Skirt Factory* on the newly exposed wall of her building. Jossie dreamed of a house with a round room with shelves for her books, knowing that she would write her long-planned novel there. When she found the exact house a few months later, she bought it; now her books are in place and the novel is flowing. After supporting her family for years after her husband's stroke in his early thirties, Jane went to a psychic. "I'm desperate," she said, "can you help me?" "You will write," the woman answered, looking into her eyes. Jane, who had never thought of writing, was baffled, and felt she had wasted her money. But when she saw a writing course offered near her home, she immediately signed up; today, she writes and teaches writing full-time. *Have you ever followed a hunch? If so, how did it work out? And if not, why?*

What I've Given Up to My Tribe. In her book, *Rich Is Better*, Tessa Albert Warschaw suggests an exercise in which we list what we were required to do, forbidden to do, and permitted to do as a child. Then she asks that we make the same lists about what we require, forbid, and permit ourselves to do as adults. Most of us are amazed when we see that our lists are much the same. We grew up in tribes, clans, families—and to reclaim ourselves, make our own rules, takes thought and effort. Listing the rules you grew up with, and considering whether they still have a place in your life, is a good beginning. Ask yourself what you allow yourself to question—and what you don't.

If I Didn't Feel Guilty, I would . . . This is the one we women are prey to, big-time. Be aware that breaking with the values of the past, the way our mothers and grandmothers did things, may induce guilt—or what a therapist friend calls "the useless emotion." Indeed, we can even feel guilty about achieving more than our forebears—being the first in our family to go to grad school or Europe. But guilt, like shame, is a feeling that we can shout down, until it creeps away, whimpering in a corner. List what you'd do if guilt wasn't a factor. *Important:* Many of those rules, especially those to do with our "responsibilities," knee-jerk nurturing, hold us back from that sparkling highway to our destiny.

If the Ball of My Rage Unraveled. When I was mad at Zane, I wrote that he "was a ball of static," an image that felt just right. What would you say or write if you let yourself go, and what's the worst thing that will happen if you do? As women, it's hard for us to disappoint others, or even to *appear* to be adversarial. "Every year I try to convince myself that, yes, I really do want to cook that big Christmas dinner. But then I'm in the kitchen, up to my elbows in stuffing—and fuming while everyone else is having a great time," Jalaine confessed to the group. This year, she and her artist daughter are in New York for the holidays, going to shows and taking in some galleries. Then there are the moments when we feel compelled to speak out, despite the consequences. Rehearse beforehand and if those stoppers *sick, bad, crazy, selfish, stupid,* or *ugly* appear to intimidate you, swat them over and over with your new labels: *courageous, honest, amazing,* and *beautiful.*

ADVENTURE BOOK THERAPY: HOW SOME GUTSY FEMMES HELPED ME LEAVE MY OWN FEARS BEHIND

According to the dictionary, "awe and reverence" are among the meanings of the word *fear.* And there's nothing like reading nonfiction books that thrill us with the exploits of women who are wilder than we are to crush our own trepidations to smithereens. Just recounting the stories of these courageous authors thrills me afresh, making me feel I can do anything.

Indeed, I have a shelf of such books, which I use to inspire myself. And whenever possible, I pick authors and subjects whose risks are more extreme than any I'm likely to embark on myself. (Though not always: in my own true-life adventure story, *Sleeping with Soldiers: In Search of the Macho Man,* I work as one of the first women aboard an offshore oil rig, and learn more about living among tough guys than many women learn in a lifetime.)

Among my favorites is *Desert Places,* in which Robyn Davidson (who had already thrilled me with *Tracks,* her account of training three wild camels and walking 1,300 miles of Australian outback alone with them) travels for a year with nomads in the Indian Desert.

In *Granny D: Walking across America in My Ninetieth Year,* Doris Haddock, activist for campaign reform, treks from the Mojave Desert to New Hampshire to make her point, wittily regaling us with her aches, pains, and even flirtations along the way.

I also devoured the recently reprinted *Travels with Myself and Another,* in which intrepid journalist and war correspondent Martha Gellhorn (the beautiful first wife of Ernest Hemingway, or U.C., Unwanted Companion, as she calls him throughout the book) takes up such breathtaking tasks as searching for Nazi submarines in a rickety hired boat in the Caribbean during World War II.

In *Shutterbabe,* Deborah Copaken Kogan starts off by describing a large man in the back of the truck in which she rides on her way to a war zone, sitting on her backpack and crushing her tampons. Throughout the book, Kogan, single and in her early twenties, describes her adventures and misadventures, many sexual.

As I sat in bed reading *Looking for Trouble: One Woman, Six Wars, and a Revolution,* I was aghast—and delighted—at foreign correspondent Leslie Cockburn's account of more than precarious moments in Somalia, Afghanistan, and Nicaragua, searching out truths in places where the State Department had forbidden her to go. Once, seven months pregnant, she had to have an extra large flak jacket made: another time, she leaves her six-month-old baby behind, only occasionally flinching or wondering what she is doing there.

At one point, she calmly answers her nine-year-old's question about what would happen to her if both her mommy and daddy (also a war correspondent) were killed, by saying that plans had been made, that she and her brother would be well cared for (contrast *that* kind of over-the-top parental fear with those to which many of us are prey). My only question as I read was whether she had room in her backpack for moisturizer.

The queen of traveling alone though she has children must be Alexandra Fuller, who, in *Scribbling the Cat,* goes home to Zimbabwe, once Rhodesia (from Wyoming, where she lives with her husband and two kids) to visit her parents, and ends up traveling for weeks with a former Rhodesian soldier who is not only—along with his buddies from the war—suffering from a severe case of testosterone poisoning, but is also crazed by his experiences. In the process, Fuller shares quarters with an overattentive lion kept as a pet by one of these guys.

Fuller's first memoir, *Don't Let's Go to the Dogs Tonight,* shows how she got that gutsy. In it she describes growing up in Rhodesia with her ex-pat British parents; at age nine, she learns how to break down and put together an automatic rifle, in case her parents get killed and she has to fend for herself.

In *Nothing to Declare*, Mary Morris lives for a year, getting to know the natives, in the town of San Miguel de Allende, Mexico; in a later book, *Wall to Wall: From Beijing to Berlin by Rail*, Morris discovers that she's pregnant while traveling alone on the Orient Express—which must be the ultimate place in which to experience morning sickness!

The journey Hannah Nyala describes in *Point Last Seen* begins partly because of her desire to protect her children and herself from the all-too-familiar territory of abuse at the hands of the man she married at seventeen. When her husband drives her and their one-year-old deep into the desert, he forces her to leave the truck at gunpoint, then drives away with the baby. Despite his predictions that she will die there, Nyala saves herself by following the tire tracks back to civilization—an experience that leads to her work as a rescue worker and tracker in the Mojave Desert, a mission through which she leads us, step by riveting step. Along the way, she gives us a piece of advice that also applies to writing: "Don't become a tracker if you're not willing to do the dirt time."

In *An Indian Attachment*, British writer Sarah Lloyd, casually making her way around India, meets a young Sikh on a train and takes him up on his offer to visit his village; she ends up living there with him and his family in their mud hut for a year, until, despite his expectations that she will remain as his wife, she decides it's time to go back to England. And in *Castaway*, Scottish author Lucy Irvine answers an ad asking for a woman to spend a year on an uninhabited Pacific Island and ends up spending a disastrous twelve months with a man she comes to hate, even before starvation set in (outcomes don't have to be good to exhilarate us).

But some of my favorite heroines haven't been so extreme; in fact, they could be you or me. In *Without Reservations,* Alice Steinbach writes postcards home to herself, describing her experiences, including her fears while traveling abroad alone for the first time after a midlife divorce. In *Natural Opium*—her marvelous description of how the best travel feels—Diane Johnson, novelist (*Le Mariage* and *Le Divorce*), writes of tobogganing in terror down a steep slope in Switzerland after a dinner party at which it's announced as the only way down.

Nor are my inspirations confined to first-person accounts of the twentieth and twenty-first centuries. In her classic *The Wilder Shores of Love,* published in 1954, Lesley Blanch writes "four seething . . . studies in headlong nonconformity" (as *The New Yorker* said at the time) of Victorian women who found their destiny in the East, including Isabel Burton, the plump, obsessively in love sixth wife of the notorious Richard Burton of Arabia (one of his twenty-seven languages was said to be "pornography"), and the outrageous Isabelle Eberhardt, who drank, smoked hashish, and, dressed as a man, illicitly entered mosques despite her sex.

Other English woman adventurers of the time were Gertrude Bell and Freya Stark. In Janet Wallach's biography *Desert Queen,* Gertrude Bell—after failing to nab a husband during her three "seasons" on the London scene—does everything except what was expected of her as a female of her station. Calling herself "the Female Lawrence of Arabia" (also the title of one of her books; she was a good friend of T. E. Lawrence) and fluent in Persian and Arabic, she was able to influence sheiks and tribal and religious leaders, and is said to have been the catalyst for present-day troubles in the Middle East. It was she who drew new boundaries for the region on a piece of tracing paper.

Freya Stark, the peripatetic heroine of Jane Fletcher Geniesse's *Passionate Nomad*, wandered alone in the Middle East, from Persia to Yemen, discovering lost cities, learning Arabic, and, along the way, creating an anti-Nazi intelligence system. Eventually she received awards from the Royal Geographic Society. Most important, she lived to tell about her experiences— and to inspire us with her boldness.

While some of these books may be out of print, the inter-library loan service at your local library, Amazon.com, eBay, or other sources will doubtless make it possible for you, too, to thrill to these women's exploits, along the way expanding your own idea of the possible.

CHAPTER FOUR

WHEN I'VE STEPPED OUT IN FAITH

How Patience, Perseverance, and Some Other Virtues Your
Grandmama Taught You Can Help You in Writing and Life

1.

COME TO THE EDGE.
We can't. We are afraid.
COME TO THE EDGE.
We can't. We will fall!
COME TO THE EDGE.
And they came.
And he pushed them.
And they flew.

—GUILLAUME APOLLINAIRE

I like to tell new Zona Rosans about how Madeleine Albright,
young and newly married, gave birth to twins who had to stay
in an incubator for eight weeks. Did she mope around, waiting
for her babies to come home, decorating and redecorating the

nursery while dealing with the aftermath of birth, as many of us would have done? No, she used that time to take an intensive Russian language course—this, years before she knew of her illustrious future as secretary of state.

I also talk about my daughter Lulu who had such moments in her own life. She spent the year she was twelve, even before she was diagnosed with epilepsy, scarfing down books on the brain like some girls her age would consume Judy Blume novels (she also spent part of that year teaching herself German well enough to have a pen pal in Germany). Little did she know that she would later become a neuropharmacologist, specializing in brain research, and after that, a psychiatrist treating the diseases that begin in that amazing organ—as well as a world traveler who speaks five languages.

Last, I describe how supermodel Jerry Hall got her start. While she was growing up tall and gorgeous in Texas, with a gorgeous mom and two equally gorgeous long-legged sisters, Jerry's dad was a brutal alcoholic, but her mother kept things together, making all three girls beautiful clothes via her talent for couture sewing. When Jerry won seven hundred dollars in an essay competition at age fifteen, she told her parents she wanted to go to Paris—to which her dad screamed, "*No way!*" But her mother colluded with her, secretly making her a to-die-for wardrobe based on the latest Paris fashions, and before Jerry knew it, she was off to the City of Light, superstardom, and the likes of Mick Jagger, never to come home again except to visit her precious mom and sisters.

As the Zona Rosans look at me, puzzled—what was the relationship between these stories?—I ask them to describe in writing three important moments in their own lives, when, like Madeleine Albright or Lulu, they experienced precognition, or unconscious guidance about something they might need in the future. Then, look back for a moment of epiphany. And last, write about when they stepped out in faith, as had Madeleine, Lulu, and Jerry Hall, not to speak of Jerry's mom.

As the Reverend Desmond Tutu, speaking at Emory University, said of Moses and his followers beside the Red Sea, someone had to step in first before the waters would part.

In this chapter, we address the biggest challenge of all—that of stepping out in faith and actually doing something. If that thing is writing, it's about why we write, how we write, and what we do with our writing when we're through. More important, it's about how we persevere when the inevitable obstacles appear, whether or not we receive the encouragement—praise, recognition, even publication—we all hope for. Sometimes it's about the carelessness of just letting ourselves be swept along—the times when we forget that time is short, that the moment is *now*. At other times, it's about long-established habits of thinking and feeling that may be holding us back. But it's really all about one thing—*character*, and how it works for or against us in view of achieving our writing and other dreams.

As Lance Armstrong titled one of his books, *It's Not about the Bike*, it's about us.

2.

You are what your deep driving desire is.
As your desire is, so is your will.
As your will is, so is your deed.
As your deed is, so is your destiny.

—ANONYMOUS

Why Riding Your Horse in the Direction She's Going Is Not Always a
Good Idea. Ronnie came up with such great concepts, embodying
them in images that were so visceral that just hearing her describe
them gave me a gut wrench, as we say in the South. As when she
told us, the day after her divorce was final, her idea for "Breakfast
at Epiphanies," or the box of crayons God had handed her, including the black one she was holding that day in Zona Rosa.

It was one of those ideas that had come to her while ironing someone else's husband's shirts. At first, right after her husband asked for a divorce, and still in the grips of the torture of
his passive-aggressive machinations, she had scribbled some of
her ideas in longhand, but she hadn't had time yet, she said, to
write this one down, nor to tackle the learning curve of using
the computer her stepson had rebuilt and set up for her. Instead she had a literary vision that she kept embroidering and
re-embroidering in her mind. "To write all the time!" she had
replied when I asked about her ideal life.

"Take them off! Take them off right now!" chorused the
other Zona Rosans, more concerned that Ronnie was still wearing her wedding and engagement rings than that she hadn't
written down such a great idea. The cacophony went on to become a debate on whether wearing wedding rings at all was a

good thing (I hadn't worn mine for five years, I told them, and I had felt much freer, more myself without them.)

But I was wondering why it was taking Ronnie so long to make the small efforts that I suspected would add to her healing. Why wasn't she writing down her great ideas? Was it the anger she was still resisting facing? It seemed she was like Carol, an adult student in my class at Lynchburg College in Virginia, who had told me that her ideas were "like golden globes, shining in the distance," and that she knew she could access them, but she chose not to do that now. I recalled how I suspected that Carol was afraid that looking at her ideas too closely and actually getting into the messy process of putting them on paper would somehow take something away from them as fantasy—a place she could go whenever she needed to.

I had long before learned that if I could find a concrete image for my discomfort when I was suffering, my distress would quickly leave me no matter how dire the situation, embedding itself within the image; as soon as it became raw material, something I could work with, my pain moved outside me and onto the page. Many of these images came to me in dreams, which I recorded each morning in my journal—an activity that would enhance their writing skills, I told the Zona Rosans, since dreams were usually so weird that writing them down in exact detail was an exercise in precision. Once, I had even been able to begin a whole book about the painful circumstance of my two adult children's illnesses, after dreaming and recording that I was being fucked by an ugly green frog with a barbed penis. It was a source of healing that I found I could depend on. And as a writer, I especially revered the words on the page, the way they contained what I had once felt and imagined.

But what about Ronnie and Carol? Was merely acknowledging their images, visions, genius, enough for them? Could they get the same result *sans* all the work? Were the evenings Ronnie was now spending with her new lover, drinking at the local watering holes, watching him play pool, more healing than sitting in front of her computer, putting her brilliance into words?

Yet knowing the truth of one of our credos, "Revision revises us," I thought they would probably be more blessed by making the effort. In *The Path of Least Resistance*, Robert Fritz describes how we often set a goal for ourselves, then take a path that inevitably leads us in a different direction. Stephen Covey, author of *The Seven Habits of Highly Effective People*, says the same thing: "Don't take a map of Chicago if you want to go to New York."

For a while, Ronnie was riding high on her writing. But alas, as the months went by, I also watched as the sex object began to take precedence. She was a natural caretaker and a superb cook, and soon she was making his lunch for him before work, and cooking gourmet meals each night. On the weekends she had to rest up, go with him, say, to his pool tournament, and shop at Best Buy.

It wasn't the first time I felt frustrated at watching an infinitely talented woman let her best stuff slide gradually—ever so gradually—down the drain in favor of the Bondage of the Pink. As Dr. Benjamin Spock wrote, "Women are subordinated inch by inch." And usually, we don't even notice it.

3.

The price of anything is the amount of life you exchange for it.

—HENRY THOREAU

A Rain Check Life

Have you ever been shopping to buy something advertised at a special price, only to find that the store is out of it? But they're willing to give you a rain check? A brightly colored little paper that you can turn in later and purchase that specific product at the advertised price when they restock . . . ?

The life I was supposed to have was all sold out, so the universe gave me a rain check . . . Could it have been a foolish marriage at nineteen? Dropping out of college to support my husband who was to finish first, then I'd go? When the marriage officially ended four years later, he still hadn't finished his two years. Could it be not being able to keep a child because I'd been immunized for German measles, not knowing I was pregnant? Could it be those twenty-five-plus years I spent working at something I was good at, but that I didn't really like?

Usually rain checks are only good for a couple of months. I've kept mine for years. This may not have been exactly what I would have chosen for myself, but there is still time to change. I'm going to the store and turn in my rain check for the life I'm supposed to have.

When we read Jan E.'s piece at a Zona Rosa meeting a half-dozen years ago at Carol O.'s house, we were excited, recognizing what we assumed was a breakthrough. Because the piece makes us think, I've read it aloud to many Zona Rosa groups since.

But when I heard several years later that despite her

epiphany, Jan hadn't worked toward what I assumed were her writing dreams, I felt sad.

"She hasn't written anything since," reported Carol O., who had kept in touch. "While during the same period I've written two books, written and published numerous short pieces, and gone back to school."

I didn't know Jan well enough to assess why she hadn't gone forward with her writing. Was it an inner "no," telling her that writing wasn't the path for her after all? Was she one of the "yes, but" people, who always have a reason why they can't do it now? Or, as Martha Beck describes in her book *Finding Your Own North Star,* was she unable to imagine it—step by step— therefore she couldn't do it? When Jan wrote to me years later, she said she had become a full member of her Indian tribe and was doing crafts—that anything creative satisfied her.

Yet my pang at hearing about Jan's state was a familiar one, since even the most talented people often refuse to take the actions that would as surely lead to their goals as a super-accurate road map. We even have an exorcise for it: "What Do I Gain by Not Doing What I Want to Do?" And some of the gains we've come up with range from the trivial to the self-protective, from more time to watch TV, shop, or play with others to not having to deal with rejection.

Indeed, I'm prey to yearning after those trivial gains myself, such as this morning when, instead of writing this chapter, I thought how nice it would be to sit around watching the *Oprah* and *Dr. Phil* shows I've taped over the past few weeks. (When I did allow myself a peek during breakfast, what I saw—women who'd swapped lives, husbands, and kids on *Oprah*—made me jump up, ready to pursue my destiny, which right now is this book!)

There was a clue in her piece as to why Jan hadn't gone forward: she might have been mulling too much over the past. In Zona Rosa, we're not allowed to look back, unless it's to give ourselves credit for what we've already done—even if it was only getting to a writing workshop for the first time! As fiftyish actress Catherine Deneuve said, "I'm too young for regrets"—a great motto for all of us, whether we're twenty-three or ninety-three.

And as for Carol O., she had long before developed the Carol Credos:

I allow myself to write when I have an idea, at any hour of the day or night, anywhere, at least to get the idea down.

I allow myself to jump over the beginning if I'm stuck and to write whatever scenes or words or images that grab me, in any order that they come.

I allow myself to write with a dirty house. Especially if I have a burning idea. Writing is more important.

I allow myself to use weak words in order to get an idea onto the page as quickly as possible. I will not critique myself on the first draft. I can use the word "bad" or "very" or any other word to keep the flow going.

I allow myself to cry over a rejection, even a small one.

I allow myself a certain amount of avoidance tactics—cleaning, phone calls, e-mail, putzing—whatever I need for a certain amount of time—especially when I'm writing "truths" and I'm scared.

I allow myself to realize that ninety percent of writing goes on inside my head. I might be working on a concept, scene, dialogue, or theme for months before a word is written.

I allow myself to view my writing as a treat . . . it's my martini at the end of the day

4.

What we should do is write as though we're already dead.
                                              —NADINE GORDIMER

The Test. First, let me say that I would consider a lifetime spent writing worthwhile, even if we never published a word of it. As Zona Rosan Carolyn said, "Talking about writing is talking about how to live." And the healing I have seen in Zona Rosa through the years, and the way writing has helped me heal my own life, makes the act of writing seem like nothing short of a miracle. Indeed, I believe, like Alice W. Flaherty says in *The Midnight Disease: The Drive to Write, Writer's Block, and the Creative Brain,* that writing is *the* supreme achievement—and not because we may publish, or be on *Oprah*, but because of what it requires of us, which is nothing short of the best spiritual and mental gymnastics in the world. When we are writing, we are enjoying that magnificent organ, the brain, in a way to which only reading compares, and that, too, may pale beside it. (When people tell me they're great readers but have no desire to write, I always wonder where all that excitement goes.)

When I look at the first page of my journal each morning, where I list writing projects spanning the next ten years or more, I feel rich—in fact, I call my ideas for future work "money in the bank," as in mental and spiritual prosperity.

While others might experience this as pressure, I find pleasure in contemplating all those years of writing ahead. The measures I take to protect my body have everything to do with wanting the life I have to go on—and on. (My sister Anne and I are both health freaks, with vitamins and fresh fruits and veggies in proximity at all times; and though Anne is better at getting to the gym, sex and walking, as I constantly remind myself, are good exercise, too.)

Many thinkers have called writing an act that flies in the face of death, a chance at immortality. I chose writing—or it chose me—because I thought of it as something I could do forever, or at least as long as my brain is intact, as has been proven by many authors. I remember the shaky handwriting on the postcard I received from Nancy Mairs, one of my favorite memoirists, just before multiple sclerosis forced her to begin using a voice-activated computer. Jean-Dominique Bauby, the French editor of *Elle*—totally paralyzed at age forty-three—wrote *The Diving Bell and the Butterfly* by flicking his eyelids to indicate the letters of the alphabet to his patient assistant.

And every time we do an exorcise on the spot in the Zona Rosa I see a miracle. Moments before, we may have looked like sane, normally socialized women sitting in a room with little on our minds than chitchat during which the tinkle of voices, as usual, is reaching high C. Moments later, even the most reluctant of us are bent over our notebooks, madly scribbling, as though there wasn't time enough in the world to record what's inside us. Within fifteen minutes, these on-the-spot authors are raising their hands, vying for the time to stand and read aloud from their pieces, some of which inevitably take our collective breaths away.

I had learned long before, in my own writing life, to live by the acronym over my desk, JUST, or Just You Start Typing. I knew, too, from experience that the moments when I felt most resistant, most reluctant, were often the moments when the tide was about to come crashing back in—that there was no way, unless you are in a coma, and maybe not even then, that the mind is truly an empty room.

That our minds and souls are never really empty has been proven to me over and over when we write together, which makes me ask, *What happens to all that stuff when we're not writing it down?* I suspect that it's still there somewhere, churning and twisting, until it poisons our spirit, causing Carpal Tunnel of the Soul. And I, like many of the Zona Rosans, experience writing as a form of prayer, protecting us against that spiritual poison of not looking at and expressing ourselves.

5.

Flops are a part of life's menu and I'm never a girl to miss out on a course.

—ROSALIND RUSSELL

That said, there are also many writers in Zona Rosa who wish and deserve to publish the books on which they've worked so hard. Yet trying to get published for the first time is a lot like being back in junior high school. If you think your fear of rejection was bad back then—Does my hair look right? Is everyone looking at that spot on my forehead? Did he tell his buds what we did in the backseat last Friday night?—just wait until you start putting your "babies"—those babies that contain your deepest feelings, best ideas (to date), and all the skill you could muster at the time—out into the world. Like being in junior high school, it's a time of both change and exhilaration. We're uncertain of ourselves, but we're also excited about the possibilities.

At any given moment, many of the Zona Rosans— courageously, year after year—are writing first, then second and even third books, before finding a publisher. If there is a true test as a writer, this is it: continuing to believe in yourself, despite not yet having received validation from the world.

Janice, who had given up a high-profile career in South Carolina politics to marry a man with five children, one severely disabled with a terminal diagnosis, calls beginning to write her biggest risk yet: "No one writes fiction with a faint heart. You do it without a map and with the knowledge that even if you had one it wouldn't help. You don't do it because . . . you expect to get any kind of reward. You do it because there is something inside you that wants out."

One of the more painful parts of teaching creative writing is seeing genuinely talented people give up too quickly. Too often, questions from others—especially significant others— about whether we've been published or how much money we've made off our writing (and their expression of disbelief when we answer "none") get us off track. These days, one of the first things we do in Zona Rosa is rehearse some flippant answers for those nosy questions, in order to protect our dream.

Ruth worked on her clever yet poignant novel about growing up as the child of Holocaust survivors for five years, then received seven rejections from agents, the last of whom said she should cut back on the book's "*Police Academy II* humor." Instead of considering the agent's suggestion, Ruth flung off an angry letter in return, then quit writing to become an aerobics instructor, after which her stockbroker husband, who had never wanted her to write anyway—obviously, there was no money in it—gave her a diamond ring and took her on a trip to the Bahamas.

Even born writers like Adrienne and Courtney, with manuscript after manuscript under their beds, are paralyzed by fear of The Test. Adrienne even felt this way after having a novel published by a major publisher, and watching it fall through the cracks. Others, like Courtney, fall in love with their books and won't let go of them for ten years or more.

Kathleen M., a spirited redhead, was a reporter for an Afghan paper when her first husband was in foreign service. When not abroad, they enjoyed an exciting life in Washington, where he was a White House correspondent for Reuters News Service, and where Kathleen worked in foreign policy for the likes of Senator John Sherman Cooper of Kentucky (during the Vietnam War he was the first Republican senator to come out against the war), and as press secretary for the Joint Economic Committee chaired by Hubert Humphrey and Lloyd Bentsen. In 1972, she published *Spies behind the Pillars: Bandits at the Pass* under the name Kathleen Trautman to good reviews, a party at the National Press Club, and a second printing.

Now she and her second husband, a retired lawyer and part-time actor, live part of the year in Savannah and part in their house in the Dordogne area of southern France (as she described her lifestyle, we gasped with envy). But when she wrote a tender novel about a young Afghan girl after 9/11, she couldn't find a publisher, ended up self-publishing, and has been depressed about her writing prospects ever since. (I'm happy to report that after just one month in Zona Rosa,

Kathleen had hired a computer coach to help her get online—something she had resisted to date—and she was looking at redesigning her book's cover, as well as going back to her novel in progress.)

"I don't think they know how hard it is," my daughter Lulu commented at our retreat in France, thinking back over her childhood when I was a beginning writer. "I remember a lot of rejection." But like the pain of childbirth, all I recall is a time of excitement, rush after rush, peak after peak—a time when I felt fully alive, no matter what else was going on, my children and I bound together in a world of creativity. They cooked from *La Cuisine est un jeu d'enfants,* or *Cooking Is Child's Play,* a French cookbook illustrated by Jean Cocteau that is introduced with the words, "Children and artists disobey." Lily's specialty was "Souffle au Fromage," and the kids made eggshell collages, gluing the eggshells I saved for them to shirt cardboards with Elmer's glue, while I wrote the poems that began like small pregnancies in my head. We were in love with the arts, and writing was not a career, but a process, part of a lifestyle, and a source of joy.

Nevertheless, I was stunned with happiness when a small literary magazine accepted three poems; as the kids swam in a lake near our house, I sat watching them as though in a dream, still unable to believe that someone actually wanted to publish words I had written. "No expectations, no disappointments," a therapist friend had said to me, and I had taken that as my motto, leaving me free to enjoy that delicious sensation that Carol O. calls being "on the verge." Later, as I collected the inevitable box full of rejection slips, their effect quickly melted before my passion for creating the perfect poem—or at least the best poem I could.

Along the way, I learned that my single protection from the slings of rejection was a certainty deep inside me about my own personal criteria for a good piece of writing, something I would only develop over the years by reading and writing, and thinking about reading and writing (more about how to do this in chapter 9). If our writing comes up to our own high standards, as often as not rejection is not about us. When we take the attitude that "everything drives to the good of the work" and not to our egos, our dealings with the outside world become easier. In fact, we may even get some good advice along the way.

6.

Your work is to discover your work and then with all your heart to give yourself to it.

—BUDDHA

"My victory [a prestigious short story publication] was soon followed by a defeat," wrote the ever-effervescent Carol O., in one of the notes with which she keeps me updated as to her progress. "I received a stinging rejection letter for my book" (about caring for her mother at her home during her terminal illness). Ouch!

"I wrote about it, of course"—Carol O. has learned the value of putting our most painful feelings into words—"and moved on, but I've certainly lost my virginity when it comes to understanding the complexities of the book publishing industry. It's a tough market and without a name, it's very, very hard. The proverbial Catch-22: How do you get a name without a book or a book without a name?!"

Later, in her usual upbeat way, Carol described what she

was learning from her experiences: "All of this proves to me that my wandering in the wilderness was necessary, and that I've probably opened doors, created opportunities, and learned many valuable lessons . . . Nothing's wasted. I view God as being very economical—everything has a double/triple duty . . . I think my life is unfolding just as it should."

Yet it's a test for which those who've had successes in other areas aren't always prepared. Tracy, whom we met in chapter 1, deals on a daily basis with Tourette's syndrome and depression. But before she quit work to stay home with her two kids, she had also won the Best Writer of the Year Award three years in a row for advertising copywriting in Atlanta. Thus when after six exuberant months she finished her highly imaginative life-after-death novel, *The Bone Orchard Society*, and three months later received her first "no thanks" from the handpicked list of agents she had researched, her spirits plummeted. She could have given up then and there, had it not been for our support and her resilient spirit.

At Zona Rosa, we celebrate finishing *anything*—much less a major writing project—with applause, wine, and Foods of the Goddesses, rather than waiting around for the delayed gratification at the far end of the process, getting published. Which means we're pretty much celebrating and drunk on joy all the time (not to mention just plain drunk).

There's a little trick I recommend, one that I've found to be used by every writer I know: focus on new work-in-progress while you market what you've just finished. "You just keep writing, and you get better and better," prolific mystery writer Nevada Barr told *Writer Magazine,* citing the importance of going on to something new.

Yet it is a test through which virtually every published author has struggled. You may have heard about instant successes, such as the Italian sixteen-year-old who published a best-selling book about her sex life. And you've probably also been told what is usually closer to the truth, that what looks like "instant success" usually started with much hard work years and years before. Most of us first heard of Helen Fielding with the success of *Bridget Jones's Diary*, but Fielding had been churning out her clever, single-girl columns in London for years. In perhaps the greatest quick-lit-success story of our lifetime, J. K. Rowling of *Harry Potter* fame (and fortune—she's now richer than the queen!) had been living on welfare, writing for herself for ages, and had virtually given up hope of publication when it all began.

And we have plenty of examples of literary perseverance on our own shores. I like to tell the Zona Rosans about novelist Janice Daugharty, who wrote twenty-two novels on her farm in South Georgia before having a manuscript accepted by Harper-Collins. About Candace Bushnell, who didn't even have the $300 to pay her rent, and only three dollars for her dinner—at which point she broke down in tears in the grocery store—just before she started the *New York Observer* column that would turn into *Sex and the City*, making her rich and famous.

Or how Alexandra Fuller, author of bestselling memoirs *Don't Let's Go to the Dogs Tonight* and *Scribbling the Cat*, both drawing on her upbringing in what was then wartorn Rhodesia and is now Zimbabwe (and a school of hard knocks that undoubtedly added to her feistiness), ignored her school career counselor's sarcasm about her ambition to become a war correspondent ("She gave me a look as if to say, 'You couldn't write yourself out of a Tupperware party, let alone a war zone,'" Fuller wrote in *Vogue*). After being displaced to the milder wilds of Wyoming with her American river-guide husband and two small children, and incapable of even using a microwave (there had been little electricity, temperamental plumbing, and no phones in their little stone hut in Zambia), she stuck a Post-it to her computer that read, I WILL WRITE MY WAY OUT OF THIS HELL, where it stayed, drying and peeling, then lying amid the dust bunnies, while she wrote nine novels. "So I stopped writing novels and wrote the truth," she explained, referring to the riveting accounts for which she was finally recognized.

Charlotte Miller, an Alabama accountant and single mom, wrote for years with little encouragement until one every morning after her son went to bed—until, on a roll, her trilogy of early-twentieth-century novels, beginning with *Behold, This Dreamer,* were published within three years by a small press, then interest was shown by two big New York publishers. When she came to Zona Rosa to read from her newest, she told me that I was the first person who had encouraged her, back when she had been an anonymous person in a large Zona Rosa group, and after another writing teacher had called her work "unpublishable."

We were excited at our Atlanta meeting when I announced that Joshilyn Jackson, author of *gods in Alabama,* would be our guest. We remembered Joshilyn's visit the year before the book was published, and how she had told us about her moments of despair regarding her writing. When her second novel didn't sell, she already had a small child at home, and—pregnant with her second—decided, fuck it, no more of this! But her agent, who had believed in her all along, sent her a Christmas gift and said he refused to allow her to give up. And now, here she was on a major book tour, her hot new novel getting mucho press and with audio rights already sold.

Because our talents are often at a much higher level than we originally imagine, getting published is a goal to which I've seen even the most unlikely people—women who at first said they were coming to Zona Rosa to facilitate their journal-keeping, or to write a family history for their children—become committed. The same woman who wouldn't think of buying Prada, indulging in a massage, or running up her cell phone bill, much less investing in the stock market, will speculate with years of her life because of her belief in the story she has to tell. (And for women who've lived through truly dire circumstances—you'll meet some of them in chapter 6—writing is the piece of cake that becomes their salvation.)

7.

Three kinds of souls, three kinds of prayers:
1. I am a bow in your hand, draw me lest I rot.
2. Do not overdraw me, I shall break.
3. Overdraw me and who cares if I break!

—NIKOS KAZANTZAKIS

When Anne, Marsha, and Pamella found themselves with near-finished books and knew that they needed to make revisions, they formed their own Sub Rosa group to keep one another on track, calling it AOL, or Ass on the Line. At the time, Anne had written two unpublished nurse mysteries and was now finishing a memoir of her near-death experience as a nurse turned patient; Marsha had spent four years getting up at four A.M. to write her novel before going to work at her job in the prison system. And Pamella had already, in her enthusiasm, made the major boo-boo of sending her novel—about a privileged Atlanta woman who, driven mad by her perverse and abusive cardiologist husband, became an "atypical theft offender," shoplifting to sublimate her rage—out to 130 agents before the book was ready. Now she was aware that it was soggy in the middle, like a cake that didn't quite rise, but that wasn't about to stop her from starting over. (She later told me that when I mentioned in an offhand way that I had already been writing for twelve years before I had a book published, it had given her strength.)

One of our most difficult writing assignments in Zona Rosa is to write a log line, or what some call an "elevator speech": a brief, succinct, preferably imagistic, description of your book of the kind you can use in a phone call, a letter, or an e-mail to a prospective agent. (The term comes from Hollywood, where producers are said to have attention spans of thirty seconds or less.) Mark Twain famously remarked, "I would have written something shorter if I'd had more time," and the log line is deceptively hard to write; some of us work on them for months, as we do our query letters.

And we inevitably learn something along the way. For example, Amanda, who has authored and published a number of quirky feminist short stories, had worked for three years on her novel about a ten-year-old girl who imagines herself to be a Confederate general as she's traveling to Civil War sites with her bipolar, suicidal mother, whom she has to care for. But when the time came, Amanda, fine writer that she is, couldn't get the query letter right. Month after month, she came in with a new version, but none of them seemed to truly capture her unique story. Until she had a breakthrough and suddenly realized what was wrong: she needed to tell her protagonist Catherine's story in first person, present tense, and keep the flashbacks in third person, past tense. (If you're wondering what this means, I'll help you find out in chapter 9). As is typical of Amanda's professionalism, she immediately dove in to make the needed changes: "When I can find a way to make something better, I have to do it." When she got the novel right, the perfect query letter fairly tripped from beneath her fingertips: the next month, an agent asked to see the whole manuscript.

Indeed, speculation is the name of the game when we commit ourselves. No book has been written, no poem or essay put to paper, no letter even penned to the editor without it. When we sit down to write, and put down those first words, and then keep on, day after day; when we attend a writers' conference, or a workshop like Zona Rosa, we are taking a flyer, investing in ourselves—just as when we buy a typewriter, a computer, a file cabinet, or even just clear out our husbands' socks to make room for our files.

Thirty-five years ago I bought my first typewriter, a stand-up L. C. Smith manual (on which I would write three books, and which now sits on a table, a monument, in my hallway) and paid for it in installments of $17.95 a month, then, six months later, a metal typing table for the same price. Ten years later, I rented a room a few miles from my house (and kids) for the summer, where I tacked up a big white poster board with the names of my finished poems, and those I planned to write to complete my second volume in progress (like many writers, I hadn't found a publisher for my first book). That was when I learned that it took me a forty-hour week (that included some lolling on the bed, reading, and sometimes crying about my love life) to write two long poems. I had also rented the room in hope of romantic trysts with my soon-to-be-ex third husband; the marriage didn't work out, but the poems did—all that repressed sexual energy?—becoming my first published book. Here was another lesson on learning to focus on what I could control, which was not my spouse, but my writing hand. (In fact, it may have been then that I developed a skill I now consider invaluable: dismissing negative thoughts in favor of thinking about the project at hand.)

It was also then that I learned that investing in myself, my dreams, gave my psyche the message of my own seriousness of purpose—that I and my writing were worth it.

Since then, it's something I've seen happen with the Zona Rosans time after time. Whatever else might be going on in their lives, every time they invest in themselves, they come into the room with new enthusiasm, a glow about them, like a label that reads *I'm Worth It* splashed across their foreheads in hot pink ink.

8.

I shall not fear, fear is the mind-killer.

—FRANK HERBERT, *DUNE*

In my first book about Zona Rosa, I described what I then saw as the Five Fears that hold us back. Because they were so ubiquitous, I gave them acronyms. Among those first fears were FOP, FOF, FOC, and the two FOSs, as in Fear of People (What will *they* say?), Fear of Failure (all that wasted time—not to speak of our smashed hopes), Fear of Chaos (the turbulence that churns up inside us when we write from our gut), Fear of Shame (that flush we all feel at showing our stuff, especially for the first time), and Fear of Success (and what it might cost us).

Some of our fears have to do with our mental health, such as Fear of Craziness. "Why do I only feeling like writing when something bad is going on?" newcomers often ask, along with its subtext, *Is something wrong with me?* Since writing is healing, it's natural that we begin writing when we're feeling pain, I answer. But if we keep writing, we soon begin to love the process itself—sometimes to the point that nothing short of catastrophe can tear us away from it (or until you actually wet your pants, as I've been known to do).

Now I've heard dozens of fears, with new ones described to me at almost every workshop, and I've also learned they are really just one big blob—that the human mind is ingenious at finding reasons to quiver before the challenge of telling one's truths. And because they're so ubiquitous, yet useless, I've put them in Appendix B, where you can check them out or not.

Indeed, most fears are easy to understand, once we know the facts—such as Jodi's Fear of Pain. Jodi had been a low-level Mafia wife, a situation she barely escaped with her life and sanity, and which she was describing in her novel in progress. I wondered why the book seemed so flat, lacking in the tension that must have been inherent in her situation, until we sat together in rocking chairs on the front porch at a Zona Rosa retreat, and she told me the *whole* story. She described, among her many trials, going back to work as a waitress, still bleeding after a hysterectomy, to support her three kids and get the family back on its feet after her domineering, abusive husband sold their house and moved into a swinging singles complex. As soon as she reestablished their finances, she had taken him back into the fold. "I've never told anyone this before—it's too painful," she said, her eyes shining with relief when I asked why these realities weren't in her book.

Some fears are so one-of-a-kind that they surprise even me. "I'm afraid—in fact, I've already talked with my therapist about this," Loretta said, tremulously, over the phone from Alabama. She had recently attended a Zona Rosa retreat in the North Carolina mountains, where we had discussed her novel-in-progress—all thirty pages of it—begun after years as a mother, professor, and wife to a prolific fiction writer who had recently been nominated for a Pulitzer. "What if I win a Pulitzer, and Bill doesn't—and it ruins our marriage!"

"Just go ahead and write the book anyway. We'll worry about that later," I said, amazed at her confidence. I'm happy to report that five years later, Loretta was our special guest at our Atlanta Zona Rosa, on the road with her first—and wonderful!—collection of short stories, her fears far behind her.

Indeed, when we examine our fears, the bottom line is often the fear of loss of love. Sometimes we mask our truths with flowery words, which leads me to reiterate that sentimentality is the death of art. "I can't write that until (whoever) dies," newcomers almost invariably say. Those we fear offending may be any family member, or all of them en masse, but the most frequent one is Mother. A close second is "What would my children think?" to which I answer, "That you're human!" Indeed, fiction writing may have partly evolved as a way around these fears. We hope that if we mask our feelings in fiction, our secrets won't shine through.

Pat Conroy calls his novels fiction but everyone who knows him knows the truth, as he himself tells it whenever possible—an endearing quality to those of us who grew up among the cocky Good Ole and Not-So-Good Ole Boys of the literary world.

"If you can't do that, you might just as well stop now," Pat advised the Savannah Zona Rosa group, at the inevitable question about offending his subjects. He said his sister Carol wouldn't speak to him for ten years after he wrote *The Prince of Tides,* but he told her that it was his life, too.

"If they didn't want us to write about it, they shouldn't have acted that way!" I usually say, paraphrasing writer Anne Lamott. If they still look doubtful, I quote poet Ezra Pound, who said, "Fundamental accuracy of statement is the sole morality of writing." I also tell them that in my own life, I have never held back on writing about those closest to me, and that no good relationship had ever been made worse by telling the truth—after all, the bad ones were already bad anyway.

The myriad ways we come up with to sabotage ourselves—to avoid stepping out in faith or continuing to persevere—show how amazingly creative we are. In my first book about Zona Rosa, I wrote about Office Max addiction, and the Anna Quindlen Syndrome, as in "If I can't be as successful as Anna Quindlen, why bother?" But there are many others.

Some of us suffer from GIG, or Got It (Too) Good, which means too many trips abroad, massage appointments, and the absence of what writer and journalist Joyce Maynard calls the Wolf at the Door Syndrome (or the need to make a living), which makes it too easy to put one's talents on hold.

(Joyce, by the way, has made her living as a writer since age eighteen, when she appeared on the cover of *The New York Times Magazine,* which featured her article on being a student at Yale. Along the way, she's done whatever it takes, often supporting not only herself but her three children and, before their divorce, her ex.)

Some of us indulge in TMP, or Too Much Pride, in which we resist learning from others. When someone comes in upset that so-and-so just came out with a book on the same subject as the one they're writing, I recommend that they read it immediately. They usually find that it's nothing like their book. There's also the idea that reading novels will make you unable to write novels, reading poetry will make you unable to write poems, and so on, when in fact studying your chosen medium may be the only way to learn. Some also have a hard time listening to others' suggestions, however loving, with an open mind. Accompanying this is often the ubiquitous "Yes, but" syndrome, in which one counters said suggestions with all the reasons why they can't be used.

Others are afflicted by MOT, or failure to trust the Movement of the Tides—that creativity comes in and out of consciousness, and there's always more to come, however blah we may feel at the moment.

And then there's Attitude, which, like L'Oréal, comes in a number of shades. The only way we can deal with it is by completely stripping our current color to its roots, then starting over again. Here are a few attitudes that could do with some re-coloring:

The Pouter, or Cutie Pie: *You write so well—won't you do it for me while I dictate?*

The Prima Donna: *I want a guarantee of publication and an appearance on* Oprah *before I write a word.*

Girls Just Have to Have Fun: *I can't run my life for writing—it's too short. And besides, there are too many men out there who need my attention.*

The Perfectionist (think Bree on *Desperate Housewives*): *I can't do anything unless it's perfect. Anything less isn't worthy of me.*

The Constant Caregiver: *I just have to do all these things first. Then I'll write (or do whatever else it is I want to do).* Even nonworking, childless widows who live alone can do this one, just by entertaining constant house-guests!

Who, Me?: *Who would be interested in anything I have to say? And besides, my favorite shows are on TV this morning, this afternoon—and tonight.*

9.

If we wait until our hands stop shaking, we will never open the door.

—NAOMI NEWMAN, ACTRESS

"What if I get unblocked, then find out I don't have talent?" newcomers often ask, intimated by what they see as the high quality of writing in the group. "What if you have talent and you don't get unblocked?" I usually say. Then I remind them that the best writers among us started where they are now.

It's like when people ask me if they have talent before they've actually written anything. Beth came up to me after I spoke at a business women's group in Savannah; "I quit coming [to Zona Rosa] because I didn't have any talent," she said after thanking me for my talk. "How do you know? You never wrote anything," I replied gently, then invited her back. As the months went by, and she didn't reappear, we struck her off the list again.

Over and over, I've seen people of talent give up too

quickly (while conversely, those with perhaps less natural talent, but more ability to persevere, win out). For proof that talent is not necessarily inborn, I need only look at the five-year diary I filled up when I was eleven, which consisted mostly of whether I had seen my boyfriend Troy in the hall at school, and other, mushier stuff. When I started writing in my twenties, I was a high school dropout who couldn't pronounce Oedipus Rex, and, to the delight of the Ph.D.'s in my writing group, called an exclamation mark "an ejaculation point." But I had read a lot of books, and I knew where my destiny lay.

Rhoda is a prime example of someone who actively used her creativity to find new ways to keep herself from writing. She had won a prestigious short-story competition for women over fifty-five. But at the Writers Colony at Dairy Hollow, where Anne and I were spending a month, the other writers complained that Rhoda was disrupting them with her constant invitations to go astray by spending the day at a nearby lake or the World's Biggest Wal-Mart, eleven miles away.

But when Rhoda wrote her self-sabotage list in the Eureka Springs Zona Rosa group, she admitted to her flaw. I commented that the only sabotage techniques she should keep on using were going to the movies and having the stupid love affair—at least they might give her creative ideas:

Rhoda's Self-Sabotage List

Cooking giant meals

Shopping for anything

Laundry when I have too much to wear

Teaching remedial comp classes

Rereading novels for classes

Typing art lectures for my students

Writing my own Cliff Notes

Driving people places

Ghostwriting

Going to the movies

Office Max

Going to the beach

Having stupid love affair

10.

I have been absolutely terrified every moment of my life and I've never let it keep me from doing a single thing I wanted to do.

—GEORGIA O'KEEFFE

Say Yes to Yourself, and No to Others—Even Significant Ones. In France, Mary Catherine made us laugh by saying she planned to "ask" her retired husband for more writing time. What she didn't know yet was that, like making self-derogatory statements, using the words *try* or *should*, or asking permission from others to do what we want to do for ourselves, are no-no's in Zona Rosa.

A few days later, Mary Catherine had a major breakthrough in which she read a piece about "a secret that I've never told anyone," a frustrated yet magical love affair. From then on, everyone noticed her new relaxation, and later she told the Savannah Zona Rosa group that those two weeks in France had been the happiest of her life. And yes, she has learned to clean up her language—no more "shoulds" or "tries"—and, yes, she shared her intentions to write with her husband when she got home.

Some claim that habits form grooves in the brain, and that change is hell. But in Zona Rosa, we see change happen all the time. As therapist Earnie Lawson explains, change begins with thinking, not feeling—that if we place thinking at the top of our pyramid, with feeling and acting at the bottom two corners, we're likely to succeed.

In a *New Yorker* cartoon, a woman tells her husband that if he brings her meals and she stays in her study at her computer, it will be just like she's at a writers' colony—a scenario so unlikely that we all laughed. But we can at least make our boundaries clear—and give our significant others a chance to support us. The best thing I've done for my writing over the years is to make clear to my husband and my kids that, yes, I'm going to do this, no matter what.

Bestselling novelist Mary Alice Monroe started writing while on bed rest during her first pregnancy, giving birth to both her first child and first book at the same time. She told us about the sign she keeps on her office door that reads BLOOD OR FIRE!, shorthand that her kids understand as the only reasons she's to be disturbed while she's writing.

Indeed, bed is a place where a lot of great things happen besides the obvious. On our first date, in one of those shivery moments of precognition, Zane, an army paratrooper, walked into my study to see a page with the words *Sleeping with Soldiers,* the title of my book-in-progress, on a page stuck into my typewriter. I had written it the day before we met and had intended it metaphorically. It also said loud and clear that writing was a part of my life, and that if he wanted to be part of it, he would have to respect that.

It turned out that besides being a real-live soldier, Zane was also a frustrated writer who loved to read and had scored high in English and literature on his SATs. Soon he was happily bringing me coffee, even breakfast in bed while I wrote in my journal and notebooks each morning. He not only accepted, but admired that I regularly spent hours sitting in front of my manual Hermes—computers, much less laptops, were still a twinkle away—and that I would undoubtedly be spending much of the future doing the same. (The best gift he ever gave me wasn't diamonds or furs, but a massive fireproof file cabinet that meant I no longer had to keep my precious first drafts in the refrigerator.)

11.

Nothing is worth doing except what the world says is impossible.
—OSCAR WILDE

"What's the story you're going to tell yourself about why this didn't work out?" Dr. Phil asked a group of couples during a week of intensive group therapy.

"Well, that's the story you tell yourself about everything in your life," he told his captive audience, making the point that we often make excuses in order to avoid doing the work necessary to change ourselves.

And since writing is a life of constant change—a continual peeling of the layers—it's a good question to ask ourselves when, after that first flush of enthusiasm, we are tempted to give up on our writing, letting it wither and become just another of those abandoned but temporary passions, like the South Beach diet, or going to the gym five mornings a week—even though when we were on the diet or going to the gym, we were beginning to see results.

Knee-jerk Reaction #4: Letting the days, years, months go by without finding out what your true destiny may be, then calling the results FATE. Letting procrastination rule, rather than deciding how much of a player you want to be, then making a plan and following through.

PILATES ON PAPER

What Am I a Genius Of? And what do I plan to do about it? In her book *Confidence*, Rosabeth Moss Kanter says that confidence is more of a predictor of success than any other factor; Stephen Covey emphasizes the ability to visualize—to imagine ourselves doing that thing well—as does life coach Martha Beck. Dr. Phil is also good at making the complex simple. On his show, he gave four questions to ask yourself in deciding what you want, and whether you want it enough to get it: *1. What do you want?* (This is the hard one.) *2. What do you have to do to get it? 3. What are you willing to do to get it?* (Possibly the most important one.) *4. How will you feel if you get it?* Or as Maxine, a hairstylist and friend of Zona Rosa, says, "When people ask me what I think they should do with their hair, I ask *how much maintenance do you want?*"

Why I Haven't Yet Stepped Out in Faith. Now that you know, or sort of know, what you want, I'm sure you're coming up with bunches of reasons not to follow through by stepping out in faith (as Zane said he did every time he stepped out of a plane in a parachute). Ask yourself what you gain by not doing what you say you want to do—more time to shop, watch the Style Channel, bake your own bread, perfect your abs (including the time it takes to drive to the gym), drink margaritas with your girlfriends, peruse Match.com, play with your kids, plus read every new book that calls out to you? Your list, I'm sure, will be endless, and all of these things are neutral, if not good. But as Grandmother Lee used to say, "You can have a lot of the small things, and none of the big things. Or some of the big things, and a few of the small things." As Stephen Covey paraphrased the French proverb, "The good is often the enemy of the best." Now list the possible gains you might make by stepping out in faith and going after what you want. Which of your lists promises more fulfillment in the long run? (I know, I know—when we step out in faith, there's always speculation involved; and those other pleasures are, well, so immediate!)

What Hospital Do I Keep Myself In? Still paralyzed? In her book *The Comfort Trap, or, What If You're Riding a Dead Horse?*, psychologist Judith Sills says there's "an electric fence of anxiety" between your current situation and your goal, and that "overcoming avoidance is the No. 1 life problem." We don't have to be ill to be in a hospital of our own making, one circumscribed by the white-padded walls we've designed for ourselves. Nor does change necessarily mean abandoning our significant others. It more often means looking at our own attitudes. Are you a Self-Protector who doesn't want to see and know too much, especially about stuff that might shake you up? A Conveniencer who puts convenience above all? How else are you limiting yourself? Again, to quote Stephen Covey—he's great on this stuff, isn't he?—"Some of the most transformational things we do are the least efficient [such as] making art, having a child, creating a relationship." Covey also recommends that "as you engage in these activities, just be sure that in your paradigm, your compass is set toward your true values."

How Can I Lead a Less Balanced Life? By now I suspect you realize you were made for much bigger things. But you may still be feeling the fear of what will happen to your life if you follow through. "Are you sure that's anxiety—or just excitement you're trying to tamp down?" a wise therapist asked Zona Rosan Danielle, as she was about to leave for the prestigious Iowa Writers' Workshop. Excitement goes along with any creative endeavor. But along with its sister, obsession, excitement has gotten a bad rap, and the Myth of Perfect Mental Health is rampant. "Good has come to mean thin, quiet, blond, silent, obedient, not messy, not loud," Eve Ensler told *Health* magazine. In her book *Exuberance,* Kay Jamison says that many of us are suspicious of those who convey too much enthusiasm, which sounds about as much fun as being afraid of chocolate or sex. Despite excitement's bad rap, you might want to rearrange your priorities—and get some of it for yourself.

What's Holding Me Back? Zona Rosan Virginia coined the term *LIG, or Life in General,* or the stuff of everyday life, and it's our biggest source of excuses for why we don't do what we say we want to do. Yes, LIG happens—so often that it should be a bumper sticker. And during periods of crisis, it happens on an even bigger scale, which may be why the Chinese symbol for crisis means "opportunity." But what matters most is whether or not you've decided to let yourself be sidetracked when it inevitably does.

❊

And if you really want to make a clean sweep, write about it in "If I Did Triage on My Life." To reduce your fear, remember that it's just an exorcise. Then visualize in detail an emotional and spiritual moving day, even though the follow-through may take years, or never even come. Still, it's good to know when and how you might—and that you have the option. And, as a last resort, it's energizing to at least consider "Where I'll Run Away To and When." It *is* possible, whether we think it is or not.

BOOK THERAPY FOUR: IMMERSE YOURSELF IN STRONG WOMEN

This is a good time to read some books about women of character, like *Jane Eyre,* Charlotte Brontë's creation who, time after time, stepped out in faith and did the right thing without losing her center for a moment.

Louise Colet, the nineteenth-century subject of Francine du Plessix Gray's biography *Rage and Fire,* was a pioneer feminist, Gustave Flaubert's lover and muse, and his central model for *Madame Bovary.* Flaubert, eleven years younger than Colet, was brilliant but a mama's boy who lived in relative luxury (when he suffered a breakdown in law school, his treatment was the usual one for the well-off, a sea voyage around the world). Colet, on the other hand, preferred to make her own way. She became, along with George Sand, one of France's most famous women writers and confidante to some of the greatest men of her generation. She was also a self-supporting single mother who refused to share her home with a man lest it compromise the principles of liberty by which she lived. Toward the end of her life, she took on the Vatican, writing a text deploring "the vicious influence of monks and priests," and also traveled as an international correspondent, becoming a witness—ever-controversial and increasingly unwelcomed by "the male club"—to the inauguration of the Suez Canal, the Paris Commune of 1871, and other historical events of her times.

Or go back to the eighteenth century to savor the life of our feminist foremother, Mary Wollstonecraft, as portrayed in Frances Sherwood's biographical novel *Vindication*. Throughout we reel at her vivid account of an oft-brutal, messy life in a heady time. Born in England, and lover to such figures as William Godwin and Thomas Paine, Wollstonecraft lived in Paris and befriended leaders of the French Revolution; along the way, she exposed society's underlying injustices and authored the landmark *A Vindication of the Rights of Women,* in which she called marriage "legal prostitution," adding that wives "may be convenient slaves, but slavery will have its constant effect, degrading the master and the abject dependent." Ringing a modern-day bell, she accused her sisters of being "docile and attentive to their looks to the exclusion of all else." When she died of childbed fever at age thirty-eight (the doctor's hands were unclean; asepsis was still unknown), she had just given birth to a daughter, Mary, the future wife of the poet Shelley and the author of *Frankenstein*.

And read anything by Jane Austen, whose women characters are nothing if not staunch. "Her heroines are brilliant contradictions to the put-downs with which men attempt to claim ownership of women," explained Maggie, Zona Rosan and

Jane Austen scholar. "She explains how different women in different situations in different stages of their lives use their womanly power to find a good life with a loving husband."

Finding a husband may not be your goal—you may aspire to higher things. But as Karen Joy Fowler wrote in her bestselling novel, *The Jane Austen Book Club,* "Wasn't it Kipling who said, 'Nothing like Jane when you're in a tight spot?' "

CHAPTER FIVE

IF I TOLD MY JUICY SECRETS

How the Power of the Pink Keeps Us Laughing,
or Why Even Serious Babes Still Want to Have Fun

1.

Laughter is carbonated holiness.

—ANNE LAMOTT

I Don't Need Therapy—I've Got Zona Rosa, someone suggested for
a Zona Rosa T-shirt. During the '70s, I loved to sing along
with Sister Sledge and "We Are Family," in which the singers
claim their girlfriends as sisters. On an unconscious level, I
must have already known—despite my reputation as a bombshell and my addiction to men—that sisterhood was my destiny, and that it's not only fun, but healing.

Since some of us are used to circles in which women compete, using secrets as weapons, newcomers to Zona Rosa often
don't yet know how much fun it is to let your hair down and

be part of a group of dynamic femmes who are also totally supportive, whatever our quirks and differences.

In Zona Rosa, we can let our Inner Diva or even our Inner Slut hang out, because unlike our grandmothers and a few of our more conservative members, we don't judge one another by our sexual behavior or other choices. And because we'll be talking frankly, this chapter is definitely not for network.

At our Zona Rosa retreats, or Pajama Parties for Grown-Up Girls with Smarts, we see one another without makeup, in our jammies, and with our hair down—and after a while, without our secret shames and vanities, learn that we can be known as we really are and still be loved. Even at our wildest, sexiest, neediest, or, on the contrary, most fearful and conservative, we're still okay with the group.

In February 2005, *First* magazine listed the top fifteen high-tech gadgets we would love to have, including "a mirror for your bathroom that shows how beautiful you are on the inside." In Zona Rosa, we become that mirror for one another.

We are born girlfriends who know that even the most serious women just need to have fun. In fact, the more focused we are on meeting our goals, the more we need to have it, and the more we enjoy it, since via our hard work we've truly earned the right to cut up, even at our own expense.

Indeed, the music of women's laughter when I wake up is one of the things I love best about our retreats. "That's good," I said when someone facetiously suggested the word *silly* as a part of our logo, "because being silly is good for us as writers."

"Life should not be a journey to the grave with the intention of arriving safely in an attractive and well-preserved body, but rather to skid in sideways, chocolate in one hand, wine in the other, body thoroughly used up, totally worn out and screaming, *WOO HOO*, what a ride!" read an e-mail Zona Rosan Gray forwarded from a Very Good-Looking, Damn Smart Woman.

The idea that we must be humorless, not to speak of angst ridden, in order to be serious women and writers is one that we disprove every day in Zona Rosa. I don't know whether research has yet been done on what makes men more humorless than women—a *Time* magazine piece said we laugh more— but the idea of the booze-driven, suicidal writer that comes down from the male model isn't necessary, much less desirable. Indeed, I've discovered that we learn most easily in a relaxed, even levity filled, atmosphere.

At times, of course, all this girly fun is just a gloss, a way to re-create and energize ourselves toward meeting our more serious purposes. As Mireille Guiliano says in *French Women Don't Get Fat,* we don't laugh because we're happy, but we're happy because we laugh. Laughter paves the way for supporting one another's strengths in writing and life, and helps us find ways to deal with the rest. It can also lead to sharing ourselves on a deeper level.

Along the way we discover that the more we are ourselves, the closer we become to others, whatever our differences; and that giving up whatever facades we've been wasting our energy on creates the kind of atmosphere in which writing breakthroughs happen naturally.

As mystery writer Nevada Barr wrote in an article in *Family Circle,* "Every woman needs three things—a pair of flip-flops, a denim jacket, and girlfriends!" And I couldn't agree more.

2.

I'd like to meet the woman who invented sex, and find out what she's working on now.

—ANONYMOUS

The buzzword in today's business world is MARKETING. However, people often ask for a simple explanation of "Marketing." Well, here it is:

You're a woman and you see a handsome guy at a party. You go up to him and say, "I'm fantastic in bed." That's Direct Marketing.

You're at a party with a bunch of friends and see a handsome guy. One of your friends goes up to him and, pointing at you, says, "She's fantastic in bed." That's Advertising.

You see a handsome guy at a party. You go up to him and get his telephone number. The next day you call and say, "Hi, I'm fantastic in bed." That's Telemarketing.

You see a guy at a party, you straighten your dress. You walk up to him and pour him a drink. You say, "May I?" and reach up to straighten his tie, brushing your breast lightly against his arm, and then say, "By the way, I'm fantastic in bed." That's Public Relations.

You're at a party and see a handsome guy. He walks up to you and says, "I hear you're fantastic in bed." That's Brand Recognition.

You're at a party and see a handsome guy. He fancies you, but you talk him into going home with your friend. That's Sales Rep.

Your friend can't satisfy him so he calls you. That's Tech Support.

You're on your way to a party when you realize that there

could be handsome men in all those houses you're passing. So you climb onto the roof of one situated toward the center and shout at the top of your lungs, "I'm fantastic in bed!" That's Junk Mail.

When the ever-witty Martha sent this riff to make us laugh, we all agreed (after we stopped laughing) that it described the worst of diva—or was it desperate?—behavior.

❀

Nor did our laughter stop there—indeed, except when tragedy strikes, it's usually nonstop. Many people have described making art as a high-end form of play, and playing is also what we do with our friends.

Like laughter, sex is energy for many writers, including me; often when we're on a roll, we find ourselves turned on. So it's no surprise that we talk about sex a lot in Zona Rosa—no holds barred. I've learned that we're earthier and less shockable than some might think.

"I can have an orgasm just from vacuuming!" Martha W. protested when I read "housework" on the list "Things We Think We Have to Do But Don't" at the New Orleans group. And when I visited her house, I saw that it was indeed immaculate.

True, some of us might roll our eyes at something so over the top. Such as when I told them about *I Shock Myself*, sculptor Beatrice Wood's memoir, penned at age 101. ("She died at 105, her heart 32," wrote a reviewer on Amazon.com.) The model for the woman involved in the menage à trois in the classic film *Jules et Jim*, Wood wrote that she loved being older because she could look at younger men and imagine how they would look naked without them suspecting.

A frisson zipped around the room when I brought in the *New York Times* interview with Jane Juska, author of *A Round-Heeled Woman: My Late-Life Adventures in Sex and Romance,* her story of long-distance sleeping around via a *New York Review of Books* personals ad placed at age sixty-six. "I'd like to have great sex with someone I like before my sixty-seventh birthday, which is next month. If you like to talk first, Trollope is fine with me," it read. We also liked her honesty when faced with such questions as how men responded to her aging body—and the photo in which she was plump and graying, and looked at least her age.

But when I mentioned *The Surrender,* Toni Bentley's account of salvation via anal sex—she was a ballerina who was accustomed to stretching her limits—an "ugh" went around the room. Only Deborah, who had written a section on "How to Use Anal Beads" in her *Cook and Fuck Book,* showed a flicker of interest.

Everyone was supportive of dark-skinned beauty Sheefa's story about a one-night stand during a trek to Machu Picchu—except lesbian Allison, who said, "Why do women do things like that to themselves?" Which led the more conservative women in the group to later complain about what they saw as Allison's prejudice against straight women, rather than Sheefa's sexual choice.

When Sue, a large gay woman who was a white witch, brought in a piece that was more graphic—and, replete with bondage and various tools, more objectifying of women than anything I had ever read by a man, including Henry Miller— even I couldn't bring myself to read it aloud, and I asked her to do so. As she concluded, a long silence filled the room—until someone called out from the back, "Not enough foreplay!" and we all broke up.

Virginia Woolf said that the older women grow, the more they like indecency, and the elders in the group were often the most irreverent about sex. After "wandering" into the local sex-toy shop, Leah, seventy-six, suggested to the young male owner that he sponsor Elderhostel tours to his store. He had welcomed her suggestion, she said, and we all thought her story would make a great column for the local alternative paper. Maggie, eighty-six, married for the first time at age fifty to a man fourteen years her junior, wrote about her love-and-sex life, "just so you'll know I always had one!"

When Deborah brought in her essay "The Dildo Patrol," we learned about the Chocolate Thriller, the Love Wand, Bathing Buddy, Glowboy, the Nubby G, and Nipple Nibblers. *Men have strip bars. Women go to try to learn to better satisfy their needs,"* she wrote in defense of one Joanne Webb who was arrested for having "passion parties" (sort of like Tupperware parties) in violation of Texas Penal Code 43.23, which prohibits the sale of any obscene device for stimulation of the genitals. *Hey, you would think those old geezer cops and judges who frequent the titty bars would be happy to go home to a wife all hot and ready for some action. . . . Men have their power tools—why shouldn't women?*

I wasn't convinced the women were buying the sex toys in order to heat themselves up for the "old geezers." But we looked at one another in amazement when we learned that in Georgia, where many of us live, it's against the law to have more than six vibrators in your possession. "I have to wonder who thought that was important enough to make a law about it!" said Brenda, a grandmother four times over.

We screamed with laughter when Katherine read from a review of *The Technology of Orgasm: "Hysteria," the Vibrator, and*

Women's Sexual Satisfaction, by independent scholar Rachel P. Maines, on the turn-of-the-century "vibratoriums," where women were brought to orgasm by doctors (no nurses allowed) to relieve their "hysteria." The treatment included stimulating the vagina and labia of the afflicted patient in order to induce "hysterical paroxysms," during which a patient might thrust her pelvis, cry out in pleasure, and appear to lose consciousness, and which was thought to return the uterus to its rightful place. The treatment was often protracted, and some patients were seen weekly for an indefinite period. We identified when the reviewer reported Maines as saying that women typically roared with amusement at her lectures, while men sat uncomfortably beside them.

Then there was our infamous—and ongoing—Blow Job Survey, instigated by Virginia's poem titled "Get Your Hand Off the Back of My Head." Many of us agreed that it's strictly a male invention, and while useful in pleasing our man, also a possible tool of subjugation. As Kim Cattrall said on *Dr. Phil,* "They don't call it a job for nothing." Thus I was thrilled to bring in E. Jean's column from *Elle* on the subject; to my mind, E. Jean was an honorary Zona Rosan and our fairy godmother re stuff between the sexes, leading to our exorcise, "If I Was a Love and Sex Columnist, or, What I Learned from E. Jean Carroll and Others."

"According to my mail, the number of chaps who had *not* received a good oraling in the past 24 hours amounts to only five, or six if you count Ken Lay," E. Jean wrote in response to a letter from a woman who had been, well, generous with her favors, and had signed off Thought I Was Pleasing Him. "My dear Miss Thought! Elegant Readers! We are busy women. I am issuing an edict: *From this moment on, no man receives any special pleasuring until he proves he's worth it.*" ("Then hardly any guy would ever get it," Zane said when I read him the column.)

But some of us looked as though we, well, enjoyed it. Claudia and Anne, who were former nurses, seemed less put off than some. "It depends on your squeam factor," said Anne, who often jokes about how prudish I am. And Deborah, for one, felt having the BJ in her repertoire added to her oeuvre. In the "How to Give a Blow Job" treatise in her book, she was the mistress of tact, describing how even those of us who were reluctant could simulate the act enough to please.

And others defended our right to tit for tat. "He should have a show about men who won't reciprocate!" Jill protested when she heard about Dr. Phil's show on a woman who refused to put her mouth near her husband's penis.

Sometimes our talk turned serious, as when one woman who had had breast cancer and felt self-conscious about her unreconstructed breast revealed she hadn't yet had sex with the husband who supported her through her surgery. Lynn confessed that, unlike some of us, she had felt powerless, rather than empowered, in her past sexual relationships. "Whenever I had a bad time," she said, "there was usually a man around."

One night around the dinner table at the farmhouse in Provence, Lulu asked for a show of hands as to who preferred sex alone, and who with a partner; we were evenly divided, five and five. I told them that it was a good thing we were in France, because in Georgia it's against the law for more than six women to occupy a house, as it might be a brothel—a law we broke annually at our beach retreats.

When we realized we'd finally exhausted the subject of sex, we talked about our plan to swim nude, forming a synchronized flower, all wearing ruffled pink bathing caps and nothing else, for our book jacket photo. (Pamella soon found the perfect pink-petaled cap on Headwear.com and brought it to me at our next Atlanta Zona Rosa meeting.)

Because of our love of swimming *sans* suits, facilitated by drinking wine throughout the day, it had gotten harder and harder to collect the Zona Rosans for the afternoon workshops in Provence. Lynn came up with the perfect term—"Herding Cats"—from a cartoon: "Geez, I hate this job," says a cowboy as he tries to herd acres of languid felines, and it became our catchphrase, meaning we had to get down to business.

On our next trip, when Air France lost mine and Pamella's luggage, we were given, along with profuse apologies, wonderful little cases that included a white T-shirt, toothbrush and paste, shampoo, hairbrush—and a condom! "Well, at least the French know what's important in life!" we agreed.

3.

If I had my life to live over, I'd make the same mistakes, only sooner.
—TALLULAH BANKHEAD

What's Love Got to Do with It. One of my biggest non-secrets is my bad taste in men. I've almost always picked them—except for the architect—for reasons of the heart or groin: long eyelashes, steel-blue eyes, hard biceps, or an adventurous spirit and a quick wit, rather than because they were the "good husband material" that Grandmother Lee prescribed.

Remember the nationally televised photo of the marine in Iraq with dirt on his face, a cigarette hanging from his mouth? Women from all over the country wrote wanting to meet him. Later, when I was on *Donahue* with my book *Sleeping with*

Soldiers, a defense of my attraction to the macho man, women rushed up to me afterward to say they felt the same way.

Zona Rosan Kathleen, whom you will meet in chapter 6, and I bonded over our attraction to bad boys. We admitted that sensible, moneymaking types—bankers, stockbrokers, and accountants—weren't even on our radar. She had had the wild boy in the band, her bad boy husband, Scott, and the police detective who was helping her to solve what she believed to be Scott's murder. I had had Zane, numerous struggling artists, and a large cast of, well, *others.* (While reading this, Zane has asked me to insert here that he has the largest penis and has given me more orgasms than any of the rest.)

Anne, who has always been more sensible than I am, has been married to my handsome brother-in-law Larry for forty years. She chose him deliberately, partly because he was so different from our boozy daddy, and not, she claims, for his blond hair and blue eyes. I've been married four times, the last time reluctantly, spurred on by not wanting to lose my sexy sweetheart Zane when he gave me an ultimatum just like women sometimes do. Since then I've adopted what I call the A.A., or "one day at a time" theory of marriage, and despite all, we've been together for over two decades.

My earlier philosophy was similar to that described in *Secrets of the Flesh,* Judith Thurman's biography of Colette. In it, Thurman cites my favorite girlie-to-the-end sensualist's reason for not seeking out men who were like herself. " 'There's only one person in this world you can count on, and that's yourself,' [her mother] Sido told Colette at the time of her divorce from her first husband Willy, and she took this advice to heart. . . . A man really worth loving would be an invitation to perdition [that is, annihilation], and she doesn't want to put temptation in her own path." Toward the end, Colette was cared for by her devoted, seventeen-years-younger husband, Maurice.

"Southern men love to be called 'boy,'" Loretta said, referring to the way the kind of men we'd grown up with prefer to remain juveniles, preferably delinquent ones, as long as possible. Casting her baby blues, she tilted her head in a way that made her blond braid curl around her neck coquettishly. At fifty-something, she still looked like a girl herself.

"Yeah, a man will pat your ass. But a woman will save it," Susan J. threw in. And joking around, especially about men, marriage, motherhood, and our other commonalties, makes us aware how alike we are beneath our differences.

When Merri Lisa Johnson came to read from the radically feminist book of essays she edited, *Jane Sexes It Up,* some of us realized for the first time that, yes, we *were* feminists, and that we could tolerate hearing about lesbians and strap-on dildos if they came in the right package, like the intelligent and ladylike Lisa. Indeed, she had such a classiness about her that she could probably read anything aloud and have it come out sounding positively Victorian. "I thought it was going to be pornographic. But as she talked about the book, I saw what she meant," said Honor after her reading. I wondered what she would have thought had she known Lisa was also a contributor to *Homewrecker: An Adultery Anthology?*

I had used the same tactics on tour for my oft-controversial books, when I wore a button-up, long-sleeved pink dress with a cream lace collar, and jousted with interviewers in a soft voice. The great thing about the Power of the Pink is that it's perfect camouflage for our wilder choices and our outstanding brains. Or as a Harley-Davidson ad read, "They don't have to know your bed has a dust ruffle."

4.

65: Percentage of women who say what they want to change most about their homes is their husband.

—AARP Magazine

The Female Chauvinist Society
(Yes, Camouflage Does Come in Pink)

A study in Wisconsin showed that the kind of male face a woman finds attractive can differ depending on where she is in her menstrual cycle. For instance, if she is ovulating she is attracted to men with rugged and masculine features. And if she is menstruating, she is more prone to be attracted to a man with scissors shoved in his temple and a bat jammed up his ass while he is on fire.

Thus read the e-mail I shared with the Zona Rosans.

In May 2004, *More* magazine reported that the main cause of stress for midlife women is their marriages. Researchers have also shown that women who live with men lose power in the relationship when they marry them, since the men then begin to be less concerned about resolving conflicts. That the Zona Rosans' feelings about men were mixed was evidenced by the kind of humor that put us in stitches, because what stresses us out also makes us laugh.

Some of us have supportive husbands, doting husbands, wild husbands, and sexy husbands (or significant others, and even secret lovers). One of us who prefers not to be named has been married eleven times ("She's been married more times than I've had dates!" exclaimed another Zona Rosan). Then there's our darling Deborah: "They couldn't control me," she confided of her five exes. Since we're obviously not about to pull a Lysistrata, rejecting men sexually until they shape up, humor helps us avoid marital paralysis.

We laughed at learning that getting married is called "committing suicide" among the Indian women of San Cristobal, Mexico. We liked anecdotes like the conversation in which one woman tells another, "Her husband left her," and the other woman asks, "How did she get him to do that?" I told them about the T-shirt I had seen on New Orleans' Bourbon Street that read, sounding suspiciously like marriage from a woman's point of view: *I Will Work, Clean and Cook for Sex*, and I quoted a line from *The Botox Diaries* by Janice Kaplan and Lynn Schnurnberger: "Hey, I'm married. I stopped thinking about sex a long time ago."

And then there were the one-liners: "Why do I have to get married? I didn't do anything wrong," I read on a Savannah bumper sticker. "I want our relationship to go back to where it was before we met," said the caption in a *New Yorker* cartoon. "Now you may begin your insane experiment," the minister tells the bride and groom in another.

Even Amanda, who lived happily with Julie, guffawed when we talked about men; in her family, she said, *she* was the one who did all those dastardly things. And Shakespeare, despite being a man, knew a thing or two about why women might not prefer the married state: "It would be a fine husband indeed to be better than no husband at all," he wrote (not that he was against sex and romance—he just knew they don't always go hand in hand).

Ronnie said the thing that had driven her crazy about her ex was his passive-aggressiveness, or, as Dr. Phil says, "When you just can't get hold," in other words, get a response. And apparently enough of us had known the type to laugh out loud at

Men Are Clams, Women Are Crowbars, a book title I had seen on a supermarket rack. Or as comic Elayne Boosler said, "I know what men want. Men want to be really, really close to someone who will leave them alone."

At our retreat in the South of France, Nancy complained that we joked about men when they weren't around to defend themselves. "And you think they don't talk about *us*?!" Janet asked in disbelief. We were bonded in our right to laugh about men. One of our favorite ongoing jokes was that many of our husbands genuflect to Don Imus's ugly mug, his high-testosterone pronouncements on television each morning, while we had never met a woman who liked him, as proved by an ongoing Zona Rosa survey.

One of the truths about us was we were mostly old enough to see that love was an act, not a person, and that it usually meant more responsibilities as much as anything else. We also were old enough not to feel we had to marry and have children to be happy. In fact, some of us who were mothers had found that despite motherhood's satisfactions this "fulfillment" had cost us a great deal. Indeed, the Empty Nest Syndrome appeared to cause only momentary pangs among women with well-filled minds and lives.

Women have always intuited that these matters were not exactly as advertised, but the culture has plenty of means, including policing by other women, to keep us in line. That's exactly what we *don't* do in Zona Rosa—instead, we laugh, using humor as the hat pin with which to burst our bubbles.

5.

Interviewer to eighty-something-year-old woman: "Can you tell me when a woman starts to lose interest in sex?" Woman: "You'll have to ask someone older than I am."
—CONTRIBUTED BY ZONA ROSAN MARIANNE L.

Back When I Was Eighty-Three. "I really like who I am. And I really like aging . . . if it didn't lead to death, it would be perfect," Eve Ensler, creator of *The Vagina Monologues* and *The Good Body*, told the *New York Post*.

"Today, epidemiologists predict that a woman with no sign of cancer or heart disease can expect to live to the age of 92," Gail Sheehy wrote in *More* magazine.

Jeanne Ray, author of *Julie and Romeo,* a delightful novel of an affair between over-sixties, told me how she got her idea: "I was in the supermarket, and I saw all the magazines with headings like 'Sex over Forty,' 'Sex at Fifty,' and so on, and I thought, What about sex over sixty? Are we supposed to be dead?!" Jeanne, a former Nashville nurse, also just happens to be literary novelist Ann Patchett's mom, and when Jeanne's book came out to glowing reviews, Ann wrote an equally funny piece for *The New York Times Magazine* in which she described the strange dilemma of having her mother suddenly become more famous than she was.

"No way!" everyone exclaimed, laughing, as one woman after another at a Zona Rosa meeting in Savannah told her true age. Barbra had used the term "elderly" in writing about a woman near some of our ages, and we had all protested. Nor did we find the popular word *crone,* as in "wise woman," acceptable. "How about 'experienced'?" I suggested, then asked them to write about "How Age Affects My Thinking: Ingenue, Femme Fatale, Experienced Woman, Wise Woman, Or Heaven Forbid, Crone?"

We joked about hot flashes—was the room too hot or too cold? Or about standing on line to the one bathroom in my house. Any symptom was fair game, as in an e-mail from Martha:

> California vintners in the Napa Valley area that primarily produces Pinot Blanc and Pinot Grigio have developed a new hybrid grape that acts as an anti-diuretic and will reduce the number of trips an older person has to make to the bathroom during the night. They will be marketing the new wine as Pinot More.

At one time my dream of being old had to do with poetry, cats, and a garden. Later, it was to live off oysters and champagne like the author Isak Dinesen. Now, at eighty-seven, Maggie is my own personal role model for aging. Indeed, she seems to get younger every year. When she bobbed her gray hair, her Kate Hepburn features shone forth. But it was her exuberance, her passion that truly lit her face. Every month, I paged through her new poems and essays in progress—she had more vibrant ideas than almost any of us—thinking what a perfect example she was of living fully until the moment of our deaths. Or, as her husband, Charles, said, "We're going to live forever—or die trying." When Maggie read from her poems—many of them on the subject of death—during dinner on our last night in France, everyone was silent for moments afterward.

At our retreat in Tuscany, we all feared for her health, convinced that it was her raw food diet and eating too many turnips that was making her ill. "It's *not* the turnips—it's something I'm processing *emotionally!*" she protested when I sat by her on her bed, admiring her bone structure and thinking how girlish she looked. When the cute Italian doctor came from the village, he pronounced her okay, even though Anne, a nurse, had told him about the turnips. "And he didn't even have a thermometer!" Anne exclaimed, leading us to think that perhaps Italian doctors tend to treat by charm alone.

Around the table during the break at our Atlanta group, Maggie, as usual eschewing the wine, munched sunflower seeds and avocado halves, while the rest of us pigged out on fried chicken, Death by Chocolate, and worse. But Maggie, her brain clicking away, was probably getting younger by the moment. Indeed, had she not considered it sexist, she probably could have joined the South Florida Follies in which women her age dance across the stage and do splits in burlesque costumes.

And where does that leave those *old* men of fifty-five or sixty who don't exercise and diet like we do? Like "a wet leaf clinging annoyingly to the leg," as Japanese women were quoted in the *New York Times* as calling their retired couch potato husbands.

6.

Do you see that tree? Do you think that tree isn't pretty because it doesn't look like that other tree . . . ? You've got to love your tree.
—AN AFRICAN WOMAN NAMED LEAH TO PLAYWRIGHT EVE ENSLER

How Plastic Is My Surgery. "Ugh! I would never do that," my assistant Caitlin said when I described the operation.

When I saw myself on CNN after I had written an article on the twentieth anniversary of The Pill, I decided the time had come to, as some of us prefer to put it, "get some work done"—those circles beneath my eyes, inherited from my father, were just too much. I've always been vain, and while I knew I didn't have to be beautiful to be a great writer, I still wanted to look as good as I could.

"Go for it!" said Meryl, who had had work done herself.

Despite Ora's beautiful face, she had gained a lot of weight after her marriage to the naval officer she met through Dial-a-Sailor. I knew that she had once been svelte; I had seen the photos. When she told us about her decision to have a gastric bypass, we all encouraged her—except for Anne who, ever the nurse, knew the bloody realities only too well. "After three surgeries, I am more beautiful—and happier—than I have ever been," Ora wrote me a year after her bypass, despite its initial complications. Of course, we Zona Rosans loved Ora all along—especially when she brought her special butter-soaked pineapple dessert.

For some of us, admitting to going under the knife was still one of the harder secrets to tell. Even Deborah, ever open, admitted to a bit of chagrin at telling us about her two boob jobs, Gortex-filled lips, and permanent eye-and-lip liner, as well as the pain involved. The only time I cringed was when she talked about her Brazilian wax jobs, which an *Oprah* guest had pronounced 80 percent as painful as having a cesarean. But Deborah, a true believer, said that all her men friends—what's masculine for harem?—liked her baby-smooth pubes. Besides, it solved the problem of that first graying pubic hair she'd written about in a poem—which she read aloud to a crowd at an Atlanta arts center, proving herself once again to be the queen of openness.

When it came to the body, it sometimes took us a long time to share confidences. Gray looked adorable in her short pleated skirts, Mary Jane clogs, and long tunics. "Nobody's seeing *my* body!" she burst out when we talked about swimming nude, as we had the year before. Since Gray was far from shy, I wondered at her apprehension until she told us about the two cesareans that had left her abdomen bisected by scar tissue and her dream of having a tummy tuck. Gray had always held two or three jobs at a time, so when the Slings of Good Fortune touched down in the form of an inheritance (and a long overdue divorce), I suggested she no longer resist. Soon she was giving us photos of the new boobs she had gotten as an added perk.

In the final analysis, the Zona Rosa survey on whether we would turn to the knife and other invasive procedures showed that we were split half and half. "Why isn't the way we are as we age good enough?" said Leah, despite her own face- and boob-lifts. Susan, who had long held the French perspective that included beautiful but untouched icons like Jeanne Moreau and Simone Signoret, swore she would never do it. "But what about Catherine Deneuve?" I said, thinking of her preternaturally smooth and gorgeous face. While reading a biography of the British beauty and author Lady Caroline Blackwood, I pointed out a photo taken near her death at age sixty-five. Since she had been younger than many of us were at the moment, I couldn't believe she had as many wrinkles as she did, and worse, to my shallow mind, that she had allowed it. "But she was British, and the Europeans don't do plastic surgery," somebody said.

There *was* one thing about which we agreed: we all shrunk back in dissent when I brought in an article on surgery billed as "vaginal rejuvenation," agreeing our vaginas were good enough as they were.

The constant scrutiny we gave our other body parts led to an exorcise, "The Story of My Hair, Neck, Stomach, Boobs, Ass, or Whatever." "One of the sweetest things about this retreat is that I'm not looking in a mirror all the time to check my stomach," wrote Claudia, who is both beautiful and honest about her fear of turning into her mother, who died "wearing what the doctor called an abdominal apron."

The idea of excess blubber, and of going against the Beauty Rule, as we call what society seems to expect of us, is just about as terrifying to some Zona Rosans as wearing mismatched outfits. Indeed, there may be no word in the South considered more vile than *tacky.* Anne and I were brought up in the tradition that says, as did Billy Crystal as Fernando, and before him, Coco Chanel, "It's more important how you look than how you feel," which made the idea of "letting ourselves go," as our aunts would say with a shudder, as mortifying as those dreams in which we appear in public naked.

In fact, the better shape we were in, the more we seemed to talk about improving ourselves. At our beach retreat, size 2 princesses Deborah and Sissy discussed their "food issues" over bags of M&Ms, while their suite-mate, 250-pound Bonnie, sat on the couch reading the newest Harry Potter. "I wouldn't have to just lose weight—I'd have to lose a whole other person!" Bonnie suddenly burst out. I ached for her, and while she seemed content with her single-girl lifestyle with her books and the cats about whom she wrote delightful stories, I also wished she could find a way to enjoy her body, just as it was. When I saw the Big Dance Troupe made up of plus-size women on *Entertainment Tonight,* I immediately looked them up on the Web and sent her the address.

When we began showing up at the retreats *sans* makeup and

in oversized T-shirts, we found a new level of intimacy. It was interesting how appealing the usually glamorous and mascaraed Pamella looked with her brows and lashes shimmering their natural platinum. "It was that exorcise, 'If I Thought Like a Guy,'" she said. "After I wrote it, I decided to just get up, grab a cup of coffee, and leave the house, like Mike does." Now Anne and I, too, go out on occasion without a stitch of makeup—though the day we dress in the wrong colors may still be a long way off.

Wendy, brunette and statuesque, has a hunky blond husband just her height named Jock, who obviously adores her. She also has a Kirstie Alley–like self-awareness that won't quit: "I'm imagining all the ways I will wear my size 12 jeans again," she wrote. "I mean, if there's a famine and I lose weight and I can find (them), buried under the size 14's and 16's."

Next Wendy described a memory that made many of us look at one another in recognition:

> I can probably pinpoint the exact moment my eating disorder turned the switch to "on." My father, my brother and I were going home . . . and we came to an old bridge that said "No Trucks Over One Ton." Grinning, my father pulled the Falcon over, and said to my brother, "Hey, bud, we better let your sister out!" I was thirteen. I weighed maybe 120 and was five feet eight. . . .

"But you know what I found out?" she said, returning to her usual wit. "[Men] don't see that. What they see is a pretty sure thing. . . . A living, breathing woman who, if he plays his cards right, will give him a blow job once in a while. Cellulite? Men can't spell cellulite, much less see it. . . . They're just wondering whether their penises are a lot, or just a little smaller, than the guy before them."

Sick of the Beauty Rule at last, we all applauded when Ronnie read the bear story:

> In my next life, I'd like to come back as a bear. When you're a bear, you get to hibernate. You do nothing but sleep for six months. Before [that], you're supposed to eat yourself stupid. . . . You birth children who are the size of walnuts while you're sleeping and wake to . . . cute, cuddly cubs. . . . Your mate expects you to wake up growling. He expects you [to] have hairy legs and excess body fat.

It reminded me of the time some friends and I went to a bar in a remote part of Wyoming, and one of the cowboys slouched over his beer turned to look at us and said, "Look at that bunch of wimmen—and every one of 'em beautiful!"

7.

There is no duty we so much underrate as the duty of being happy.
By being happy, we sow anonymous benefits upon the world.

—ROBERT LOUIS STEVENSON

Habits of Happiness. Because we get to know one another so well in Zona Rosa, I began recording what I saw as our Habits of Happiness—those little secrets for living that each of us has evolved, and from which the rest of us can learn.

For one of us it's the generous spirit revealed when she paid her sister Zona Rosan's fare to France, so they could spend that time together: "I knew how special she was when she came over with a bunch of flowers while I was going through a rough spot soon after we met," said the recipient of her gift, and throughout the years they have been there for each other. Lynn likes to walk on the beach with her dog, stopping to read a meditation book, or draw with the colored pencils she carries in her backpack. When Carol O. was tending her dying mother, she stroked her dogs and cats: "I had my fingers in fur all the time." When Courtney, fifty-eight, told me she had taken up roller skating alone at her local rink, I laughed out loud, delighted by the image of her swirling past the preteens in her high-top skates. It was a reminder of Courtney's perpetual girlishness.

Marsha displays an enviable serenity, even, it turns out, when she isn't feeling that way, such as during the time her job changed from the one she had conquered over the years to one that meant a much more frantic pace, at odds with her natural temperament. Yet years of four A.M. yoga have kept her centered, and her slender frame flexible and sinuous; the gorgeous clothes from Nordstrom's with which she adorns it—"my weakness"—accentuate a waistline that most of us would die for. Indeed, she conquered the onset of arthritis via exercise, and she's attracted to workouts that require balance, such as the trapeze course she took, though just the idea of walking across space on a rope made the rest of us gasp. While reading from Marsha's exquisite novel-in-progress, I observed that the balance she sought physically spilled over into her writing as well: there is nothing that can hurry Marsha, ever. She does whatever it takes, however much time it might require.

Pamella gets up at five each morning—"It's so great to see the sun rise and have that special time alone"—and never flags during the day. When she wears her "butt pants," as described on *Oprah,* it's easy to see what her early mornings at the gym have done for her body. Like my cat Amber, Pamella can also sleep just about anywhere; she doesn't mind sleeping in the living room or on the sleeping porch when we run out of room at the retreats. She has even trained herself—to the envy of many of us—not to get up to go to the bathroom during the night. "One night I woke up and said, no, I'm not getting up. And then I never did again." And Pamella is just as persistent at working away at her novel-in-progress; once she makes her mind up, it's a done deal.

Doris is possibly one of the most focused women I know, and that focus is never on the trivia about which the rest of us obsess, such as men, sex, clothes, or weight. Instead, she's thinking about funny events in her life, past and present, her scholarly pursuits, and amusing anecdotes that reveal a mind ever in the present. Quiet and gentle, an actress in local theater as well as a writer, Doris turns in humorous, surprising essays each month. Her dry, almost English wit reminds us of a combination of Dame Edna and Miss Marple, and has us laughing aloud before we even finish her first paragraph.

"Bubbly" doesn't begin to describe Jill's joie de vivre, which she maintains despite the things in her life that are hard for the rest of us even to hear about. As we sat on the patio in France, she wore the pink beret she had barely taken off since she bought it at the market, her blond curls emerging from its edges, and talked about a painful, even shocking, discovery about her husband, and what she did next. Instead of keeping what many would see as a shameful family secret, she immediately announced her plight to everyone in earshot, from her mom to her pastor to her therapist to friends. "Everybody knows that if something is going on in my life, the whole world is going to know it!" she explained, hugging her knees and laughing as she described her method of reducing her stress by reaching out.

Needless to say, my sister Anne has also long been my inspiration. I called her "Cinnamon Roll" when we were little because she was so sweet, and sharing Zona Rosa has made us even closer. We have always talked about everything, from recipes to poems, sometimes within the same paragraph, as in "What's that cooking?" and "What are you working on?" And while we have different lifestyles—she likes to hit the gym early every morning and to knit while watching a movie with Larry each evening, and I like to get to my desk first thing and eat at night from a tray in bed, surrounded by books and new magazines—I have learned everyday courage from her, especially since her diagnoses of lupus and Crohn's disease.

I'm sure their lessons will go on and on—and never have I learned so much so effortlessly and with so much pleasure. When some of the Zona Rosans got together to brainstorm their ideas for a title for this book, their choice was *Blood Sisters*. For in Zona Rosa, immersed in what Susan J. calls our "estrogen-soaked atmosphere," even the most unlikely of us become sisters.

8.

The connections between and among women are . . . the most potentially transforming force on the planet.

—ADRIENNE RICH

The Secret Sect. In 1993, not too long after the Velvet Revolution, Anne and I visited Prague and my friend Diana, who had given up a tenure-track job at a college in Massachusetts to move to the city of the man she had fallen in love with during her research for her political science dissertation. Diana's journalist boyfriend regaled us with stories of before the revolution, a period he called Golden Totalitarianism, when he and his pals, unable to make money, made art: music and poetry. They also typed out or copied by hand forbidden books—among the most popular in English were Jack Kerouac's *On the Road* and Joseph Heller's *Catch-22*—to pass out among themselves, an act for which one could be imprisoned. "We were all so close," he said with longing. When Anne and I were taken by a writer-friend to a private pub where the former revolutionaries still met, and where we had to press a buzzer and say who we were in order to enter, the air in the underground room was thick with laughter and cigarette smoke. They were a secret sect, their spirits obviously intact after years of struggle.

Later I dreamed what I think of as my archetypal Zona Rosa dream: in it, the Zona Rosans and I are held prisoner by Nazis in a supermarket in which the shelves are filled with pink packages. We stack the packages higher and higher, and fill the space with a blinding violet and fuchsia light, thereby defeating our enemy when they return.

"This is an important dream," I wrote in my journal. "I and other women fight an oppressor using our femininity. . . . The oppressor is real and life threatening and *male*." Surrounded by fuchsia and lavender lights, bathed in the deliciousness of the Power of the Pink—we were real-life wonder-women, bonded and strengthened by our friendship.

9.

French is for secrets, English for stories.
—POET AND NOVELIST RUTH KNAFO SETTON

Southern Women Are Like French Women, and French Women Are Like Cats. When I worked in Poetry in the Schools, a second-grade boy, already fascinated by the other gender, wrote—with some help, on that paper with wide lines—that "women are like pocketbooks." For the rest of the class period, I caught him more than once trying to unclasp my purse. But he was right: when we open up, we're as full of secrets as our handbags.

In Greek, the word *mystery* means to close the mouth, which, as Lewis Hyde explains in his book *The Gift*, may refer to the secrecy to which initiates of ancient religions and secret societies were sworn. It may also refer to the belief that ultimately a mystery cannot be spoken of or fully explained. "Shown, witnessed, revealed," writes Hyde, "but not explained."

Or, as I sometimes said to kids when I worked in Poetry in the Schools, "I don't have to understand you to like you." This also helped them see that we don't have to fully comprehend a poem or a painting in order to enjoy it—in fact, we may delight in its mystery.

In Zona Rosa, we've learned that it's not only fun but healing to share our secrets, and that while we're doing so at our retreats, we're bonding in special ways, refreshingly free of what cardiologist and author Larry Dossey calls "time sickness"—the obsessive belief that there's not enough of it, and that we must hurry, always hurry. As we become closer, we're also preparing to talk about the *really* hard things in our lives, as we will in chapter 6.

Indeed, the beautiful, zany, secret-filled Zona Rosans confirm one of my favorite theories: *southern women are like French women, and French women are like cats.* My fat cat Amber is peering down at me from the top of a file cabinet as I write this, and I see afresh that she has her own Habits of Happiness. She doesn't conceal her efforts at grooming and beauty. She asks for what she wants, and persists until she gets it. She is mysterious, and always a good listener. She knows she's beautiful—no matter what. And she doesn't expect to become famous—she just *is.*

Knee-jerk Reaction #5: Thinking that we can't be serious women, and still be girlie and have fun. Imagining that we have to maintain a certain image of ourselves, even around our girlfriends.

PILATES ON PAPER

In Praise of Shallowness, or Some Trivial Things I Really, Really Love. "A man just doesn't understand what a bedspread can do for a woman!" a Zona Rosan in North Carolina said, quoting her new daughter-in-law. When author Barbara Hagerty visited with her beautiful book, *Handbags,* we all but slobbered over the full-color photos. In Sophie Kinsella's *Shopaholic and Sister,* Becky's downfall is the 2,000-euro Angel bag she sees on the cover of *Vogue,* and which is only carried by celebs. "You've *got* to get these stilettos from Neiman's with lip prints all over them, like our logo!" Pamella exclaimed, and my mouth watered, though I could imagine the price. When my novel *The Hurricane Season* came out, I bought the most ex-

pensive costume jewelry I had ever owned—huge swinging star
earrings, embedded with rhinestones. I bought them in a hurry
to wear to a book party that night. But then the stars began to
inspire me—when I wore them, I *was* a star. Despite the press
otherwise, "shallow" things—beautiful clothes, 200-count cotton sheets, feeling thin or pumped, a delicious new novel, having a pedicure or massage, a flirtatious look from an attractive
man, or having a piña colada with girlfriends—do make us
happy. What are some of the things you enjoy whenever you
can? What are some pleasures you could give yourself but
don't? And what are some you can list with the intention of
giving them to yourself at the first possible moment?

Little Altars Everywhere (and My Magical Rock). Have you
ever had an object that made you happy, just by knowing it existed? Life coach Martha Beck suggests clients under stress carry
a soothing object in their purse or pocket. And while I don't always carry them on my person, I have all kinds of magical
things—at the top of my list are my cowgirl boots, embossed
with red roses and bought from a thrift shop, one given me by
Susan J., the other by Carolyn, with a card on one reading "for
kicking ass" and one on the other "for stomping butt." And then
there is my vast collection of shoes arranged around my bedroom where I can see them, along with a dresser top covered in
scarves, jewelry, and darling little bags—I like things out where
I can see them. I have a musical pink scepter that I wave to bring
the Zona Rosans to order, an ordinary rock painted gold and
thus given magic powers by my eight-year-old niece, Faye, and
baskets full of photos of the Zona Rosans—the refrigerator is already covered with them—that live on a small table in my dining room. "This is your altar," Ronnie said, dusting around it,

and indeed, it makes me happy just to look at it, as does seeing the stacks of books everywhere, and Lily's huge paintings—the eyes of the cats who are her subjects, staring down at me from the walls. *Make an altar for yourself by creating a space for some of your favorite things.* Listing some of them first is a good way to start. Then look around and find a special place for them.

My Romance with Women's Magazines, and Other Secret Vices of Serious Women. Grandmother Lee read *Seventeen* magazine until she was in her seventies, claiming she was looking for fashions to copy for Anne and me. But I always suspected she was really indulging the teenager inside herself, and I obviously inherited her magazine gene. All it takes to make me forget the pressures of the day is to climb into bed with a stack of magazines, from *Vogue* and *Elle* to *Star* and *First.* Or, as otherwise serious Zona Rosan Robin said, "I love to go to a doctor's office—then I have an excuse to sit and read magazines." Although even the ones I adore predictably and rhythmically repeat themselves, I always find them comforting, addressing as they do the realities of our lives as women. Indeed, I call it "research"—I've learned as much of what I really need to know from reading women's magazines as from any other source (ask a man if *he* knows how many carbs are in a handful of pasta, the best way to communicate with one's significant other—they could use this one—or the Web page address for stitchnbitch.org). The magazines I love often contain some top-notch writing, not to speak of the visual feast of page after page of sumptuous photographs. *What unwinds you like nothing else?* Name the ways, whether getting on the phone with a friend, playing with your dog, or taking off in the afternoon for a first-run movie—the more ways you have, the better.

❋

Which leads us to **Listomania.** I love de-cluttering my dresser drawers. While writing this book I've kept myself going with the fantasy of all my jewelry and scarves arranged in perfect order. But my primary stress reliever is making lists—of the things I'm *not* going to do while getting this book written (like de-clutter those drawers), and the things I *will* do as soon as I'm through— like visiting Lulu at her new house in Phoenix, ordering something luscious from the Victoria's Secret catalog, and getting someone hunky to tote the eighteen boxes of books setting at my elbow into the attic. One of my favorite lists is *Life Repair 101: Clean out my purse. Polish my shoes. Balance my checkbook. Get a picture framed. Have alterations done. Get rid of stuff. Put clothes in order. Get rid of a bad man.* Another is *Money in the Bank,* by which I don't mean money at all, but the good stuff in my life: *Writing done and ready to go out into the world. Friends who help—and help and help. Places to go, pals to visit, and a packed suitcase. Skills I've developed over the years—like teaching and public speaking. My looks, style, and health (and some pretty clothes). My genetic blessings—e.g., intelligence, optimism, and thighs disinclined to cellulite. Freedom from stress (when I can arrange that). Experience with a capital "E."* And last, but not least: Zona Rosa and the Zona Rosans. I write all these lists in present tense, whether I have them all at the moment or not. I've also been known, when angry with Zane, to list my reasons for pique, then present them to him the next morning before breakfast—not merely to make a point, but to de-clutter my brain, so that I can get on with my day. Now begin some lists for yourself. If you wish, start with something simple, like listing your favorite clothes, then making a plan for putting them at the forefront of your closet. The possibilities are endless, and Listomania may become for you, as it is for me, a favorite tool for centering.

Your Picture of Success. On the other hand, you may already have just about everything you need for happiness and don't even know it. My idea of success was once having fresh-cut flowers in the house and being able to buy all the new books I wanted. Now that I have those, it's seeing a good movie the moment it comes out, having subscriptions to all my favorite magazines, and the Sunday *New York Times* out on the dining room table all week waiting to be read—all, easily achievable. In her book *Just Enough: Tools for Creating Success in Your Work and Life,* Laura Nash posits that there are four "spheres of life"—happiness, achievement, significance, and what we leave behind for others. She says that having just enough in each sphere is more fulfilling than having way too much in any one of them. She further explains that workaholism, the cult of celebrity, and the out-of-proportion amounts paid some people lead us to ignore the very spheres that might give us the most pleasure. "You are going to enjoy a cup of coffee a lot more if you're not worrying about whether it's the best cup of coffee you can get," she told the *New York Times,* and recommended finding a level of "just enough." She describes her dad, who lost an arm in World War II, and saw his disability as giving him more time for jazz, poetry, and the other things he loved. "No one can maximize all four things," she said. "And no amount of success in one area will buy you satisfaction in the others." How do you stand on the four spheres as described by Ms. Nash? Draw a pie—colored pencils are always fun, especially if we choose the shades that we feel go with that part of our lives, such as pink for happiness, magenta for achievement, yellow for significance, and green for what we leave behind. *Just be sure to indicate the good stuff you already have.*

BOOK THERAPY LITE: BAD BOOKS I HAVE LOVED

How long has it been since you've stayed up all night reading simply because you couldn't stop? It's one of life's great pleasures, and surely among the most harmless.

One of our Zona Rosa exorcises is to write about "Bad Books I Have Loved," which, like childhood books, always hold a special place in our hearts because of the way they made us feel back then. I don't know how *Forever Amber* or *Peyton Place*—shockers when I was a teenager—have held up. But when I reread *Dragonwyck* by Anya Seton, I found it as titillating in its repressed way as I did at twenty-one; I turned the pages faster and faster as the heroine fought her attraction to her sexy and sexist patroon husband who, virtually a stranger before their marriage, had brutalized her (in unspecified ways, of course) on their wedding night.

And then there's my secret stash of Victoria Holt novels, in which heroines are strong and feisty, and find true love after overcoming great obstacles. I was relieved when I found out that a Ph.D. I met at an academic conference loved them, too.

"My two worlds rarely come together because . . . academics tend to deride romance; romance readers often ignore literary fiction," Mary Bly, a college professor who teaches English literature and writes historical romances, wrote in the *New York Times*, going on to say that romance novels actually validate female desire. "These days, however, a romance heroine is likely to toss her own bra, and if buttons are skittering on the floor, they're quite possibly shirt studs."

When I'm driving somewhere to speak or teach, literature lite in the form of well-plotted yet undemanding novels, like those by Barbara Taylor Bradford or Sandra Brown, fill the bill. In the car, I can listen to most anything—the simpler, the more *Lifetime* TV-ish the better.

Chick lit, good or bad, is just about always to my taste. It can't be too silly for me because if I've chosen to read it, I'm already in a certain mood. Did Helen Fielding, before her vast popularity, wonder how her character Bridget Jones's habit of writing in her diary using initials to stand for almost everything would go over with the general public? Fortunately for us, Ms. Fielding didn't fear creating an inane heroine.

There's no bottom line to what we women can appreciate when it comes to humor, and I love to laugh out loud, whatever the cause, such as at *The Botox Diaries,* in which a character declares, "I don't care what the magazines say, forty is the new eighty." I also love dish, as in *The Nanny Diaries* and *The Devil Wore Prada,* and I could have eaten with a spoon *Sex and the City* creator Candace Bushnell's *Four Blondes* and *Trading Up*—in which shallow women don't necessarily come to a bad end.

Obviously, plenty of stuff is out there to satisfy our longing for shallowness. Like Godiva chocolates—which, by the way, go very well with any of the above—we can enjoy them without fear of losing our way or our basic seriousness of purpose. Like Martha Beck, I believe that most of us have a built-in limit when indulging the superficial; also that we'll pop back after having our fill, refreshed and ready to go back to work. So go for it—bad books you love may be just the Jungle Gardenia cologne you want sometimes instead of your usual Chanel No. 5.

CHAPTER SIX

"IF I'M REALLY HONEST,
I'M NOT ACTUALLY OKAY WITH…"

How Writing plus the Power of the Pink Helps Keep Us Sane
When the Worst Happens

1.

God writes straight with crooked lines.

—PORTUGUESE PROVERB

"If I'm really honest, I'm not actually okay with being slaughtered," one cow says to another in a macabre but funny *New Yorker* cartoon. We Zona Rosans all loved this so much that the first part of the sentence became another exorcise in which we encouraged ourselves to share our deepest fears.

When I was asked to be on a panel titled "When Life Interrupts Memoir," I realized that the title could have been the story of my life. I started out as a writer, and then, just as I felt I had gotten off to a good start, things happened that were beyond my imaginings.

In this chapter, we'll discuss the traumas that attack us out of the blue, creating a Before and After in our lives. We'll consider things so big that denial is no longer a possibility, and the reality of what we are dealing with fills our days and nights. We'll talk about the moments when our hands are sweaty and terror clutches our hearts, making us look back on simple pleasures as though they were in the distant past.

We'll discover how trying to conceal or run from our despair only makes it fester, in danger of hardening into the stone in the breast, the burden of the untold story, even Carpal Tunnel of the Soul. We'll learn to live out the adage that the truth will set us free.

We'll learn how those of us who already have writing skills or some other art practice in place are at an advantage in dealing with the inevitable. Indeed, writing practice—writing every day when life is normal, even boring—may be our best insurance against an uncertain future, more important than long-term care or wealth, because as long as our brains are intact, we can write and create.

Along the way, we discover how to compartmentalize, prioritize, nurture, and even pamper ourselves during even the worst of times. We also find that we need our girlfriends more than ever.

✻

Motherhood—with its heightened joys—is often the source of our greatest pain, and the most unexpected, since no woman holds her darling newborn dreaming of a traumatic future. In *A Potent Spell: Mother Love and the Power of Fear,* Janna Malamud Smith points out that women always feel responsible for their children, no matter how old they become; also that motherhood itself fills us with anxiety because of our need to keep our children safe.

Even in this time of high-powered glamour moms, there's no way we can protect ourselves from this most basic of fears—and our devastation when things go wrong. Or, as someone wrote, "Having a child is like having someone else walking around in the world with my heart in their body."

Some of the women in this chapter came with a burning story to tell, even several years later—sometimes it takes that long before we can write about it. Others felt they must do *something*, even in the midst of shock and loss. And some of us were already in the group, simply living our lives, when we suddenly found ourselves knocked for a loop.

You'll meet Ann, Jill, Jalaine, and others who, as successful adults, found themselves confronted with situations so over-whelming that they erased for a time everything but the large-ness and intensity of the foreground. You'll hear how they faced unusual illnesses, unexpected deaths, and devastating things with their kids.

In Zona Rosa, we learn that what besets us, and what we thought was unique, is simply part of the human condition. The question becomes not "Why me?" but "Why not me?" And while I wish that this chapter could be shorter, given the nature of existence, we have more examples than we would wish.

Whatever its cause, the women in these pages responded to their anguish in different ways. Some, with courage and a passion for truth, dive without hesitation into self-excavation, using writing as a tool. Others respond, either immediately or after the fact, with irony and humor. Some even manage, despite their circumstances, to reach out to others and become advocates. Almost all experience a deep-ened spirituality, the search for meaning becoming a crucial part of their lives. And almost all find that writing is a tool

for healing. Some—in what for them is a healthy response—
use writing as a way to distract themselves.

And sadly, some, not realizing that it's when we're in the
grips of grief that we most need such gifts, deny themselves
the support of the group, citing their depression as a reason not
to write or to come to Zona Rosa.

Whatever route we choose, we are there for one another. As
a friend e-mailed, "Girlfriends listen when your lose a job or a
friend . . . when your children break your heart . . . when your
parents' minds and bodies fail . . . when the men in your life let
you down." We also become one another's inspiration. As Zona
Rosan and nurse-to-the dying Pat says, "It is an honor to be
with them at that time."

This chapter is about the beauty of sharing everything—
and about how, over and over, as we share our stories, we realize afresh the truth of literary critic Austin Warren's statement
that "Art . . . makes that pleasant to contemplate, which would
be painful to experience, or even, in life, to witness."

2.

Break my heart, so love can flow more freely.

—SUFI PROVERB

The Miracle of Creativity, and How It Blesses Us in the Worst of Times

September 11, 2001. At 6:30 A.M., I drive Fred's gunmetal
Lexus toward my job fifty-five miles away. I meditate on the
uplifting vision of my children's book about my three children and a butterfly, picturing it scattering out over the world,
bringing a gift to children. Briefly, I think of calling Fred in

New York on my cell—we often talk as he walks to the subway going to his Wall Street job at the 104th floor of the
World Trade Center—but I decide the e-mail I sent him
would start his day, and I will talk to him later. Sometimes I
call him at work and picture him—six foot five in his custom-
made suit and Brooks Brother striped tie, standing in the middle of the busy sprawling office. And I say in baby-talk, "Are
you Mama's baby?" And he always whispers, "Yes—I'm
Mama's baby!"

"Mother, I don't know if I'll live to be an old man," Ann's
twenty-seven-year-old son Fred told her at the family's lake
house in New Hampshire in August of 2001. "But if I walk
through this door, and never breathe another breath, I will
have had a perfect life," he went on, indicating the screened
door, the fresh blue lake bathed in butter yellow sunshine.
Ann, who teaches art in a South Georgia high school for most
of the year, was there to spend time with Fred and his beautiful fiancée, Annelise. "They looked like movie stars," Ann later
wrote. "I squinted, drinking in every detail of his handsome
John-John Kennedy-like face, desperately trying to picture
him as an old man . . . I couldn't."

Throughout her visit, Ann fingered the Tiffany silver heart
Fred had given her with the words "I love you" engraved on the
back. The three of them had recently made a sunset cruise,
arranged by Fred, on the Hudson. "Time stood still as the sun
beamed from behind a silhouetted Statue of Liberty and in the
distance the elegant twin towers graced the New York skyline,"
she wrote. Fred's two sisters were ensconced in their own lives,
Ann's difficult divorce from Fred's wealthy father, Fred Senior,
was in the distant past, and she was happily remarried to Mike,

an English professor. She was a happy woman, and she had just had a perfect visit with her perfect son.

Now, this September morning, I'm talking to the arts program coordinator at our high school in Waycross, Georgia. It's nine-twenty A.M. A woman walks in from the left and tells us, "The World Trade Center has been hit by planes!" "Oh, no!" My heart stops. "My son works there. Where were they hit?" "At the top," she replies. Time freezes. I grab my cell and dial Fred's number—it just bleeps. I call his office phone—the same. Then I get out my address book and fumble to find Annie's home or business number, but I can't get her either. I knew Fred was in New York . . . I knew he was an early bird. I had just talked to him on Saturday, September ninth. "Mom," he told me, "you know how much I love you, and nothing will ever come between us—nothing!" My last words to him were "I love you."

In a bubble of skewed time, I drove through small Georgia towns toward my family home where my husband and I live. "God, please let me know. Please let me know what has happened to my Fred!" I prayed. At that instant, in an indigo sky, on the edge of a graying white cloud, I saw an angel. First, it was the right wing . . . then the form . . . followed by the left wing. As the angel lingered, I struggled in vain to make out the features on the oval face. There are no words for this moment . . . for my heart knew . . . a mother knows when her child is not on this earth.

Ann was single when we met, a tall brunette beauty with long dark curls tumbling down her back, the kind of woman other women might envy—if they didn't know what was really happening in her life. She was going through a brutal divorce, and soon after, a hysterectomy. Her little Savannah flat was just down the street from mine, and we became fast friends. She became part of the original Zona Rosa group, and we were both involved in an Adult Children of Alcoholics group; we also led successful workshops together for 12-step groups called Words and Pictures—she led the visual art exercises, I the writing. And even then, she had a spiritual bent. "Faith, Hope, Charity," read the left side of a note she handed me one day; "Certainty, Intention, Help," read the right. I remember how impressed I had been when she refused pain medication after her surgery because of her commitment to sobriety, but I also perceived her as fragile because her emotions always seemed to be on the surface. (Later, I would realize what a strength this was.)

We had also had our differences. She was a vibrant artist, and I impatiently encouraged her to show her work, but getting the recognition she deserved didn't seem that important to her. I was also living with Zane, who definitely wasn't booze-free. After a while she moved out of town with her new husband, whom she had met at a 12-step group. Sometimes she would call to report that her high school art students had won yet more prizes for their work, or I would receive a postcard from the lake house in New Hampshire where she and Mike spent the summer months. But it had been a long while since I had seen her.

Now as I sat down to call her, I wondered how we would be able to talk about something so devastating that I—a friend who only barely remembered the cute, curly-haired boy—hadn't been able to absorb.

But instead of being wrung out with grief, as I had imagined, I hung up feeling blessed by our conversation, and amazed by Ann's resiliency. With an innate wisdom, she had known intuitively how to protect herself, and what she needed to survive. She had not seen *any* of the TV coverage of the towers collapsing; nor had she followed any of the news coverage: "When it starts to come on, Mike makes sure I don't see it." She said that the tomato sandwiches her twin sister, Martha, brought her in bed, and their crying sessions together in the hot tub, were all that kept her alive at first.

I had always noticed how, in her writing, Ann went straight to the perfect visual image to express her feelings. (One poem, for example, was about how she felt like a sour, neglected washcloth beside her twin, whom she perceived as being washed in Downy and tenderly folded by their mother.) Now, since she was an artist, she had already begun to think in images, not the images of the towers collapsing and what had happened inside them (she later told me that she never let herself go there), but of Fred and what his life had meant. Almost without a pause, she had begun to create a narrative from what had happened, as though she were already glimpsing where the experience would take her. She would first, as a tribute to Fred, finish writing and illustrating *Freddy & Flossie Flutterby,* the children's story she had told Fred and his sisters over and over, about a boy who longed for a "betta place."

"I painted the paintings and wrote down the story for four years, from 1994 to 1997, when I was in Zona Rosa. Having that body of work saved my life when my darling Fred died," she says.

Ann's friend and sister Zona Rosan Pat, who went with her and her sister Martha to see Ground Zero, says that Ann sat caressing the book she had written for her lost son. "It was like when I visited the Vietnam memorial," said Pat, who was dealing with her own demons by writing her story of life as a nurse during that war.

Today, Ann is back in Zona Rosa, inspiring the rest of us as she writes the memoir she started after publishing the brightly illustrated children's book and creating the foundation called Betta Place in Fred's honor. She is able to talk about Fred easily now, and with pride. She also believes they are still in touch and regularly talks to him through a psychic. Fred's handsome face splashes Betta Place posters and handouts, and something larger than her grief has taken its place.

Through Betta Place, 12,015 schoolchildren, eight school administrators, and 111 teachers are dedicated to making changes that will have long-term positive effects on the effort toward world peace. One of the schools involved, Golden Door Charter School in Jersey City, New Jersey, saw the terrorist attack; another, P.S. 53 on Staten Island, lost 218 of its town's residents that day, many of them firefighters. Ann's schedule is heavy with speaking engagements to educators, describing and teaching the concepts she has created for use in Betta Place, Inc., such as "flashlighting," in which we keep the light—the focus—on ourselves, rather than on judging others, as well as the symbols worn on the sleeves of Betta Place shirts, indicating a student's special talent.

At our last meeting, Ann brought a copy of *Lucky* magazine in which the willowy Annelise modeled skinny jeans. She read Annelise's account of her and Fred's courtship, adding that that morning, Annelise had gone back to kiss him goodbye where he lay in bed with the hairdryer going—a childhood habit because he loved the warm air—"And he said I love you, with the most perfect look of peace on his face." Annelise lost not only Fred that day but her brother, who also worked in the Twin Towers, and, despite the difference in their ages, she and Ann have bonded over their grief.

We all feel energized every time we see Ann—instead of being reminded of an agonizing event, we are inspired by the way her creativity spills over into everything and everyone she touches. She is the perfect example of character and creativity combined with a sense of destiny; and the fact that with them, no matter what our situation, our light can shine.

Or, as she wrote at the top of her last manuscript submission, "Life may not be the party we hoped for, but while we are here we might as well dance."

3.

What the caterpillar calls the end of the world, the master calls a butterfly.

—RICHARD BACH, CONTRIBUTED
BY ZONA ROSAN JILL ANGEL DAVIS

Finding Meaning in Suffering, or Outreach Is Everything

"There are things worse than death." The doctor paused. "I want you to know that I will deny this conversation to anyone and forever."

We sat once more in the hospital conference room outside PICU. The doctor looked at us. Bill and I looked at each other and then back to him.

"The amputations and the brain damage." He grimaced. "That level of disfiguration for life. While I am doing this test tonight, while the hospital is quiet, I have the opportunity to let him go. But only if you both agree."

Bill and I looked at each other again. Disfiguration? I thought. I didn't care what Christopher looked like. I did care that he lacked any function for enjoying or appreciating life.

"We all have to be in agreement," the doctor continued. "I

cannot have another doctor come in and accuse me, 'You killed him!' At this point, medical intervention is not prolonging your son's life; it is prolonging his death. I will leave you and come back after rounds. You must both agree."

The door to the conference room closed behind him.

My eyes returned to Bill's.

"What are you thinking?" I asked.

"What are you thinking?" he countered.

"I think that God is calling Christopher home and this man is his chariot."

"I see no reason to do this now. We have plenty of time."

I took a deliberate breath. "We should do this now because God has sent this man of mercy and Christopher will be able to slip quietly away. He doesn't even know us."

"I can't say yes in this way," Bill argued.

"In what way?"

"Pushing him over."

"Pushing him over? So, you think he's going to get well?"

"No."

"How much more does he need to suffer?" I asked. "This is letting him go without further suffering."

"There will be opportunities."

"This is an opportunity!" I whispered in a hiss. "Enough already. I will not watch him gasp for breath with pneumonia!"

"Some suffering will have to be involved."

"Some suffering has been involved." My voice rose. "More than enough suffering has been involved. For the love of God, let him go . . ."

"I know that letting him go would be best for him, but"— Bill paused—"I cannot because of fear of God."

"And I can because of love of God."

A light tap sounded on the door. The doctor entered. He looked at us.

"We cannot agree," I said.

"You can have more time to think about it," he offered. "I will put the test off until tomorrow morning."

I went to Christopher's bedside. I took a photograph. I wondered if it would be his last. He was so peaceful. He looked like a rag doll that someone had been playing doctor with, all of his limbs bandaged and swaddled in hospital blankets. No amount of mommie kisses would help this.

I couldn't hug him back to me.

I couldn't send him on because his parents could not agree.

God, I begged, please take him home. Take this decision away from us.

By the next morning, another doctor had become involved in the procedure. The opportunity was gone.

At forty-three, Jill has had to bear more than any one woman should have, but you wouldn't dream it if you met her, she's so bouncy, bubbly, and perpetually up. But if you read pages from her memoir or hear her speak you are destined to feel tears rise to your eyes—and be stunned by both her survival skills and her resiliency.

Jill is one of those who needed a period of several years to absorb what had happened to her before she could write about it. "But I did write about the first six days, when he was being misdiagnosed, right after we went home from the hospital, because I was afraid I would forget. Also, I was afraid that if I forgot something, it would mean I loved him less."

When Jill's son Christopher, an angelic-looking three-year-old, developed a fever, she assumed it was just another of those childhood things, and guilt-tripped her reluctant husband, Bill, into coming home early from his office at a nearby university so she could take Christopher to their pediatrician. The doctor concurred that her son's fever was nothing to worry about, and after prescribing antibiotics, said Christopher would probably be better in a few days.

Instead, Christopher—to Jill and their doctor's surprise—got worse and worse, until by day six, he was airlifted to Children's Hospital in Birmingham, where he was diagnosed with Rocky Mountain spotted fever.

But by then, it was too late. Christopher was in a coma, brain-damaged and blind, and the doctors insisted that his fingers and feet be amputated inch-by-inch in order to prevent gangrene spreading through his little body. After four months, Jill, Christopher, Bill, and the kids went home to spend the three years it would take for Christopher to die—a time during which his seizures became near constant and he frequently screamed in distress.

At the hospital and during the first weeks of crisis, Bill, twenty-four years Jill's senior, had made it clear that he was one of those men who didn't handle hard stuff well. Jill, on the other hand, was a high-energy mother who had been home-schooling her children. Back at home, everything fell to her, and she made the decision to take Christopher with her everywhere, ignoring those who stared in curiosity or revulsion.

Among her funnier and more macabre stories was the one in which a visiting minister to her church glared at her after his prayer, thinking she was allowing Christopher to cry out and otherwise misbehave. Then there was the time she insisted on taking him to the water park and riding down the water slide with him in her lap until the manager of the park told her adults weren't allowed to ride the slide. Then when she let Christopher—to his delight—slide down alone and he twisted to arrive head first, the woman told her the children had to slide feet first. "'He doesn't *have* any feet!' I finally told her," Jill said.

During those three years, it took every bit of psychic energy, faith, and strength Jill could muster to take care of Christopher and keep things as normal as possible for her other two sons. She put her anger with her husband on the back burner. Then four months after Christopher died, she found herself pregnant again, a condition that she believed was significant; when her new son was born, they named him Daniel:

> Christopher had been in the hospital six weeks. We asked a volunteer to sit with Christopher while we went out. We... hit the dollar store [and] I made a bee line to the book table. There I saw... Danny Thomas's book, *Make Room for Danny*... about how Danny Thomas's child got sick from a rat [bite].... I read about Jude, the patron saint of the hopeless. I thought about this man who had made a promise to God and who had kept it in a big way, eventually building a huge children's hospital ... as the shrine [Saint Jude] deserved.... I knew I would one day have a son and name him Daniel Jude.

Jill and Bill had a romantic courtship—she the vivacious blonde, he the older, reserved professor of philosophy. Indeed, she had proposed to him by writing a letter to Garrison Keillor that Keillor read aloud on *A Prairie Home Companion*. But seven years after Christopher's death, Bill had already developed Stage 4 prostate cancer, and had been chemically and surgically castrated. Nevertheless, she confronted him, telling him—in possibly the understatement of the year—that she was no longer happy in the marriage. "If he hadn't gone straight to a marriage counselor, I would have left him. But he did."

When Daniel became the age Christopher had been when he got sick, Jill was finally hit by a long-overdue case of post-traumatic stress syndrome. She began therapy with a male therapist who first told her she was smart and sensual—then segued into seduction. Bill had just been diagnosed, and attracted to the therapist and sexually frustrated at home, Jill's anxiety escalated. "It was like having a lifeguard save your life—then come up afterward and put a lip-lock on you and finger you beneath your bathing suit," she said. She began seeing a new, woman therapist, but when her former therapist, in danger of being exposed, e-mailed her breaking their ties, Jill's internal conflict became so great that she imploded with self-hatred, and made a suicide attempt.

"I cracked up. But I also went on. I took one day a week off when I did nothing but lie in bed, surrounded by books. My favorites were about people who came back from suicide attempts and did something significant with their lives. Like Kay Redfield Jamison, who wrote *An Unquiet Mind*."

When Jill heard of another writer's piece on Asperger's syndrome, she suddenly realized what was wrong with Bill, and why he had been so unresponsive through the years. In Zona Rosa, we laughed, saying that a lot of men are like that. But Jill insisted that Asperger's, a form of autism, was the answer to why Bill had been unable to respond to or handle stress through the years.

Today, Jill's essay on her ordeal with Christopher, "The Paper Promise," is used by counselors and other grief professionals as a handout in hospitals for parents of terminally ill children. If there is one word that would describe her best, it is "clear"; she is so intelligent and honest in everything she does and says. She courageously—and to controversy—reads to large groups

the section from her book (quoted here) about her and Bill's agonizing argument when they were offered a chance to let
Christopher be euthanized.

And Jill is still able to laugh—which was demonstrated
when she described the day her new vibrator, complete with
G-spot stimulator, came in the mail, and how she had kept her
curious kids from opening the package. "At least I'm still vi-
brating," she said with a giggle.

4.

If you don't bring forth what is within you, what is within you will kill
you.

—THE GNOSTIC GOSPELS OF ST. THOMAS

The emotions we feel when in extended shock are not always
what we would suppose or choose. Jane was in her early thirties
and pregnant with her second child when her young husband
suffered the devastating stroke that left him unable to speak
but for a few words, as well as with a permanently dragging leg.
In order to support her family, she became a successful accountant. She also found moments of happiness with her husband, despite his disabilities: "He could say a few words—like
the day he called me over to the window to look out onto a
winter lake. 'Ducks, Jane, ducks,' he said." But after the Zona
Rosans gasped in admiration at her strength and good humor,
the two children raised to successful adulthood, Jane admitted
to rage and depression—and a feeling of being cheated—until
writing came into her life and saved her. She and her husband
now have less money, but Jane now has her dream job, writing
and teaching creative writing full-time.

Carolyn, a poet who is always honest, and therefore refreshing, admits to the rage she felt while watching her husband Bob die of Lou Gehrig's disease; worse, she felt during
that time that her art had also deserted her:

> I was still working [teaching English and creative writing at an
> inner-city high school] and having so many conflicting feelings
> about living and dying. It got to where I was merely trying to
> survive on no sleep and constant care of him. The only outlet I
> had was cooking. I'm a good cook, and I could get away from
> the horror of the disease by making him his favorite meals
> while he could still eat. . . . The basic writing I did during his
> illness was e-mails to my brother and Susan J. [her dear friend].
> Susan saved all the e-mails and gave them to me after he died.
> The words . . . are full of angst and anger. My love of life had
> been taken away by this ugly disease. The words, once lovely,
> became harsh. . . .
>
> As I planned his memorial service, I found the sweet words
> again. . . . The words came back to me, and I wrote a poem.
> We took his ashes out on a boat; my cousin John . . . read the
> poem and my son and I scattered his ashes and threw rose
> petals on the water.

At Bob's funeral, we were all concerned by Carolyn's ex-
haustion. But we were happy again when she was back at Zona
Rosa, sitting in her regular seat at the end of my yellow couch,
a sheaf of new poems in hand. She said that having writing in
her life before Bob's illness had given her something to look
forward to, and asserted her belief in the healing power of the
written word: "Writing makes you immortal. It's that simple."

And that's the way it is in Zona Rosa. We were with Joy
during her ovarian cancer, then with June as her beloved sister

died of multiple brain tumors. And later Carolyn would be there to comfort Susan J. as she lived through her husband's bout with non-Hodgkin's lymphoma.

5.

You must stay drunk on writing so reality cannot destroy you.

—RAY BRADBURY

"I should subtitle my book, 'How My Inner Comedic Bitch Beat Back the Demons and Saved My Life,'" says Kathleen, whose mordant wit I loved from the moment we met. "I'm convinced that my congenital sense of sarcasm and dark comedy is what got me through my decade from hell. Laughter was the only thing that pulled air into my lungs and kept me breathing, and I was always—and still am—on the lookout for my next fix."

Kathleen is fond of saying that her husband, Scott, was the only person she's ever known who has been banned from Kmart. A well-known attorney and mover and shaker, Scott once owned a club that regularly booked the likes of Odetta and Steve Martin in Athens, Georgia, where they lived and where Kathleen once played bass with a local band. A former alcoholic and heroin addict, Scott was clean and sober when he and Kathleen met, and she was sure she had met her soul mate. Nine years later, he had relapsed with a vengeance, and his six-figure income plummeted as "he started skipping A.A. to watch O.J. on TV." Soon he was driving 120 miles round-trip each day to a methadone clinic in Atlanta, and had tried to forge a narcotics prescription at the Big K pharmacy.

This took place three years before Scott's suspicious death, which is the subject of her oft-hilarious book, *Trials of a Dead*

Lawyer's Wife. By then Scott had developed a $400-a-day habit, and in a court-mandated treatment center, he met nurse-addict Brandi Scruggs. Within twelve days, he was sent home to continue to twitch in withdrawal, while Kathleen sorted through the $16,000 in bills for the cash advances on credit cards he had fraudulently obtained in her name. "My mother insisted that estrogen replacement therapy would solve all my problems," Kathleen wrote of that time. Before long, Scott was living in a luxury apartment with Brandi, and Kathleen's mother was diagnosed with inoperable lung cancer. Four weeks later, Scott was dead—but not before he had bequeathed his remaining estate of half a million dollars to Brandi.

As Kathleen, a divorce mediator, started to investigate, she discovered that Brandi had been on the scene at two other mysterious deaths, leading Kathleen to ask for a post-funeral autopsy and to begin the quest for the truth about Scott's death that would inform her book.

And then, as though the gods were sending her exactly what she needed, Goat, an old boyfriend from the past, now a vice cop, e-mailed to say he still loved her, and soon, after she discovered he had once arrested Brandi, they were a team, searching out the truth. Think Cybill Shepherd as former model turned private eye and detective Bruce Willis in *Moon-lighting*, except that Kathleen and Goat *were* having an affair!

Kathleen admits that, contrary to her book, Scott's downward spiral and their divorce weren't quite as funny while they were actually going on.

"The agony was terrible—it wrapped around me like an anaconda and just about squeezed the life out of me. . . . I wasn't keeping a journal back then—I was operating on much too primitive a level—but I found myself constantly scribbling down my thoughts and observations and experiences on whatever scrap of paper was at hand. I also saved a lot of letters and e-mails and other documents, and I threw everything into a laundry basket in the back of my closet. . . . Sometimes I would sit on the closet floor and read through that stuff and cry my soul dry. I did just about all my crying over Scott . . . in that closet."

Though she had been a musician and was a creative person, Kathleen wasn't an experienced writer. But she soon became the perfect example of that old piece of advice that writers should put a woman up a tree, put a scary dog beneath it, then tell us how she gets down.

"Then when Scott died under bizarre circumstances, I knew I was going to have to write a book. I wrote a rough outline and the first draft of the first chapter about three years afterward. For the next three years, I was a Chihuahua gnawing on the ankles of the criminal justice system. . . . Having this story inside me made me feel like a pregnant elephant—I knew it would take a long time to birth the baby, but it has to come out, and I'll feel a whole lot better when I finally get through the labor."

She credits the Zona Rosans with giving her the courage to take on such a project: "Of course, I'm still in labor and sometimes it's painful and depressing to revisit the awfulness—it makes me feel like a shit magnet all over again. Then you and the magic sisterhood heave me and my traumatized muse back on the high road and show us—with love, laughter, and literary lust—how to take the next step, and the next."

Then she added a line that I will treasure for the rest of my life: "You and Zona Rosa have changed my life, Rosemary, and I love your guts!"

6.

Works of art are always products of having been in danger, of having gone to the very end of an experience to go where [wo]man
can go no further.

—RAINER MARIA RILKE

Their vacated bodies, hers in the bed, his on the floor, with the
silver cowboy pistol lying next to his hand as if a last-minute
prop person had run in and placed it just so. . . . At the exact
moment I stepped over him to get to her, a thousand-watt bulb
switched on. . . . At seven o'clock in the evening . . . I walked
into my parents' house, and less than a half hour later, walked
out with some raw material ripe for its own creation.

"Where's Jalaine?" someone asked at the Atlanta group one
night after we were all seated. Then the phone at Anne's house,
where we meet, rang, and it was Jalaine, telling me that she had
just been to her mother and father's funeral—that her father
had shot her mother, then shot himself, leaving their bodies at
their house next door to hers like a tableau for her to find.

For months, we had noticed Jalaine's stress when she, an
only child, talked about her aging parents. A beautiful, high-
strung redhead, the cords in her slender neck would stand out
as she talked. They were angry and disapproved of her divorce,
she said. Or her mother had revealed something devastating,
such as that she had been conceived only three months after
her mother had an abortion that she regretted. Then they had
become elderly prescription drug addicts—her mother had
even been admitted to the drug and alcohol unit at Emory

University Hospital. Most recently, Jalaine had gotten them into therapy with a geriatric psychiatrist.

Jalaine is a born writer who had already won awards and published a book of poetry. Because her skills were so well honed, she went straight to her desk to write the first of what would be a series of brilliant poems about their fraught relationship. "I've never been so struck by how much my poetry aided me as I was when I wrote a poem only two weeks after their deaths. It gave me hope that I could nail it down, have a picture to look at later—that I wouldn't forget."

The other way she dealt with her pain was working on the fourteen wooded acres on which she lives, hacking through kudzu, a vine that can become as thick as a tree trunk.

Still, it would be three years before she could begin the stunning memoir *Bone Slave: Redeeming the Lurid,* in which she weaves the truths of what happened into a work of art. And even then, publication is not her goal as much as the search for truth and clarity:

> People die of fakery more than anything else. I have been up-
> held in fakery all my life. . . . Fakery under the guise of hon-
> esty learned from my parents . . . who faked their own
> deaths . . . yet . . . found themselves as a matter of fact dead.

"Even now, I'm letting it cook," she told me recently, ever determined to be accurate and measured in her account.

In 1987, Jalaine marched against segregation in racist Forsyth County, Georgia, and had written about the march for *Atlanta* magazine. This was a mission she espoused early on, when she asked why there were no blacks at the First Baptist Church of Tucker, which she, Anne, and I attended as girls.

Because of her "insolence," she had been dropped from the church rolls, and her lifelong mission as Disturber of the Peace had been established.

A sexual and psychological adventuress, she had never recognized or bowed to class boundaries, and now she embarked on two passionate affairs with black men, one her father's landscaper, Melvin, as "other as they get," as her therapist put it. Finally, she realized the futility of this means of escape. "I cannot fuck them back to life," Jalaine wrote at the end of a poem. "And now I realize that sexual acting out is as normal to grief as people bringing food for the wake," she told me recently, reflecting on the wisdom of her body and psyche at that time.

"Anything we bury stays in our bodies and creates havoc," she added out of the psychological savvy she had gained from twenty-five years of therapy and thirty years of writing. Like her beloved cats, Jalaine also feels the need to curl up and isolate herself when she's processing her feelings. And while Jalaine is less of a group person than some of the Zona Rosans—"I charge in solitude"—she has lifted many of our spirits with her writing, while dealing with her own pain.

7.

Will there be songs in the dark times? Yes, there will be songs in the dark times. There will be songs of the dark times.

—BERTOLT BRECHT

The Solace of Sisterhood. The poet Robert Frost advised writers "not to join too many gangs." But our gang of female outlaws is of the best kind. We can't go through these things for one another. But we can be there.

We're at our most intimate when we're at the Zona Rosa retreats, or Pajama Parties for Grown-Up Girls with Smarts. There, at lunch on the patio, or around the dinner table, there's time to talk about everything. Mostly we talk about the fun things, but we also, bit by bit, share our stories.

We learn about the states of one another's marriages, who has aging parents to care for, and how things are with our kids. Often we find ourselves spilling secrets we thought we would never tell anyone—and then we almost always feel relief at sharing them.

And even in the sunny South of France or at our beach house near Savannah, the news from home isn't always good; when one of us gets such a call, it's hard to conceal our real feelings—nor do we try. Surrounded by our sisters, we have our own built-in support system, and the group dynamic pushes us toward truth, a truth the rest of us listen to without flinching or judging.

We've also been especially blessed in having older women in our groups. Some have inspired us, then have passed away. Others are still among us, sharing their wisdom. At our last dinner last fall in France, we sat mesmerized as Maggie, eighty-six, read from her poems, many of them dealing honestly with death. I asked her for a copy of her entire collection to have beside my bed so that I can start the day inspired by her wisdom.

In Italy, Janet and I walked through the olive groves outside our villa, each of us in the grip of fear for our daughters, but soothed by each other's presence. Janet's adult daughter had suffered a brain bleed that had left her disabled. I had left a crisis at home and was seeing the geometric patterns at the out-skirts of my vision that sometimes came on me during stress. Nancy, who had them too, had just reassured me that they were "just painless migraines," rather than the imminent stroke I imagined. When we went back inside to join the others, Janet hypnotized me and gave me the self-hypnosis tapes that I would come to depend on in the months to come.

Nancy has never let the chronic vertigo that had become part of her life keep her from joining us at our retreats in Europe; sometimes, she walked holding one of our arms until the medication took effect. She was also dealing with difficult problems at home with one of her six kids. At our beach retreat, Sarah lovingly peeled and chopped fresh ginger and steeped it in hot water to make tea for Claudia when she became sick with an upset stomach.

That great purveyor of mental health, Russell Crowe, told *Interview* magazine that after becoming famous, he craved "the solace of collaborative companionship." When we're dealing with life's difficulties, it's healing to be among women who love us. Research shows that people will be patient with our problems and try to help for a while, then they get fed up. But it's not that way in Zona Rosa, where we are given all the time we need.

Nor do we have to be permanently devastated by what life "unfairly" throws our way, as has been evidenced by many women in the public eye: Jane Pauley went public with her bipolar disorder. Suzanne Somers turned her breast cancer into the search for knowledge that turned into her book *The Sexy Years*. As a young news reporter, Barbara Walters supported her disabled sister. Jane Fonda suffered a famous father who couldn't or wouldn't express his feelings and the censure of a nation during the Vietnam War, and turned her experiences into her memoir, *My Life So Far*. Life coach Martha Beck wrote about her decision to give birth to a Down's syndrome child in *Expecting Adam;* and, in the face of threats, recently wrote about the sexual abuse she endured as a child in her Mormon family in *Leaving the Saints.*

Oprah, whose girlhood sexual abuse and poverty are well-known, considers these events God's whispers: "What appears to come out of the blue first comes to you as a whisper, then a voice, then a brick wall, and then the wall falls down on you—until you pay attention . . . ! When you're in it you just have to go through it. Later you have perspective and you can see the lesson." Nor does she believe in indulging the survivor's guilt that can afflict those of us who have carried on: "We're saved for a reason."

One of the thrills of Zona Rosa is seeing our sisters come out of the dark and back into the light. Last month Janet, who had learned firsthand the agonies of brain damage from her daughter's ordeal with it, walked into Zona Rosa carrying her usual platter of her famous deviled eggs, laughing and spouting witticisms at her original rate. She looked like a teenaged sprite in her denim capris and shirt tied at her waist. "I've started going to Curves," she told us. "I weigh less now than I ever have." My heart soared, not because of her weight loss, but because she was proof of our ability to heal, and even become joyous again, after the worst of times.

"I was driving home, and I looked up at the leaves swaying on the trees," said Claire, who described her excruciating childhood in chapter 2. "Then I felt a feeling I'd never felt before, and I knew it was joy." At first, Claire was frightened and wondered if this new sensation was mania, since suicide and bipolar disorder run in her family. But we all quickly reassured her, and I suggested she read *Exuberance* by Kay Redfield Jamison.

Anne said that when she was acutely ill with what was finally diagnosed as Crohn's disease, everything seemed dead; she had no interest in anything. But she could hardly remember that time when she called to tell me about the flippy new silk skirt she had just bought: "Now I want to have pretty things!" She said she now constantly feels the kind of joy Claire described.

During our next retreat in the South of France, we suddenly saw a lighter and brighter Nancy—a simple medication, an antidepressant long prescribed by her doctor, it turned out, had been causing her dizziness. And things were better at home, too—all six kids had left home, and she and her husband were alone for the first time in years. When she published *The Fool's Path,* the first of the trilogy she had been working on for so long, she flew to the Atlanta Zona Rosa from her home in upper New York State to celebrate with us.

And, as I had discovered, there were also unexpected blessings in having to deal with the unexpected. Courtney, whom I call my southern Virginia Woolf (in her writing, if not temperament), had left graduate school and a life she loved to take care of the schizophrenic son left in her charge after an unexpected divorce. She now feels that the path she was forced to take led to her personal growth, a closer relationship with her son, and her exquisite novel.

"I've always been crazy but it's kept me from going insane," goes a country-western song by Waylon Jennings, and I remember the way colors heightened and vegetables in the supermarket seemed to come alive, jumping toward my fingertips, when I was in the midst of pain; also how poems came to me whole cloth, ready to be born. Then there was the energy generated by planning for our next Zona Rosa meetings.

Occasionally I receive an e-mail or letter from a woman who says she's dropping out of Zona Rosa for the time being because she's depressed; or that she doesn't feel comfortable in groups. These messages are sadder to me than any others, because these women, deluded into thinking they have to be on top of the world to be among us, are denying themselves the solace of the Power of the Pink. Dr. Phil, who knows a thing or two about trauma—his dad was a volatile alcoholic and teenager Phil's paper route money went not for spending money but for groceries for the family—gave concrete advice on dealing with transition: "Avoid catastrophic language . . . get out, have fun." And above all, "Develop a support system."

While Pulitzer Prize–winning author Carol Shields was dying of Stage 4 breast cancer she wrote her final and exquisite last novel, *Unless*. Nor had she lost her belief in the force for good: "[I think evil is] a kind of minor corruption of this major force. It seems to me evil is always where something has failed, and it doesn't have anything like the force of good," she told *The New York Times Magazine*.

"The dark nights of the soul are just as instructive as days of wine and roses, if not more so," Gregg Levoy writes in *Callings*. And though it's not the way we like to find our inspiration, life's darkest moments can become the stimulus for our greatest creative efforts.

8.

I cannot believe that the inscrutable universe turns on an axis of suffering; surely the strange beauty of the world must somehow rest on pure joy.

—LOUISE BOGAN

The Vintage Fur. Before I discovered my adult children's illnesses, I had a darling vintage China mink with puffed sleeves and a rolled collar. I loved to throw it over jeans or wear it with a glamorous dress—it always looked right (this was during the period when I was also wearing a peacock-feathered pillbox hat with a veil that fell over my eyes).

Then I took it to be relined and the guys at the shop told me it had been stolen off the mannequin—I always suspected they sold it to someone else for a profit, it was that adorable—and they offered me another fur in exchange. I selected an oversized fox cape with a scalloped hem, but it was never the same.

From that moment, like a race skier determined to crash, my life flew downhill. When I learned about my two children's illnesses and began my search for ways to save them, things like fur coats became the furthest things from my thoughts. My live-in relationship with Zane was tempestuous—I had finally found a boozy, sexy guy like my dad. Later, Zane's quadruple bypass and near-death from staph would add to my anguish.

I also watched my novel—for which I'd received a large advance and on which I'd pinned my hopes—fall through the cracks, when it turned out my publisher didn't believe in advertising. In Atlanta, where my children then lived, I would go to book signings or a TV studio, deal with multiple crises with my kids, then go to bed in Anne's guest room with my journal, a pint of Black Jack, and a Hershey bar. I tried to keep what was happening separate from the rest of my life—an inclination intensified by the fact that their illnesses, since they were mental, came with a stigma attached. At the same time, I also imagined that this was temporary, that there would be easy solutions, and that I would soon be back to my fun-loving single life.

Zona Rosa was just in its beginnings then, and I still felt that it was important for me as leader to appear on top of things at all times. If I had known that more than a decade of suffering and struggle would be required of me before my kids' recoveries began, that three times I would end up in the ER when my anxiety surfaced as vertigo, sweating, and nausea— the symptoms of heart attack—and that there would be two grandchildren lost to adoption and crib death, I might have fainted from fatigue. For a long time, it was as though I was standing on the strut of a plane, but instead of jumping, I was stuck there, frozen in fear.

Then gradually some of my efforts over the years on my kids' behalf—all those small, moment-by-moment, seat-of-the-pants decisions—plus their own natural talents and re-siliency, began to take root and blossom. Soon they were living near me in Savannah, and our relationships were healing. Lily was selling her paintings—I had also encouraged her to write her life story, with me as villain if necessary—and my son, Dwayne, was playing music and working out. Zane and I had learned to love each other, despite our differences, his stints in rehab. At the same time, Zona Rosa was becoming by the year a more and more essential part of my life. I also had several new books in the works, and a new agent.

Then one beautiful spring day in Atlanta, about to drive home to Savannah, I flashed stopping at the same store where I had bought the original vintage fur. When I stepped inside I was surprised to be greeted by the son of the man who had sold me the first one. "Do you have a vintage mink with puffed sleeves and cuffs at the wrists?" I asked, expecting a no.

Within minutes he was out front again, holding a pale blond near-replica of my first coat. And as I slid my arms inside the satiny lining, I suddenly knew the bad stuff was over. And even better, that I had girlfriends waiting in Zona Rosa to hear about my victory.

Knee-jerk Reaction # 6: Thinking that when the bad stuff happens, we have to suffer alone—that our sisters are only there for us during the good times, and that we should keep our struggles to ourselves. Not realizing that writing practice while things are going well can serve as life's best insurance policy, and that there's almost nothing that the arts and good girlfriends can't help us through.

PILATES ON PAPER

Listomania Redux. The lists we make during difficult times are different from those we make for fun and growth, and perhaps even more important because they can become the means to help us through the night, or even to keep us alive. "Relentless stress causes the body to respond as it does in an emergency, with a 'fight or flight' response," Dr. Redford Williams, who studies stress at Duke University Medical Center, told the *New York Times*. "When you are in this mode a good deal of the time your brain is scrambled, your thinking process doesn't work well, your judgment is clouded. It's very difficult to think clearly." But lists can help us order our thinking and our existence. The middle-of-the-night lists I made when dealing with the really hard stuff were my attempt to deal with something that I didn't yet understand or have a handle on. And looking back, I now see how ingenious they were—as some of us have learned, we're often hypercreative when we're under the most stress. One notebook, for example, was devoted to listing the current crisis on the left side of the page; what I did in response in the middle; and how effective my response had been on the right. While I had shelves filled with literature on my kids' conditions, my own lists were as effective as any other means I used to help them. Indeed, they were probably the beginning of my growing confidence in my ability to make decisions regarding their well-being myself, rather than appealing to the "experts" I had first assumed would save them. *List the Specifics of Your Trauma without Holding Back,* putting them outside yourself while describing how they affected your life. As time goes on, the situation will change, and making new lists will keep us aware of the transitory nature of even the most painful events.

Another good place to start is to list "What I've Done to Get Through the Day (and Night)." I found, as many of us have, that even in the worst of times there is always something for which to feel grateful, and I always described it in my journal, no matter what, because I knew that it was my primary conduit to sanity. I never let a morning pass without writing in it during my decade in hell, recording not only each ordeal and insight but every dream; I also got up in the middle of the night to write in it when fears beset me. I knew that solutions to my stress lay in my unconscious, that trying to solve problems without the information that dreams provide is like "a detective with only half the facts on a case," as Ann Faraday writes in *The Dream Game.* I also listed the times and situations when I had felt happiest and most alive, to keep myself aware that this was not the whole of my life, and listed ways to soothe myself, like "go for a walk . . . talk to a girlfriend on the phone . . . listen to one of Janet's tapes . . . take a bath by candlelight." I also created a set of mantras—words or phrases that soothe me—to have them at the tip of my tongue. My favorite was "On this the mystics agree: all is well." And last but not least, I always had a good book to get me back to sleep, finding that there was nothing like a woman trapped on a deserted island with a man she detested, or one feeling the rats run over her body at night in India, to make me forget my own troubles.

Are You a Thriver or Survivor? There was wisdom in Carolyn's continued enjoyment in cooking while her husband, Bob, was dying. Anne never stopped going to the gym, even when symptoms overwhelmed her and questions about her possible diagnosis were still mysterious and disturbing. Taking pride in functioning, and keeping to a regular schedule, kept me feeling strong, no matter what else was going on. Leading the Zona Rosa workshops, reading the manuscripts, and getting my own work done was a challenge I became determined to meet. I also knew that I wanted to have a life in place when it was all over (even if at times I wasn't sure it would be). How can you keep your life as normal, your schedule as regular, as possible when chaos rules? Are you unnecessarily giving up doing things that are important to you? When I arrived in Laramie, Wyoming, to teach for a semester just after my grandson had died of crib death, I zoned out in my little apartment for a week, watching TV. But the following week I went to meet my students at the university. If you find yourself avoiding activities that you know are good for you, list them, and figure out how to keep them in your life.

Write a Little Something—You'll Feel Better. Remember how Kathleen said that writing down what was happening was the one thing that kept her from going bonkers as her life turned into a series of insane events? The lucky ones among us already have writing skills in place when the worst happens. Up until this time, you may have thought of your writing as a hobby, a potential or already actualized profession, or a tool for personal growth. But now is the time to use it to soothe yourself, to organize your racing thoughts, to give order, as the poet Wallace Stevens said, to chaos. Psychologists say that the reason we take pleasure in labyrinths and garden mazes is because they represent controlled chaos. "Walk through pain to peace" is one of my friend Ann's favorite credos, and revision in writing acts in much the same way. Every time we rewrite our account of something traumatic, it distances it and calms us. The first draft hurts, but every draft after that decreases our pain, until what we once thought we would die from becomes simply a blob of raw material, the clay we've used to create art. And just as it's harder for a portrait painter to paint a smiling face, it's sometimes easier for us to express ourselves in the midst of crisis. In fact, we may find we need to—that we have a near-biological imperative to do so. As Gregg Levoy says, "Chaos precedes creation." So write a little something—or a lot—even if everything inside you wants to avoid the subject of your torment. Remind yourself that along the way, you can always stop, take a breather, and do one of the things that you've listed as sources of relaxation.

What I've Given Up to the God of Good Taste. Before we face one of life's more difficult realities, we often live under the veil of Good Taste, doing and saying what we think is appropriate, rather than what we feel. One of the things that often happens when we're in a crisis is that everything phony, everything we've believed important in terms of self-image, falls away. Janet says what she thinks and lets the chips fall where they may—though the chips she scatters are usually laughter!

Jalaine was always honest, but after her parents' deaths, every word that fell from her mouth or pen was indisputable, because truth and the search for meaning was her primary goal. That's why it's often surprisingly refreshing to be with people when they are up against the wall. On the other hand, this is *not* the same thing as talking constantly—read whining—about what is happening in our lives. Anne, I, and others have found that the less we talk about our situation, and the more we interest ourselves in others, the better we feel—but that doesn't mean we don't tell or write our truths when we need to.

What I Can No Longer Deny. "What is not brought to consciousness will be manifested in life as fate," said psychologist Carl Jung. Sigmund Freud believed that our conscious minds only contain a minute fraction of what we really know and feel. Though we sometimes may need a tablespoonful of repression to get through the days and nights, and even years, at times we're denied even that. When Anne was in the hospital after a trusted doctor prescribed a drug with inadequate follow-up, she was only too aware, as a former nurse, that her symptoms meant she was dangerously near death. When her son brought her grandchildren to visit, she feared she would never see their darling faces again. But Anne's joie de vivre today can be partly attributed to that confrontation with mortality—she knows that every day is precious. I'm sure you've heard the analogy comparing personal growth to peeling an onion. Some of us—in a quality common to writers?—dote on putting ourselves under a microscope (Jalaine, a therapy junky, says she hasn't tired of self-exploration after twenty-five years). In *O* magazine, columnist and life coach Martha Beck suggested we ask ourselves, "What do I almost know? What do I almost feel? What would I want to do if it wasn't forbidden? What am I tired of hiding from myself? What really happened, though I act as though it never did? What is it that my family and I all know but no one ever talks about?" She suggests that "beneath consciousness lies repression, but beneath repression lies wisdom." But she also says that we may need an excavating buddy, and this is where the Power of the Pink, and the friendships we enjoy in Zona Rosa, come in. And after you've done your dig, you may be ready for the next exorcise.

What I Now Believe to Be the Meaning behind My Experience. Now that you've written things out and gotten honest with yourself, you're ready to go on to the most difficult exorcise—that of finding and writing about meaning. Death camp survivor and therapist Viktor Frankl created a system of therapy called logotherapy, as described in his book *Man's Search for Meaning*. Frankl believed that we must search for meaning in the events of our lives, and that we can find that meaning no matter what our circumstances. Logotherapists also believe that we respond to our experiences in one of three ways: with false meaning (the search for sex, money, or power), transitory meaning (whatever it takes to get us through the day or night), or ultimate meaning, which gives us a glimpse of the heavens and what is larger than we are. Whatever your religious beliefs, if you have suffered, you undoubtedly have depended on and developed one or more of these sources of meaning. *How did you search for meaning in your experience, and what do you now believe that meaning to be?*

BOOK THERAPY SIX: SOME REALLY GOOD READS BY WOMEN WHO'VE BEEN THERE

It all started in 1976 with *First, You Cry,* Betty Rollins's account of having breast cancer, and the courage it gave her to leave a less than perfect relationship. Whatever card you've been dealt, there is a good book (or many) in which other women describe going through something similar. At the same time, however like yours her story may be, it will never be exactly like yours, which may serve as further inspiration to get your own down on paper.

In *Not Exactly What I Had in Mind,* Rosemary Breslin, daughter of Jimmy Breslin, uses humor—her asides on how to get spots out of laundry made Anne and I laugh aloud—to describe being struck down with the mysterious blood disease that would ultimately kill her. Suzy Becker, bestselling cartoonist and author of *All I Need to Know I Learned from My Cat,* wrote and illustrated the self-deprecating story of her brain tumor and her subsequent disabilities in *I Had Brain Surgery, What's Your Excuse?*

In *Waist-High in the World: A Life among the Nondisabled* and *Ordinary Time: Cycles in Marriage, Faith, and Renewal,* Nancy Mairs discusses not only her life with degenerative multiple sclerosis, but her and her husband's adulteries and his cancer, without a smidgen of self-pity.

Ann Patchett writes in *Truth and Beauty* about her long friendship with her suicidal, demanding—and possibly borderline—friend Lucy Grealy. Before her death, Grealy was the award-winning author of *Autobiography of a Face,* in which she describes her life with a jaw deformed by girlhood cancer. Elizabeth Wurtzel, who has addressed her addictions in more than one book, writes about her relapse to Ritalin in *More, Now, Again*. Wurtzel is controversial because of what some view as her narcissism, but I for one like her energy and honesty.

Columnist Jeannette Walls describes seeing from a cab window her homeless, squatter mom dumpster-diving on the streets of New York, then vividly recounts her deprived and eccentric childhood in *The Glass Castle*. In *When Katie Wakes*, Connie May Fowler surprises the readers of her successful novels with her story of growing up poor with an abusive mother and a deformed jaw; as an adult, she is seduced, beaten, and taken advantage of by the former radio personality her mother had long before been in love with because of his voice—he steals the $7,000 she has saved for her dental repair.

Karen Salyer McElmurray's tenderly rendered *Surrendered Child* recounts the agony of growing up with a mother with obsessive-compulsive disorder—Karen has to remove her clothes upon coming inside the house; and of having a baby at fifteen, giving him up to adoption, then finding him again many years later.

In *Because I Remember Terror, Father, I Remember You*, Sue William Silverman lyrically but mercilessly describes her years of childhood sexual abuse at the hands of her prominent father, a friend to President Truman and international businessmen; in her follow-up, *Love Sick*, Sue reveals her resulting sexual addiction, and how it led her to inpatient treatment. In *Lucky*, a book that lays the groundwork for *The Lovely Bones*, Alice Sebold describes the repercussions of her rape as a college student, including a dance with heroin use (because of her honesty and clarity, some of us at Zona Rosa prefer this book to her best-selling novel). And in *At Home in the World*, Joyce Maynard describes her seduction (and near destruction, but for

her resiliency) at age eighteen by a fifty-year-old and long-
famous J. D. Salinger. Joyce courageously wrote her truths despite threats of lawsuits from him and his "people."

There have always been those who haven't wanted women
to write their truths. But the best thing about the books I have
cited is that in addition to the comfort and inspiration they
provide, they are all beautifully written.

CHAPTER SEVEN

IF I THOUGHT LIKE A GUY

Yes, There's a Lot We Can Learn from Them!

1.

The roosters may crow, but the hens deliver the goods.

—Ann Richards

"I guess that one will be short," Charlene quipped when I told the Atlanta Zona Rosa group that I was beginning a chapter about men. We pride ourselves on being a female-chauvinist society, even a secret sect. We're also aware of the special benefits—intuitiveness, empathy, and emotional gutsiness— that the Power of the Pink bestows on us and our writing.

We've noticed that men talk about how hard writing is, while women talk about how hard life is. When a visiting male novelist came to read from his first book, he said he was behind on his second one, already under contract. "Why?" I asked, knowing he taught one course at a local junior college while his wife worked. "Well, I have a seven-year-old to get off to school, and a dog to walk," he answered lamely, probably wondering why the women in the room—among them some who had three jobs and multiple children, some whose adult kids had returned to the nest, and some working to support husbands whose careers had slumped at midlife—were giving him such icy looks. When he continued by saying he had to have a six-hour block of time to even begin writing, I could see their expressions hardening even more. Some of them struggled to find that hour or even half hour within a busy day to write.

I was glad to see that the Zona Rosans had given up what Jane Fonda calls "the disease to please," or our inclination to change our demeanor when a man enters the room. Any man with the courage to breach and stay in our mixed groups, where all ears are attuned to any hint of male chauvinism, whether written or spoken, is a brave man indeed.

In our mixed gender groups, the men sometimes report that their wives corrected and typed their manuscripts. But none of us have ever heard of a woman who was pampered in the way some male writers are. And while we may yearn for wives, the gay women among us are the only ones who actually have them.

When my sister Anne, a wonderful (and published) poet, spread out dozens of her poems on the breakfast room table so we could organize them into collections, her husband, Larry, walked through to say, genuinely puzzled, "Oh, you've been writing poetry?"

Sadly, this is the degree of interest in our writing that many of us find on the part of our significant others. But once we've made our passion and commitment clear (and they've determined it's "harmless"), the men (or women) in our lives may begin to gift us with computers and file cabinets instead of lingerie and vacuum cleaners—and, if we've protested enough, they may even leave us alone while we're writing.

Indeed, Zane likes the time alone I require. "Why don't you go work on your writing?" he sometimes says crossly, when I'm trying to talk to him over a car race on TV. But if we want a cup of tea while we're working, we're probably the one who gets up and gets it.

And since statistics show that husbands leave alcoholic wives more quickly than women leave alcoholic husbands, it's doubtful that any of us would pull a Stephen King, with a mate concerned enough about us to stage an intervention (as King's did). After all, not many of us go the route of many male writers, using our artistic torment as an excuse to dissipate ourselves. (We can't—we have too many responsibilities!)

Though I've heard that Anne Sexton gave readings drunk, I've never heard of any other woman writer doing so. But I've seen many male writers swaying at the podium, including one at a girls' school where I wasn't invited to read because of my "outrageousness," but where the male author propositioned the students from the stage. What's more, we often find that we're better writers than the visiting male writers who visit our groups as guests.

An Outdated Male Model, or Why We Became Female Chauvinists in the First Place. Before we go on, let me get something off my breast right now. I explained in chapter 1 how Mother and her failure to fulfill her promise as a writer inspired me to begin Zona Rosa. But there is more to it than that.

In my earlier books, I embraced my growing feminism. But as a woman writer, my male peers, while often my inspiration, were not always my supporters. Indeed, women writers throughout history have rarely been well treated by their male peers—*dismissive* is the word that comes to mind. As in many professions, there is an old boy (and sometimes a new boy) network in the world of creative writing.

Also, since I've lived most of my life in the South, I'm used to a certain amount of diminishment in the guise of chivalry. "We'll know you didn't mean it, honey," a soon-to-be-famous southern poet said after asking what *Fatal Flowers* was about. Then there were the male writers who responded to my work with comments ranging from "Wanna fuck, baby?" to "You just can't write like that." My favorite reaction was that of a New York editor who, after reading my first poetry collection, yelled at me over the phone, "I hated it! I felt like I'd fallen down a vaginal orifice!" ("That sounds like heaven!" said Zane when I repeated this.)

When I announced that my first book had been accepted for publication by a New York publisher, the male writers on a committee on which I was one of two women kept talking, not missing a beat and ignoring my news altogether. And sometimes, like Jane Fonda says, we even become "ventriloquists for patriarchy": "It's women like you who hold feminism back," the other woman on the committee told me when I finally confronted the same men after one chauvinistic comment too many. Also, by announcing my own success, I had failed to protect their male egos as the culture—particularly southern culture—demands.

When I became a writer, I was primarily influenced by the then-prevalent male model of what it was to be a poet. Newly in love with modern poetry, I didn't even notice that the poems I was copying into my notebooks in order to learn from them were all by men—Randall Jarrell, Ted Hughes, Theodore

Roethke, John Berryman, and Dylan Thomas. Nor did I notice poet James Dickey's sexism when he became first my mentor, then my lover. I unconsciously absorbed these men's notions of what it was to be an artist; that is, a drunk, depressive, and/or otherwise self-destructive (most of them did themselves in with booze or suicide).

Later came the women's movement, a volatile and exciting time when women countered with credos of their own, such as "Mockery is the tool of the oppressor," a phrase designed to counter the primary tool men were bringing to bear in their attempt to silence us. When I read from my poems at Louisiana State University, the one woman among five male poets, the women on campus asked for a caucus with me to discuss their treatment at the hands of male creative writing professors who denigrated their work when it became too real, saying such things as, "Julie, we can't help it if you sleep with every man you go out with!"

Before long "confessional" became the word used to slam the kind of writing I and other women were doing; that is, writing that was too real. To this day, critics still use that word in order to reduce the power of writers of whom they disapprove—just as "women's writing" is used to describe books about women's lives that exert power over women readers, and "romance novel" is the dismissive label given even to some literary books about women's desire.

In Zona Rosa we counteract such messages by surrounding ourselves with "damn smart" women, and the kind of men who appreciate us. "You don't have to isolate yourself, or be a drunk or an asshole to be a great writer," I tell the Zona Rosans. And if Zona Rosa reminds us of nothing more, that's enough.

2.

It's not the men in my life, but the life in my men.

—ANONYMOUS

That Said, Testosterone Is Still Our Favorite Cologne. According to *Health* magazine, research in which women sniffed the scent from cotton pads used to collect perspiration from beneath men's armpits shows that smelling the pheromones (disguised with various scents) from men's sweaty T-shirts raises our spirits.

In the rest of this chapter, we'll discuss, with a nod to *Esquire*, "Men We Love"—though in this case they don't have to pose in their underwear, no matter how much we'd like them to. We'll talk about the men who, like us, are more interested in the creative process than the literary establishment. We'll describe the sweethearts—the men who support and inspire us, and aren't afraid of smart women.

My original title for this chapter was "Then There Are the Guys: How They Heal and Deal, Barely Hovering at All." Just as the angels on the ceiling of the Sistine Chapel are male—Zane reminds me of a particularly muscular one—we have our male angels in Zona Rosa. These are the men who support and just plain inspire us. They are the kind we need to surround ourselves with, or admire from afar. They are also the kind we can learn from—especially because they bring us messages from the other side.

Since most of us are heterosexuals and many of us are mothers to men and boys, we like them for obvious reasons. And they like us: some, like Greg, an expatriate Brit who was the sole man in our age group with us in France, appeared to be in ecstasy surrounded by so many dynamic women, and we doted on him. "I was flirting with him, and you had to come up and start talking to him, too," Gray, newly divorced, complained when I interrupted their conversation to ask about his wife.

Some men have gone so far as to beg to visit the all-women groups, rightly suspecting that what they might hear there could help them unravel the mystery of the Power of the Pink. Pat Conroy would always tease—with a *soupçon* of genuine chagrin—that I wouldn't let him in when he visited our all-women's group in Savannah until near the end of the afternoon. Even Zane, high-testosterone guy's guy that he is, admits to being intimidated by the sheer quality of the Zona Rosa women and their writing: "They are unlike any other women I've ever met," he says.

Indeed, this chapter is a celebration of our differences, and how the men with the courage to join Zona Rosa are special guys indeed. When Nancy came to Zona Rosa, she reported that her friend Bill K., who had been the one man in our group for a long time, told her, laughing, that being in Zona Rosa had made him "write like a girl."

Or as Tom, novelist, retired orthopedic surgeon, and former Rhodes scholar put it, "If a man in his lifetime can figure out what the Zona Rosa is all about, he'll be a very happy man!"

3.

In my interest, she left no wire unpulled, no stone unturned, no cutlet uncooked.

—WINSTON CHURCHILL ON HIS MOTHER

Now for the Good Guys, and What We Can Learn from Them, Whether Sitting on Their Laps or From Afar. First, they accept help—usually ours, and even expect it as their due. Reds came into the Savannah group after his wife, Maxine, called me on his behalf. He had written a book, she said, and he hoped that Pat Conroy would rewrite it for him. Knowing that it was highly unlikely that my friend would take on such a task, I suggested that Reds visit Zona Rosa, bringing Maxine along if he needed support.

I had heard of Reds for years as the guy who had hijacked a United Airlines jet in the '60s and had been acquitted. Some people said he was rough, a good guy to stay away from, especially in a bar, where booze might trip his rage. But when Maxine walked into my living room, Reds in tow, he looked like a big, redheaded lamb.

His goal with his book, he said, was to explain how he had become the man who had done such a thing. The obsession that had led him to his crime, and his attempt to assassinate Fidel Castro, had risen from his passion for the military and his excessive patriotism, which had begun when he was sent to a military high school in Charleston as a boy. But now, because of his second wife, Maxine, and the many messes he had made during his life, he had stopped drinking; he was also a born-again Christian who worked in Haiti with Doctors Without Borders, he told us. Now he wanted redemption—and, I suspected, understanding.

After looking over a pile of news clips—one was from a *Life* magazine in which he had been featured—and hundreds of single-spaced manuscript pages, I suggested that he join Zona Rosa and try to write his story himself. "Just take it step by step, and keep it simple," I said.

And for the next three years, he did just that, sometimes coming with Maxine, then later without her. We would read new material from his story, and I would hand him back the pages from the month before, corrected in purple ink. Nor did he hesitate to ask for help; at the next meeting, he would bring the pages back, freshly typed by Maxine.

There's a certain kind of guy in the South who loves to tell tales about living on the edge, and Reds was one of those. In the prologue to his book, which we worked on until it was crisp and sharp, he goes to the Savannah airport with the goal of hijacking a jetliner to Cuba. "Tell Fidel El Rojo is coming!" he instructs the pilots as they land, referring to his nickname. The prologue ends with his jumping down onto the tarmac in Havana, only to face dozens of men with submachine guns—and, though he doesn't know it yet, months in solitary confinement, deportation to Canada, and a trial that could have ended in life in prison.

Much of what he wrote was funny—he had us in stitches with his story of, at age fifteen, driving his cousin, an "older woman," from Savannah to Macon in his uncle's car, only to find himself in the backseat having sex with her. In fact, he seemed to have a history of getting in trouble over women, such as the time he picked up a girl at an off-post bar and had a one-night stand with her, only to find out that she was a military police officer's girlfriend and an officer herself, and thus superior to him in rank—"All hell broke loose!"

But his most charming story was the one about how he and Maxine, both married to other people, and with children, had felt the intensity of their attraction to each other during an event known as a Lemon Dance—in it, couples dance with a lemon beneath their chin until it falls, and then someone else can cut in. Indeed, because of Red's nostalgia for this event, he titled his book *The Lemon Dance,* over the argument of others in the group who preferred *Tell Fidel El Rojo Is Coming.* By that time, we were all invested in seeing Reds' book come to its conclusion.

When Maxine, a hairstylist, asked if we could barter services for his tuition to the group, I said yes. From then on she came over once every month or two to do my hair. Soon, my hair was looking worse and worse, while Reds' book was getting better and better. Three years after he had started with a rough draft that made even me blanch, he won a prize at a literary conference at a nearby college.

There were also moments when his old obsession showed through. One day, he came over with Maxine, who was trying to talk him out of revisiting Cuba. "I still want to sit down with Fidel," he insisted. But Maxine and I managed to convince him that, well, it might not be the best thing to do, since he had once planned to kill the man.

Though I was sure Reds could find a New York publisher, his impatience was surfacing. "I felt like going over and beating him up," he said of a local attorney who had put him in touch with a New York literary agent who had rejected him on the basis that the book's vernacular was too rough. "Beating your contact up wouldn't be, well, *businesslike*," I said in what I hoped was an effective argument.

I was now taking care of him, too, but Maxine's dedication was only beginning. Soon she was Xeroxing copies of the entire manuscript for all of us. Next I heard she had agreed to sell their house and move to the country to provide the money it would take to self-publish the book in hard cover.

Reds' book was a big hit, especially in his hometown of Savannah; he sold many copies, vindicating himself among the people who mattered most to him. After someone picked up a copy at a bookstore in Texas and showed it to a friend in L.A., we heard that *The Lemon Dance* might be made into a movie, with Brendan Fraser playing Reds. At our next annual Zona Rosa party, Reds was the Star in the Zona Rosa, and Maxine was right there beside him, basking in his glory.

❈

When I was single I was always waiting for some guy to fix something in my apartment or take my latest boxes of manuscripts up to the attic, and usually, though they may have come over for other reasons, they were happy to oblige; indeed, it was a form of foreplay. Then I remarried and became a control freak who thought I had to do everything myself, despite having a perfectly good man on the premises.

And while I probably won't ask Zane to type my manuscripts, the lesson I learned from men like Reds is that I can ask that person who insists on living with me to do some highly useful things, and as many of them as possible. Instead of my running out for the *New York Times* every Sunday morning then going on to grocery shop, Zane now does it for me while I remain at home, writing in my journal in bed and working on my iBook. When he comes home, he finds the little list I've made of the other helpful chores he might accomplish that day. And instead of feeling irritated as I had expected, he is accepting of my simple requests—as though he had been expecting them all along, leading me to think that, despite my determination not to be a traditional wife, maybe the "honey-do" list is built into the male brain.

When I looked around me, I saw that while Anne's husband may not have noticed her massive poetry collection, Larry does keep their house humming—bills paid, wiring redone, shelves put in—in such a way that her life hums, too, leaving her plenty of time for writing and going to the gym. The nice thing about people who keep the focus on themselves is that they're not likely to be laying shit on you. I also learned that, like Connie, who adored having a hunky male assistant, I can hire someone, male or female, when I need help with writing or Zona Rosa stuff—and yes, that I'm as important as any husband!

4.

I write as though I were a person of importance; and indeed, I am.
—W. SOMERSET MAUGHAM

They Blow Their Own Horns. The modesty we women are taught is attractive rarely affects men. I sometimes hear Zane introducing himself over the phone to National Guard buddies as "the good-looking one." He says he does this in self-mockery, but since he *is* good-looking, I don't believe him for a minute.

When Charles, an ex-con drug dealer and international adventurer, showed us the newsletter he had sent out while paying his dues in federal prison, we were not surprised to see that its title, in huge letters, was **CHARLES.** It had become so popular (before prison authorities forced him to stop publishing) that even the warden subscribed—it was a better way than most to know what was going on among the men in his charge.

We already knew from listening to Charles's text for his graphic novel that he wasn't one to hide his light under a bushel. Nor, despite eighty-six-year-old Gibson's eyes widening above her trim violet suit and the violet in her lapel, did Charles soft-pedal the graphic scene in which his daughter Daphne sees herself being born.

Since being released from prison, Charles had studied

cooking with Julia Child and Jacques Pépin. At the end of our week of workshops, he and our hostess Katherine prepared us a meal that is forever engraved in my memory. After bringing out endless bottles of wine and huge platters of warm pasta tossed with fresh basil leaves, chunks of tomato, and garlic and olive oil, they served the salad, then platters of bread pudding surrounding mounds of vanilla ice cream, and the chocolate pies Gibson had made, including the delicious crust. And though Charles had once used drugs liberally, he was now in A.A. and hadn't imbibed for the past seven years; yet he didn't mind as we swilled down the red wine that went so beautifully with his meal. It was a night to remember, and none of us counted carbs.

When I met Charles a year later at a dinner party—the menu again perfectly prepared—he was still a man in transition, seeking out the best life had to offer. To my dismay, he had abandoned his cinematic graphic novel; instead he read from a poem about a recent spiritual epiphany. We all agreed he was still **CHARLES,** forever written in bold.

5.

It's kind of fun to do the impossible.

—WALT DISNEY

They Don't Hesitate. Nor Do They Take Things Personally. Brad was in his early thirties when he appeared one September at a Zona Rosa retreat at Black Mountain, North Carolina. He told us that he had tried his hand at stand-up comedy in Los Angeles when he was only nineteen, then in his early twenties had gone into business in the Netherlands with his brother; they had made so much money that he had recently been able to retire with his French-Canadian wife, Nathalie.

Now he had decided to write, using what he had learned as an international businessman to inspire others. He was excited, his dimples showing, as he talked about the manuscript for the futuristic novel, *The Bird That Flies Highest,* that he had brought with him and which he considered finished.

He hoped to find a publisher for it within the year, he told me, not put off by my gentle admonition that he had a great deal of rewriting left to do. After the workshop, he joined a Zona Rosa that included men, and by Thanksgiving he was calling me at my mother-in-law's, asking whether I would read and edit the manuscript over the holiday weekend, then FedEx it back to him that Monday: he had picked up a flyer from the batch I passed around at each Zona Rosa meeting about Robert McKee's screenwriting workshops; he planned to attend one in Los Angeles the following week and he wanted to have his corrected manuscript with him. Still skeptical, I nevertheless spent the weekend eating my mother-in-law's cooking and scribbling all over his pages in purple ink.

At our next meeting, Brad filled us in on the many contacts he had made at the workshop—including a guy from Chicago who had written scripts for Spielberg and was interested in coauthoring a script of Brad's book. The month after that, we heard about his trip to Chicago to meet with the scriptwriter. And the following month he told us about sending queries out, in what he called a "postal blitz" to 130 agents at once, and that he had received twelve encouraging replies.

"I tacked the rejections on the wall and used them for dart practice, just like I did in business," he said, laughing, then added, "Every rejection is a step toward acceptance." He didn't even send an SASE, as I had recommended, because he didn't want them to get the idea that they would turn him down.

Before long, he announced that *The Bird That Flies Highest* had been accepted for publication and would be out—could I believe it?—in not much more than the year he had cited at the Black Mountain workshop. Soon we were receiving press releases created by his charming wife and notices of a heavy schedule of book signings throughout the country. He also told me that he had another book in the works.

And Sometimes They Cut Their Losses. After *The Bird That Flies Highest* was published, we didn't hear from or about Brad for a long time. Then one day Anne ran into him in an airport, changing planes. He was dressed again in a coat and tie, and, briefcase in hand, told her that writing and promoting his book had been the hardest thing he had ever done; also that he and Nathalie were divorced. He still wanted to be The Bird That Flies Highest, but he had seen what it takes to do it through creative writing. Or maybe he just didn't have the patience we learn as wives and mothers. As Pamella sometimes says about a Zona Rosan who doesn't handle stress well, "It must be because she doesn't have children."

6.

He who mounts the wild elephant goes where the wild elephant goes.

—RANDOLPH BOURNES

They Are Fearless—Or at Least, They Act That Way, faking it until they make it.

"Afraid of what?" Eric Haney asked, puzzled, when his

wife, Dianna, a journalist, asked in bed whether he was afraid
of writing the book he had just contracted to finish, when he'd
never written anything longer than fifteen pages.

Eric, one of the original members of Delta Force, in which
there's a one-in-thirteen failure rate during training, had
jumped out of enough planes and road-marched, rucksack and
rifle on his back, through enough rough country to be certain
he could do something as simple as writing a book. He was
right: in five months, the book was finished—he credits Dianna with helping him—and in June 2002, *Vanity Fair* listed
his resulting book, *Inside Delta Force,* in "Fanfair."

"Don't let the appearance or the soft-spoken words of Eric
L. Haney fool you," J. R. Rosenberry wrote in *Connect,* the alternative paper in Savannah, where Eric and Dianna keep a boat.
"He is a highly efficient antiterrorist killer whose special, super-
secret training makes him a walking, talking lethal weapon."

We knew about Eric in Zona Rosa before we met him. Now
that Eric was out of the military and an independent operative,
Dianna told us about him on a regular basis. Though they were
married, he was as often away as not, in some foreign hot spot.

Indeed, one of Dianna's best essays was about what she
had done before she and Eric officially fell in love. After they
became friends and she realized her growing attraction, she became intensely curious about what made a guy like him tick,
and she decided to do a very risky thing: knowing Eric had
once been an Army Ranger at Fort Benning, Georgia, she got
into her car and drove to the base, where she met some rangers
who took her under their muscular wings for the day, telling
her about the life Eric had led before she met him. That evening she left, full of admiration for the bravery and honor of
the young men she had just met.

When Dianna sent her piece about her visit to Eric, he let a pal read it. "Hey, guy, this woman is in love with you!" the other man said, and that was the beginning of a relationship made even more romantic by Eric's long absences. The one flaw was when she learned that the Texas company he was working for abroad was reading her love letters, which were sent there first before being sent on to him. With Eric's support, she brought a suit, but the Texas judge threw the case out, citing the need for security.

When Eric came back to the States, and they were living together for the first time, with all the adjustment that entailed, Eric came to our Atlanta group to read the essay he had written about his time in Delta Force as part of the group who instigated and led the unsuccessful attempt to free the Iranian hostages. It was a tough piece, and though we weren't used to such a masculine perspective, we all recognized his ability as a writer.

At the time, Eric was at loose ends—unusual for him—and after sending his piece out to several magazines to no response, he decided he might as well try for a book contract—that getting an agent and selling his book idea might be just as easy. With Dianna's help, he created a packet that included a photo of himself in camouflage and with a blackened face, and the next thing we knew, he had gone to New York and signed a book contract.

After the success of *Inside Delta Force,* Eric became a CNN analyst during a particularly delicate time in U.S. history, and more recently, he and Dianna were in Hollywood as guests of playwright David Mamet, while Eric advised Mamet on a new military series, *The Unit.*

"[The military] brands itself on the soul and causes you forever after to view the world through a unique set of mental filters. The more profound and intense the experience, the hotter the brand, and the deeper it is plunged into you. I was seared to the core of my being," he wrote in *Inside Delta Force,* describing what could also apply to the obsession required to write such a memoir.

And in the meantime, his book, with its descriptions of extreme physical and psychological testing, is what we look to when we want examples of how to hang tough!

7.

Never bite off less than you can chew.

—FREDDY ADY, AT FOURTEEN THE
WORLD'S YOUNGEST SOCCER PRO

They Take Risks, Go for Broke. When I talk about women's issues, Zane is fond of responding with John Wayne's line to Maureen O'Hara, after she complained about the harshness of life in the West. "Well, life ain't a piece of cake for us men either, ma'am." But what's required to be manly might not be as repressive as what it is to be ladylike. Describing what it's like to jump out of a plane or run onto a football field and smash your face into someone else's, Zane used the phrase "reckless abandon," an attitude men may more readily espouse than we who are more involved in the nurturing and safety of others.

At a writers' conference, Bill Diehl, the author of a number of thrillers, including *Sharky's Machine,* which was made into a movie with Burt Reynolds, told the group that at one time his dream of writing had been just that. He had long been a photojournalist for the *Atlanta Journal-Constitution* when his wife planned a fiftieth birthday party for him and, knowing his dream, ordered a Baskin-Robbins ice-cream cake made in the shape of a typewriter.

That night after the guests had gone home Bill went into the dining room to see the ice-cream typewriter melting on a plate, and he realized that his life was melting away, too—that unless he did something, he would never fulfill his dream. The next day, he sold his cameras, quit his job, and began writing.

After being diagnosed with lupus, Fred Willard, too, gave up his work as a freelance photojournalist, and began doing what he had always wanted to do: write. "For a long time, I couldn't get published," he told us. "But when I let go and didn't care anymore, it finally started happening." Now Fred, who's known around Atlanta as a café aficionado and bon vivant because of his friends from all walks of life, has a following for his funky noir mysteries—think the movie *Sin City*—such as *Down on Ponce* and *Princess Naughty and the Voodoo Cadillac,* in America, France, England, and Germany.

Despite multiple diagnoses and heart surgeries, Fred is also writing screenplays, and he and his wife, Brianne, are building a study on the deck of their inner-city condo. Two weeks before we talked, he'd had a stent put in to open an artery but he hadn't lost an iota of his wit. "That will be a short one, won't it?" he said, chuckling and echoing Charlene as I described this chapter about men.

8.

The aim of life is to live, and to live means to be aware, joyously, drunkenly, serenely, divinely aware.

—HENRY MILLER

They Use the F Word—Focus. The monkey-mind that afflicts women (read, what will I cook for dinner tonight, how wide are my thighs in this skirt, will so-and-so be hurt if I put this thank-you note off another day?) doesn't seem to impinge on the male of the species' wonderful left-brain inner-directedness. Any woman who has watched a man watching a sporting event on TV knows that he is capable of tuning out just about everything but what he's interested in.

In the same way, they do what it takes. Bill, a fiftyish re-tired carpenter in a Zona Rosa workshop in Cleveland, had a happy, boyish personality; after class he would tell me about his wonderful Italian wife, his wonderful Italian mother-in-law, and the wonderful dishes they cooked. He also had an ex-citing story to tell about his grandfather, who had lived all over the world and had been involved in the world-changing events of his times. But because of the writing problems that pep-pered Bill's single-spaced pages, I thought him the least likely person in the group to finish anything soon.

He kept in touch by mail, and a year later he sent a photo of himself in Russia, sitting beside a white tiger, which I put up on my refrigerator gallery. He was there following in his grandfather's footsteps, doing further research for his book, he wrote.

Two years later, he was sitting in my living room in Savan-nah, published book in hand. He had hired a copy editor and had gotten the book cleaned up. "I just did everything you said," he told the Zona Rosans when I asked how he had done it. Then he went on to describe how he had recently gotten in touch with Arnold Schwarzenegger's agent via the Internet, and that the star (not yet governor) was looking at his book as we spoke.

"Oh, yes," said his obviously supportive wife, who was with him that day, after complimenting me on my pizza made with fresh tomato slices. "He was determined to get it right."

And They Keep That Focus on Themselves. Telly, who waited to marry until she was a successful, over-forty exec, told us that her new husband wanted her to sit in the den with him while he watched sports on TV, whether she was interested or not, and even if she would prefer to be doing something else. We quickly offered some backbone-asserting phrases, but we were not particularly surprised. Most of us already knew that men, as a general rule, assume that whatever they're doing is of ultimate importance—as in "Can't you stop writing for a few minutes and help me look up the best golf courses in Scotland?" Most of us knew, too, how near addictive the pull to please our mates, even at our own expense, can be.

Indeed, before the women's movement, even the most brilliant women often succumbed to the belief that men were more important. The famous diarist Anaïs Nin was born in 1903 and came of age before second-wave feminism (as feminism after the first suffragettes is called) and published her first book, a study of the work of D. H. Lawrence, in 1932, giving Lawrence a leg up. She later put Henry Miller's work above her own, tacking up not her own words but those of her rakish lover on her writing room wall. It was as though it was *his* energy that kept her going, both sensually and creatively.

But while living in Paris, and despite Nin and the other women in his life, including his demanding wife, June, Henry Miller kept the focus on himself with this schedule:

Work Schedule, 1932–1933, Henry Miller Miscellanea

1. Work on one thing at a time until finished.
2. Start no more new books, add no more new material to *Black Spring*.
3. Don't be nervous. Work calmly, joyously, recklessly on whatever is in hand.
4. Work according to Program and not according to mood. Stop at appointed time!
5. When you can't *create* you can *work*.
6. Cement a little every day, rather than add new fertilizers.
7. Keep human! See people, go places, drink if you feel like it.
8. Don't be a drought-horse [*sic*]! Work with pleasure only.
9. Discard the Program when you feel like it—but go back to it the next day. *Concentrate. Narrow down. Exclude.*
10. Forget the books you want to write. Think only of the book you *are* writing.
11. Write first and always. Painting, music, friends, cinema, all these come afterward.

Daily Program

Mornings:
If groggy, type notes and allocate, as stimulus.

If in a fine fettle, write.

Afternoons:
Work on section in hand, following plan of section scrupulously. No intrusion, no diversions. Finish one section at a time, for good and all.

Evenings:
See friends. Read in cafés.

Explore unfamiliar sections—on foot if wet, on bicycle, if dry.

Write, if in mood, but only on Minor Program.

Paint if empty or tired.

Make notes. Make Charts, Plans. Make corrections of MS.

Note: Allow sufficient time during daylight to make an occasional visit to museums or an occasional sketch or . . . bike ride. Sketch in cafés and trains and streets. Cut the movies! Library for references once a week.

Miller's schedule for himself is so good—so wonderfully self-indulgent—that we use it in our all-women's groups to check out just how unfocused on ourselves we've become.

Also, to her credit, Anaïs Nin didn't follow through when her analyst, the famous Otto Rank, asked her to give up her "addiction" to journal-writing. Instead, she later seduced him, using the one power she had come to depend on.

9.

Let us be grateful to people who make us happy; they are the charming gardeners who make our souls blossom.

—Marcel Proust

Men Can Be Romantics about Literature, reconfirming our faith in its importance in our lives. Over the years most of us have come to realize that men are the real romantics, and women the pragmatists. And some men have such a tender pure regard for literature that even we women are moved. I met Glynn, blond and slightly balding, in the Savannah public library when I saw him Xeroxing a long, handwritten list of books. I couldn't resist asking what it was about. It was his reading list, he said, and for the next five years, he became an important part of Zona Rosa, bringing in poems that moved us afresh every month. We could also hear the awe in his voice when he praised others' poems. Publication was the last thing on his mind. He just loved good writing.

A blue-collar guy, Glynn had been injured in a work-related accident, and was on disability; sometimes he had painful bouts with his bad back, but occasionally he was able to take on jobs doing house painting or other work. Once when I was in the market for a used car, he insisted on having his friend Ron bring one by for me to look at.

On another day Glynn knocked on my front door unexpectedly. When I invited him in, he told me that he had just been to the doctor and had been diagnosed with lung cancer. In the short time he'd had to think since his diagnosis, he had already made a plan: "I want to sell some of my poems as songs," he said, "so I can leave something to my teenage daughter." I thought of the way he smoked on the front porch during the break at our meetings. I reassured him that he would probably live a long time, at the same time thinking how difficult it was to market poems as songs.

He inspired us with his own poems, and his appreciation of our poetry, all the while giving us lessons in grace, up until the time of his death, when he left this life feeling he had done what was most important to him. " 'You worry too much,' " Ron reported as Glynn's last words—to his mother. He had called to tell me Glynn had passed away while napping on the floor at his mother's house.

A year later, I was signing books at a bookstore, when a frail woman stood before me, next in line. "I'm Glynn's mother," she said, bursting into tears.

"And he was a wonderful poet and man," I said, tears coming into my own eyes as I clasped her small hand in mine.

10.

John Muir could not keep "glorious" from popping out of his ink well.

—KAY REDFIELD JAMISON, *EXUBERANCE*

They See Themselves as Part of a Great Tradition:

I've been having lots more starts and fragments these past months of Talon's young life, as it's been easier with taking care of him to concentrate on smaller writings than my novel-in-progress, *The Eyes of the Sun*. Do you have any advice? You wrote with your children, how did you balance the craft and bigger projects with motherhood? At least I know from experience with Finn I'll be able to return soon to deeper and longer concentration. And on the plus side, these smaller pieces are fun, strong stories of their own.

An e-mail from a young mother? Not at all. Jody is one of our younger male members, and a house husband and father of two. In college he developed a software program that is still used in education today, but now he chooses to stay at home with his kids while his wife, Sarah, works as a pediatric occupational therapist.

He also records his family via his photography—ethereal images of Sarah at various stages of her pregnancies filled his Web page—and for a while, he was hanging out with pals, making a low-to-no-budget film.

Like some of us did when we were stuck at home with small children, Jody takes a night off every week to go to a local coffeehouse to do wireless Internet. "It makes me feel less isolated," he said, using practically the same words some of us use about our nights out with the girls.

Indeed, Jody, who helps the Zona Rosans and others with their Web pages (he created our exceptional one) and computer problems, doesn't need to be taught a thing about feminism—he's already there. Or, as I've heard the women in the group say more than once, "I just love him!"

One thing the male model did for men who are writers is that it made them feel that they are part of something larger than themselves. But I've learned from Jody how a man can feel he is part of that tradition, and still be completely modern, even feminist.

In the seventies, "grokking" was a term used for looking another person deeply in the eyes in order to see her soul, and

Jody, with his big blue irises, is that kind of listener. Because of his obvious sweetness, even our most conservative members listen empathetically when we read his work aloud, even though, reflecting Jody's belief in the benefits of altered states of consciousness, they're apt to be edgy accounts of young people stoned on various drugs.

"Jody, I got your submission and have read it. I don't think we'll be able to use it, however. The realist style is fine. I think it's the subject matter that we can't embrace. Just to fill you in, our managing editor is seventy-four and a grandmother, and our fiction editor is also in the over-fifty category. That first page was a bit too much. The writing is fine, however. Go ahead and try again," the editor of a literary magazine e-mailed him of a story that we had all, even the oldest of us, lauded.

When we first started Zona Rosa groups that included men, the men who joined tended to be alpha guys who assumed that they would dominate. After a while, things smoothed out, with a different kind of man joining in. "I can't believe my dad is in a group led by a feminist woman," Neil, a dentist, reported his adult son as saying. Indeed, Neil hung in with us even after the women in the group pointed out the sexism in his writing.

But there was still the occasional testosterone-induced problem. And along the way, Jody, ever tolerant, became our peacemaker. When other men in the room egged a drunken male poet on in his obnoxiousness, or a male writer read a racist piece in front of our black guests, Jody inevitably stepped in with just the right gentle comment. "Did you make a decision to read from that part of your book before you arrived, or when you got here?" he asked the racist after our guests left in an appropriate huff. "After I got here," the man said, admitting to the deliberateness of his crude act.

And it wasn't long before the offender had decided that Zona Rosa wasn't for him, bearing out my belief that I never have to kick anyone out of Zona Rosa—they just do it themselves.

While Jody's own writing became increasingly publishable as he worked and revised, he also believed that the writing itself was what made him a writer, rather than publication; also that writing was something that should be shared. A supporter of Web sites such as Scrytch, where the credo is "Appropriate when appropriate," and Creative Commons, he was part of a new tradition among younger writers who consider creative writing to be a communal affair, just as it was in Shakespeare's day. Unlike some male writers of the past, Jody's ego was not at stake, nor was his manhood. But I suspect that, someday, he will also get the recognition he deserves.

11.

My only job is to be talented, that is, to know how to distinguish important testimony from the unimportant.

—CHEKHOV

They Often Inspire Us from Afar. If I had stuck to reading James Dickey's poetry, rather than getting involved with him, I might still be his admirer today.

I loved Henry Miller's sendup of the reverence shown famous writers when, aging and living on the California coast with an array of hangers-on, he placed ads in *The Nation* asking for donations of used clothes because he was so broke.

The Zona Rosans were charmed by a story from Norman

Mailer's book *The Spooky Art: Thoughts on Writing.* In it, a young Chekhov drives his horses and carriage through the snow to visit an older, venerable Tolstoy; during the course of the evening, Tolstoy tells Chekhov that his stories are good, but that his plays are "as bad as Shakespeare's." " 'As bad as Shakespeare's! As bad as Shakespeare's!' " Chekhov exults to himself as he travels back through the snowy woods.

Sebastian Junger, whom many of us would rather meet than Johnny Depp, inspired us when he told the *New York Times* how he wrote *The Perfect Storm* at his parents' house on Cape Cod during a cold winter. "The deal I made with myself is that if you are at your desk working, you can turn the heat on. . . . It kept me working a lot. The rest of the house was freezing. . . . [otherwise] I wore a big overcoat. I wore a hat to bed. . . . If I tracked snow into the kitchen, it would be there for weeks."

And though sales of the book and film rights had generated around four million dollars before taxes, by that time, Junger remained the same simple guy, buying a remote house on the Cape, and upgrading from his two-room Manhattan apartment to a three-room one, with "a mattress on the floor, a make-shift desk, a kitchen in chaos, no television set, and a William Butler Yeats poem pinned on the wall." Always interested in the struggles of others, he now makes his living writing articles about the world's trouble spots.

Men Also Show Us What Not to Do. Don't get me wrong. Men have their own forms of resistance and they're equally destructive. There are plenty of self-defeating would-be writers out there, whether male or female; I call them the People of the Yes But. Whiners, I've finally learned, don't listen, whatever their sex.

When Martin couldn't find any takers for his novel about a well-off retired attorney much like himself—he lived next door to an Arab prince on nearby Sea Island—he assigned the blame to his belief that "all the agents and editors in New York are rich Jewish heiresses" who were prejudiced against men. This, rather than the fact that his novel about a woman who asks for support after years of living with a man very much like himself was so sexist that it would be bound to turn off any self-respecting woman (or thinking man)—a flaw about which we had warned him time after time, but he refused to listen.

Robert, a local columnist, was such a doll that I nearly fainted when he walked into our group. Then I was stunned by the quality of his book in progress, a Deep South thriller about a college girl who disappears in the backwoods of Georgia on her way to college. The prologue, in which she stops at an isolated service station during a rainstorm and is murdered by the single employee there, had us all gasping for more.

But soon Robert had decided to go a different route, cutting the prologue and replacing it with something tamer, despite our pleas that he keep the story as it was. After a while, I noticed that he left behind the pages I had critiqued for him; that and the way he rolled his eyes ceilingward when people commented on his writing became a running joke. He was more interested in drinking wine and our response to the complicated hors d'oeuvres he brought than to his work. But still I persevered, his resistance calling out my own stubbornness.

When the movie made from Dennis Lehane's book *Mystic River* appeared, we all rushed to tell Robert how riveting it was and how much his story reminded us of Lehane's. But Robert, it turned out, had a vendetta against possibly the one writer he was most like. Instead of looking to see what Lehane may have done that he could learn from, he wrote a scathing column, denouncing Lehane's writing style. When I met Lehane's editor in New York—*Mystic River* displayed as a point of pride—I doubted that mentioning Robert's book would be worthwhile.

12.

Turn-of-the-century male writers considered themselves the Old Masters. But now it's time for the New Mistresses.

—ZONA ROSAN CONNIE BAECHLER

Why I Like Tough Guys, or How the Most Unlikely Men Can Serve as Muses. An ad for Club Hedonism pictured a tanned, toned guy in a swimsuit, a panting dog's head replacing his. I found the ad appealing—and then I realized why. He reminded me of many men—and dogs—I've known.

At five, I thought all dogs were boys and all cats were girls until the day I learned the difference. A boxer puppy tore off my circle skirt, and the bigger, more rambunctious ones have terrified me ever since.

Yet in life, the more doglike—the more manly—my men friends are the better (except for my gay male friends, whom I consider "girlfriends"). As a southern woman, effete or overly intellectual men have not been on my radar (which is not to say the men I prefer aren't smart!). I adore Frank Rich's columns in the *New York Times,* and fantasized—when I was angry with Zane—about being with a man like him, until I saw him on C-Span 2. "That guy on TV has a hole in the sole of his shoe," Zane pointed out, unaware of my fantasies, and as I glimpsed the offending aperture, my bubble burst. Later that afternoon, unaware that I was writing about men as dogs, he told me that when he had been moving boxes of books to the attic, he'd had an erotic fantasy about me and had felt like barking.

Anne and I agree that our husbands are what are called "men's men"—practical and earthy rather than intellectual. Yet they have turned out to facilitate some of our best writing—with the minimum of interference or competition.

One of the things I appreciate most about Zane is that not only is he a truth-teller, he also supports me in telling my truths—even when they're about him. Given the number of pages I've written about him, it's obvious that he has been a source of inspiration—if only by being so doggy. Without meaning to, he has become my muse—though far from the abject female one preferred by some men. In fact, he may be exactly the right irritant, the right grain of sand, to keep me writing.

And that may be as good a kind of muse as any!

Knee-jerk Reaction #7: Thinking men are the be-all and end-all—more important, smarter, and more knowledgeable than we are. Or thinking of them as the enemy, to be avoided at all costs.

PILATES ON PAPER

Think Back on the Men in Your Life. Who Did You Learn From and What? Remember the Habits of Happiness modeled by the women of Zona Rosa? I've also learned a great deal from men. "You should rent a computer, get an assistant, someone to drive you, so you can think," a fan and businessman told me, in essence saying, "Take yourself and your work seriously." At the time—computers were new and barely on my radar, and it had

never occurred to me to ask for help—his words sounded foreign, exotic. He was also the friend who said, when I admitted
I'd never been to Europe, that "you've got that to look forward
to!" And though my trips there were still part of a mysterious future, I believed him. (Then he went on to describe his own ambition to become a Democratic state senator, demonstrating
another thing I've learned from men: they don't hesitate to make
big plans.) Then there were the many others who showed me the
way: among my first supporters was Van Brock, a graduate instructor at Emory University where, a literary virgin who barely
knew who Emily Dickinson was, I was in his poetry workshop.
Ignoring my malapropisms—"This line needs an ejaculation
point!"—he heaped praise on my poems, inviting me to join a
weekly poetry group studded with Ph.D.'s and professor-types.
When my first book of poems came out, rather than being scan-
dalized like everyone else, a Jesuit priest at Loyola in New Orleans asked me to come to his class to discuss their religious
imagery—leading me to feel understood and appreciated.
"That's exactly what she's writing *against*!" novelist David Mad-
den said from the podium, speaking up in my defense when a
man asked during the Q & A what I was doing after my reading,
instead of addressing my work seriously. Years later, at a book
festival, David handed me a used book by a disappeared southern woman novelist of whom I had never heard, saying, "This is
for you." When I read the book, I was so moved that I knew I
was destined to write about the author's life—and wondered
how David had known.

Next, List the Good Relationships You've Had with Men, especially the nonsexual ones. You may have been one of those
lucky women who had a great dad. Caryl Rivers wrote in *Be-*

yond Sugar and Spice that high-achieving women often identify more with their fathers than their mothers. We have disproved that time after time in Zona Rosa—a certain kind of parenting is not always an indicator of success. But if you did have a great dad, write about what you learned from him. Pamella's father taught her how to enjoy the moment—and how to get along with his demanding wife, her mother. Kathleen's dad was bipolar and an alcoholic, but he was also a charmer who "managed" the first band she was in, getting the group gigs in clubs and traveling with them until they were actually making money. Or maybe your support system included a brother, an uncle, or a family friend. Indeed, a real challenge in writing this chapter was realizing that yes, I even had reasons to be grateful to lovers in affairs that ended badly and to my handsome boozy dad, of whom Anne just sneaked me a photo in which he's tenderly holding me, aged nine months. Now *Reflect back over the men in your life, and be grateful to them* in writing.

THE NEXT-TO-LAST BOOK THERAPY: READ SOME BOOKS BY GUYS TOUGH AND TENDER

For a long time, I've kept a *New York Times* travel-section essay by Rick Mashburn. The piece described how, even though a neurosurgeon had told his parents when he was eleven that he had a progressive spinal condition that would probably kill him before he reached his twenties, he and his family had embarked on the trip of a lifetime to Disneyland, Chicago, Marineland, the Seattle World's Fair, San Francisco, and Las Vegas. His parents never talked with him about his dire prognosis, and the next summer they allowed him to take a twelve-hour train ride

alone to visit a cousin in Florida. And that was just the beginning of a life crammed with travel and adventure uncurtailed by
first a brace on his left shoe, then another brace, then crutches,
and at last a wheelchair. His parents' unspoken message, he
wrote, had been "Act like nothing is wrong. Live like there's no
tomorrow." Whenever I need my spirit to be braced, I pull the
article out and read it again.

"It's always something," Zona Rosan Kathleen says of the
obstacles life presents us, and it's good to read about men who
didn't allow even major ones to stand in their way. ABC correspondent John Hockenberry's *Moving Violations: War Zones,
Wheelchairs, and Declarations of Independence* raised my spirits
as I lay in bed after breaking my ankle in three places. The
break would ultimately require three surgeries, and a year on
and off crutches, but what was that compared to Hockenberry's
paralysis from the waist down after an auto accident when he
was nineteen, and his subsequent determination—as his physical therapist looked at him as though he was mad—to conquer
the stairs to the subway in Grand Central Station (he did it, on
his bottom, pulling his folding wheelchair along beside him,
without one person offering to help, and only a friendly word
from a passing black woman). From there he went on to cover
the world's hot spots in his wheelchair, including Beirut, where
there's no such thing as handicapped access, and young men
paralyzed by bullet wounds languish on the high floors of apartment buildings without a way to the street below. His courage,
his good humor, and his tender accounts of depending on the
kindness of strangers kept me mesmerized, and also aware of
how insignificant my own injury was.

John Krakauer, who was at Mount Everest for the fateful
1996 climb in which Rob Hall and ten others lost their lives,

hadn't intended to write a book at all, merely an article for *Outside* magazine. But fate took its turn, and he was stranded with the rest, later going on to write *Into Thin Air*, which stunned me with its poetry, its brutal truths. And, as I pointed out to the Zona Rosans, because Krakauer was already a working writer he was able to write his best-selling book in record time, the experience still fresh in his mind.

When I served as visiting writer at a small college in Bradford, Massachusetts, I quickly learned that Andre Dubus, whom I vaguely knew as the author of strong, Catholic short stories, such as "In the Bedroom," had taught at the same school and lived in nearby Haverhill. Indeed, he was a legend—a man's man and runner who also ran after women, and was given to drink, until the accident—he had tried to help a motorist on a dark freeway—that left him in a wheelchair. When I had dinner at his house, I met a guy a lot like I would have imagined an aging Ernest Hemingway to have been: morose, cynical, and serious about literature. But he could have been any way, and I would have been in awe: *Broken Vessels,* the book of essays he had published since his injury, was one of the cleanest and most beautiful pieces of writing I had read in years, especially his essay on his deceased friend, novelist Richard Yates, in which he describes Yates's decision to lead a life of simplicity, living in one room in Boston, in order to go on writing. I knew Dubus's book was destined to go on the shelf in my study at home where I kept the books that, as a writer, I found most inspiring.

Lawrence Durrell's *The Alexandria Quartet,* a mesmerizing set of four novels that cover the same story, each from a different point of view, had long been on that shelf. I devoured all four books, which included *Balthazar, Mount Olive,* and *Clea;* but *Justine,* the first, had especially thrilled me with its exotic imagery—the country is Egypt—and the complexity of its characters. And one day I read something that gave me an extra bit of inspiration: Durrell, who had been writing the books on Majorca, an island off the coast of Spain, wrote in a letter to a friend that "I just finished *Justine* and this afternoon after tea, I'll begin *Balthazar.*" It was the perfect example of just how ordinary the act of writing can be, thus demystifying what can cause paralysis. It was Durrell's words, too, from *Justine*, that helped me realize when the time came that the postpartum depression that follows the great effort of completing a book is normal.

Just before I wrote *Fatal Flowers,* I recall sitting on the couch at my daughter Lulu's apartment, crying as I read the last words of Ron Kovic's *Born on the Fourth of July,* a book that begins with Kovic, paralyzed from the chest down, being helicoptered out of a battlefield in Vietnam; while the boys around him cry for their mothers, he remembers the recruiter who only months before came to his high school to say how great and glorious it was to be a marine. In the book's last scene, after he has learned to live both as a paraplegic and with his violent memories and his guilt, he reverts to his recurring daydream of having use of his legs again and running on a ball field. As I sobbed, I dreamed of someday writing something that would move someone as much as Kovic's book had moved me. At the same time, I was aware of the book's engaging structure, the direct way he told his truths, and the simplicity of his language.

Many other male authors have inspired and instructed me. In Rick Moody's *Purple America,* I read a risky prologue that was really one long sentence, which gave me the idea of trying such a thing myself. In Tim O'Brien's *The Things They Carried,* I saw how repetition—each version with a new twist—could be used to good effect when writing about a difficult subject; in his

case, how a young American soldier who has shot a young Viet-
namese on a path repeatedly looks at the body, each time with a
new reaction, in a scene that only covers minutes.

When I worked in Poetry in the Schools, I read, to the
kids' delight, from Michael Ondaatje's verses—full of puns
and down-to-earth humor—in *The Secret Life of Billy the Kid*.
Later, when I read his novel *The English Patient*, which *The
New Yorker* called so well written as to be unreadable, I realized
how diverse—and how brilliant—one author can be. Kazuo
Ishiguro's *The Remains of the Day* made me aware that if one
writes well enough, one can write about anyone, even a fascist
British butler, and make him or her interesting—though when
I finished, I still wasn't sure how he had done it. While reading
Larry McMurtry's *Terms of Endearment*, I realized that yes, a
man *could* write stunningly and accurately of a woman's life. I
felt that way again when I read Larry Brown's *Fay;* I was inspired, too, at learning that the unpretentious Brown had been
a fireman in Oxford, Mississippi, for years before recognition
freed him to write full-time—a recognition that took longer to
come to fruition than for Chuck Palahniuk, who claimed to
have been an auto mechanic who read books beneath cars, all
the while thinking he could do better—until he did, with *Fight
Club*.

"What about Cormac McCarthy? Harry Crews?" Zane
asked, citing his favorites. Indeed, I could go on and on—I
haven't even mentioned Faulkner, Fitzgerald, and Thomas
Wolfe, whom I read early on, or the influence of male writers
who are also friends.

But I hope you are now ready to home in on your best-
loved male writers, and what you have learned from them—
and even to begin a special shelf of your own.

CHAPTER EIGHT

A CHORUS LINE OF WINNING LEGS

To Take You Where You Want to Go

1.

I am a woman who writes, and every woman here is a woman who writes. . . . I'm extinguishing the fire, but never the creative fire.

—MARILYN DAY

"I'd write a book, too, if I had time," one woman tells another in a hot tub in a *New Yorker* cartoon, in an example of the kind of comment every published author hears over and over again.

If only it were that simple—in reality, writing is a highly complicated process that requires much more than just time. But it can be simplified, and in this chapter and the next, I will give you all the writing how-to you'll ever need, including the means to go beyond whatever writing you're already doing.

As I'm sure you've noticed by now, this is not an ordinary how-to book, but a book about getting in touch with the best parts of ourselves, and how, for many of us, writing is the best possible means. It's a book about Zona Rosa and how it works, and about the dynamics we observe in ourselves and our writings during the time we spend together.

Women have always taught women, since the first cave woman found that throwing raw meat on the fire made for a new flavor sensation. Our paternal grandmother, Annie, taught my sister Anne to crochet and knit, and to play Chinese checkers. I learned to cook by watching Mother and Grandmother Lee. Instilling the notion that appearance was important (if not everything!), Grandmother Lee made me beautiful handmade clothes, and also instructed me on dealing with boys, telling me they were like puppy dogs, and not to kiss one until we were engaged—advice that with my usual good sense I ignored. Anne still loves knitting to this day, and I love cooking and clothes, not to speak of men. But what we teach each other doesn't have to be confined to recipes for pound cake, the fine points of putting on mascara, or how to "manage" men. We don't have to limit our sharing to crafts groups, or even book clubs. We can also teach each other the fine points of how to be wild women, bad girls—and artists and writers.

When I first began to write, an older artist friend advised, "Take the greatest possible unknown and say it in the simplest possible way." He was a drunk, unhappy man who was soon to die, but his words have been among my credos ever since (and no, the four food groups for writers are not necessarily, as cited in a *New Yorker* cartoon, "Pizza, The Alcohols, The Nicotines, and The Caffeines"). This chapter is a reflection of my belief that the complex act called writing can be made simple, and that there are tools accessible to all of us, even the first time we write.

I learned this firsthand when I worked in schools for a dozen years, teaching kids to write poetry: that yes, a fourth-grader can understand what concrete imagery is and what surrealism means if I break it down, make it simple enough—and, most important, relate it to something in which they were already interested. For years, I got them to write by quoting their own lines back to them—"Girls are like boogers—they take up space," or "He came into the room and I felt like a stick of margarine in a pot of boiling fudge."

In Zona Rosa, I constantly meet women who say they want to write, are writing, and have written. Since you are reading this book, I assume you, too, are writing, or think you might want to write. And if you're keeping a journal or have been doing the exorcises at the end of each chapter, you're already writing, even if you don't yet call your writing anything else, like *poem, essay,* or *story.*

"I am not a writer at this stage of the game. I did write a simple poem for a dear friend 2 yrs. ago—I'm enclosing it," wrote Jude, just before taking part in a five-day Zona Rosa workshop in North Carolina. I wasn't concerned about her lack of experience or expertise. As we tell newcomers, everyone starts somewhere, often with just a long-held dream.

In this chapter and the next, you'll discover ways to jump-start your writing, break through blocks, develop your own style and voice, and think like a Real Writer. You'll learn about quick fixes and read about the Zona Rosa credos, designed to keep us focused. Indeed, you'll find these chapters crammed with tools, and made extra fat by examples. With them, you can go as far, fly as high as you wish—or even decide that writing is not for you after all.

You will learn that all of these means are designed to simplify the writing process, which, however mysterious, even magical, *can* be broken down. And along the way, you will meet some Zona Rosans who, using these simple steps, achieved their writing and other dreams.

2.

Failing to plan is planning to fail.

—ZONA ROSAN PAMELLA SMITH

The Simple Steps. As Dr. Phil says, when solving a problem, defining it is 50 percent of the solution. Next we need to take definable, measurable steps; set time limits; and be accountable to someone—who, for us, of course, are the Zona Rosans. We are the loving irritants, the yeast, the nitty-gritty, with no toxic feedback allowed.

In his book, *Simple Steps to Impossible Dreams,* Steven Scott says it this way: "1. Define in writing; 2. Convert into specific goals; 3. Convert each goal into specific steps; 4. Convert each step into specific tasks; 5. Assign a projected time or date to complete each task."

Life coach Jennifer Louden advises that our attitude should be "I'm going for it, and I don't know if I can do it or what's going to happen, but I'm going to be in the process." She recommends designing a way to move toward a goal without being attached to outcome. Louden, who is also writing a novel, also says that "it's a challenge because I'm trying to go deeper than I ever have. Going deep is scary; it's much easier to tick stuff off my to-do list."

In a list in *Writer* magazine, Erica Jong advised that you "forget intellect. . . . Be a beginner. . . . Don't think your mind needs altering. . . . Don't expect approval for telling the truth. . . . Use everything. . . . Remember that writing is dangerous if it's any good. . . . Forget critics. . . . Tell your truth, not the world's. . . . Write for the child in yourself. . . . There are no rules."

In this chapter and the next, you'll find the means that, in Zona Rosa, we've found to be tried and true, among them:

Dream Big

Imagine Living Out Your Dream

Let the Chaos Flow

Remember That the Personal Is the Universal

Allow Yourself to Fail

Start Yesterday

Listen to Your Voice of No

Be a Diverger

Move into Process and Make It Your Permanent Address

3.

The best way to make your dreams come true is to wake up.

—PAUL VALÉRY

Dream Big. "Let's plan a week-long Zona Rosa retreat at a bed-and-breakfast," Susan suggested in her soft-spoken way, sitting on my couch in Savannah.

I didn't know Susan well—only that she was a serious writer who had spent eleven years researching her first novel, based on the life of Rosamund, real-life mistress of King Henry II. She had attended a weekend Zona Rosa workshop in Atlanta, then had become a part of our regular Atlanta group. So far, Zona Rosa had strictly been a labor of love, growing more by chance than through deliberation. Little did I know what a mover and shaker Susan was, and how important she would soon become to me and the Zona Rosans.

At that moment I couldn't have imagined that she would not only be instrumental in planning our first, then our second, week-long retreats in Lexington and Savannah—her vision—but that she would also soon have many of us on planes for our first retreats in Italy and the South of France near her new home in Aix-en-Provence.

Susan, it would turn out, is one of those people who are able to dream the (seemingly) impossible dream, break it down into predictable tasks, and deal with any obstacles, no matter how mountainous, along the way. She has the ability to pay attention to detail—and to have patience throughout, trusting in a positive outcome. And she is one of the fortunate ones who knows how long things take.

At the time we met, Susan was only a few years from realizing her lifelong dream of moving to France. She had studied French history in college and, fluent in the language, had visited the country at age twenty-three, falling in love with its culture and everything else about it. Indeed, her first vision of France had been her epiphany: she was destined not only to visit but to live and write there. After a while she zeroed in on her choice of home, Aix-en-Provence. Indeed, with her Yorkshire terrier Sophie ever riding in her purse, her stylish blond cut, and her understated style she looked as though she belonged there even before she actually moved.

But despite knowing what she wanted, what ensued was working as an editor for *TV Guide* in Atlanta for thirty-five years, making a good living but unable to save enough to realize her dream.

At our retreat in France, Deborah confessed that she was tied up in knots over her hundred thousand dollar credit card debt. In response, Susan surprised us by telling us the story—belied by her serene demeanor—of how she had faced a similar dilemma, and had determined that she would not let it undermine what she knew to be her destiny. "I would wake up in the middle of the night, thinking about the money I owed, and about family considerations," she said. "But to give up was just not acceptable. So I came up with a plan: in addition to my job at *TV Guide*, I would offer to use my skills with French language and culture to lead tour groups and organize exchange trips to France. After a while, my debt was paid off, things in my family smoothed out, and I was able to make plans to sell my condo and move to France, as I had always known I would do."

During the period before her move, Susan also worked part-time as an international travel consultant, a job that gave her even more access to the land of her dreams, as well as a lot of savvy about travel abroad. But as always, she was careful and detailed in her plans, taking into account every necessity along the way, from cleaning her condo and putting it up for sale, to planning a place to store her belongings and an interim place to live while she traveled to Aix-en-Provence to check out apartments.

Her time lines during that period, which she brought to Zona Rosa, included these activities and a schedule for them, along with her ongoing plans for her book, and later, for developing ideas for future writing. On the one she made for the period during which she was making her long-dreamed move to France from Atlanta into reality, she even included "first good hair day" and "get driver's license renewed."

And before we knew it, we were there with her for our first European retreat at a château in the South of France, enjoying her expertise in the culture and new perspectives with her ex-pat friends. ("How's *this* for a girl from a small town in Louisiana ?" writer Carol Allen said, greeting us at the door of her vast château before taking us on a tour of her famous garden labyrinth.) And when we visited Susan later in Aix, she looked totally at home, leading the typical French woman's life, walking to market each day with her rolling bag, her figure more svelte, her legs curvier than ever.

By then, her time lines reflected both her elation and a period of adjustment. But after a while, they focused once more on her writing. And in her most recent time line, she planned her writing projects—revising *Rosamund,* and beginning a new novel about the French poet Louise Colet, as well as meeting her goal of reading a few pages of Proust each morning.

"I think we should have two retreats in Europe next year, not just one. Let's have them in both Italy and France," she said last fall at our retreat in La Cadière d' Azur, near the Mediterranean. Sophie, whom we had all come to love, had died, and Max, Susan's new Yorkie–shih tzu mix and our new Zona Rosa mascot, rested as usual in her arms, seeming to nod in agreement from beneath his tan bangs.

"Of course," I said, not missing a beat. After all, who was I to doubt the wisdom of the Queen of Planning?

4.

At the moment of commitment, the universe conspires to make it happen.

—GOETHE

Imagine Living Out Your Dream. When Audrey first came to a Zona Rosa meeting, she told us the story of how she had begun her novel. Years before, as a tourist, she had visited Patrick and Sarah Henry's house in Scotchtown, Virginia. The docent had led them from room to room, then to the cellar. " 'And this,' she said, 'is the room where Sarah Henry was kept for four years, after she went mad. She died down here when she was thirty-seven.' It was like I had been punched in the gut! And the story stayed with me for years."

At first Audrey, already a freelance writer, didn't have the courage to start a full-length book. But like a pregnancy of the brain, Sarah's story kept growing inside her. "Then September eleventh happened, and I just couldn't do those silly features for a community paper anymore, after all that suffering in New York."

Audrey held her dream of telling Sarah's story—one she had only mentioned to her violin-maker husband—inside her for seven years, until one day over lunch, she confided in her adult daughter Nancy, who, as a painter, understood the power of a vision and what it takes to make it come true. "She took me that very day to the library at nearby Emory University to help me get my alumni card, show me around the stacks, and tell me how to navigate the system in order to begin my research."

By the time Audrey took part in our weeklong workshop in

Highlands, North Carolina, she was well into the book, and on the way to her dreams. And just hearing her talk about it excited us—the story of Sarah's descent from spirited girl of her times to the mad woman in the basement touched on many issues important to women: postpartum depression (Sarah's breakdown took place just after the birth of her sixth child), the frequency of deaths in childbirth and the absence of proper prenatal care and mental health treatment, as well as her husband Patrick Henry's continuing love for her, despite their devastating circumstances.

We all loved it when Audrey took time off from her novel to do one of our favorite exorcises, "My Wildest Fantasy of What I'd Like to See Happen with My Writing":

I want to finish my novel about Sarah. I want to find an agent, not right away, perhaps, but soon enough that I don't lose hope. I want my agent to pitch this to a top-tier publisher who then takes it on and assigns me to a kindly and competent editor.

Then I want my editor to be in a hot relationship with an independent filmmaker, and one night, after not-so-great sex, I want the filmmaker to pick up my manuscript and read all night and all day until he's finished. I want him to tell his lover that this is just the project he's been looking for, and that he has the perfect backer in mind.

I want my phone to ring. "Hello, Audrey? This is Robert Redford. I've just read the story of Sarah, and I think it would be a fine film. But I'm strapped for time here, and I'd need some help turning this into a screenplay. What would you think about working with me . . . No, out here . . . at Sundance . . . Well, you wouldn't be in a hotel, I was thinking more along the lines of having you stay out at my ranch . . . Oh, no, it would take a bit more time than that. Perhaps five or six weeks."

I want my husband to say it sounds like a great opportunity.

I want the back cover of my book to have an airbrushed portrait of me leaning against a gnarly oak. I want to look four inches taller, twenty pounds lighter, and fifteen years younger. I want to come out for book tours in long silk pants and Manolo Blahnik strappy heels, instead of the orthopedic shoes I'm wearing these days. I want to eat hors d'oeuvres at my book parties without spilling goat cheese down my cleavage, or having bits of spinach stick to my teeth.

I want Diane Sawyer and Katie Couric to invite me on, and I want Barbara Walters to be pissed because she didn't get to me first.

I want it all.

"I already see it happening," I said, after reading her exorcise aloud to the group.

5.

All you need is a blank piece of paper and a pencil.
—ERICA JONG'S FATHER, WRITER SEYMOUR MANN

Let the Chaos Flow, or What Will I Write About? Since creativity is a mystery, with more than a hint of the divine about it, I have no idea what you'll come up with. Or whether or not you'll become a famous writer, though I *know* you won't become one unless you start.

Probably at this very moment you're thinking, "I'm too sleepy, I must have that piece of chocolate in the kitchen, I'll just pop up and put in that load of laundry, or I'm no writer—and what made me think I was?" We're especially prone to this one when we're having a "bad writing day" and we haven't been writing long and hard enough to know how normal they are. We're all prey to this kind of self-talk until we learn to put a stop to it.

And what will happen when you start may take different forms. "It's like a fucking monkey unleashed [inside my head]," Ronnie said of her brain—not on drugs, but on fire with ideas for her writing. Or you may be more like the British novelist Iris Murdoch, who says that "the beginning of a novel is a time of awful torment, when you're dealing with a lot of dead pieces and you have to wait and wait for some sort of animation." (Please note Murdoch's willingness to wait for that moment when her material comes to life. Ronnie, on the other hand, needs some of that same patience to revise once she gets her ideas down.)

When I was teaching at the University of Wyoming in Laramie, the kids would complain that their lives weren't interesting enough to write about; that all they did was break horses, spend their summers in a shack on the range, herding cattle and birthing calves, or camping out for weeks in the snow, hunting elk to freeze for the winter—all of which was incredibly exotic to my eastern ears.

Everything you, too, need to know to start writing is right there in your brain cells, ready to be translated onto paper. As Clarissa Pinkola Estes said, "All you have to do is take dictation—then take the time to unravel the answer." As the women's magazines advise of sex, do it anyway, even if you don't feel like it—you'll soon feel aroused. When we're writing, we have to start somewhere, and all we have to do is pull the thread of the first word, the first image, and trust that more will come.

In *Blink: The Power of Thinking without Thinking,* author

Malcolm Gladwell advises that what we perceive in an instant is often truer than what we surmise after much reflection and study—too much information gets in the way of the unconscious. In *Zen in the Art of Writing,* Ray Bradbury advises that we not think while we're writing, and in *The Journey from the Center to the Page,* Jeff Davis connects writing to yoga practice, advising, "Don't forget to breathe." The brain is a physical organ, and it's no wonder that so many writers recommend long walks—which have also been shown to improve IQ—to loosen it.

An article in the *New York Times* described the discoveries in science made by amateurs. And that's what we all are when we're writing. Whatever comes into our minds is usually connected to our subject, however loosely (unless it's merely that piece of chocolate in the kitchen, and maybe even then), and we can usually include it. You may even wonder why you're thinking about such silly things—the way Jude Law looked with his shirt off in the movie *Closer,* or that recipe you saw in *First* magazine—just as you're trying to write.

But just as your unconscious is constantly selecting from the myriad experiences you have each day that move you toward your goals (once you have stated them), it is also uncovering your true subject—what you're *really* writing about—and often making connections that move beyond your wildest expectations. This also happens when we write down our dreams and suddenly see the sense of what at first seemed irrational as a perfect little story, replete with the dream's message.

In France I woke from a dream in which my cat Amber was trapped in Italy without a passport and ended up having to stay in Rome, roaming the streets with the wild cats there. My dream even had a title—*Mississippi Mudslide, or How I Became*

My Own House Cat. It became only one of the many pieces I've written based on dreams, and while I doubted that it made sense at first, it turned into a funny if quirky poem that I used in Zona Rosa as an example of how even our craziest thoughts often contain a pattern or a seed of meaning.

Some of us are blessed with too many ideas, which means we have to decide where to put our energy. Sandy said she couldn't decide between continuing to write columns for her local paper, writing more magazine articles, working on her mystery novel, finishing her collection of poems, or completing her children's book. I suggested that she list her various projects on the left side of a piece of paper, starting with those already in progress, then create columns for "cost in time," "cost in money," "possible intangible rewards," "possible tangible rewards," and "predictable obstacles." Then I asked her to fill in each category beside the project in question.

Cost in time and cost in money are often interchangeable, I explained to Sandy, since money buys time. "Intangible rewards," on the other hand, are things like compliments from friends and community, literary recognition, or a mainstream audience, while "tangible rewards" include such stuff as those all-important bucks, whether big or small, grants, and other such things. Predictable obstacles could be something as simple as her local writing group being unsupportive when she talks about giving up her column and veering off into writing a full-length book, to lack of self-discipline when she finds herself in the "mid-book Sahara," with no water or quick fixes in sight.

Sandy quickly saw that the column that gave her a local name meant little in terms of intangibles and money; that she could expand her magazine writing by going for better-paying markets; and that her mystery novel was likely to give her the

SANDY'S WAY-TO-THE-HEART CHART: DECIDING THE ZONA ROSA WAY

POSSIBLE PROJECTS	COST: TIME & MONEY*	INTANGIBLE REWARDS**	TANGIBLE REWARDS**	PREDICTABLE OBSTACLES
Newspaper features—E	1 day	Immediate local recognition, writing practice	$35 per piece	None
Magazine features—E	1–3 weeks or more	Broader recognition, upgrade in writing skills	$90 (current fee at *Lexington* magazine) –$5,000	Competitive at upper reaches; will need to learn to write and send out queries
Poetry	Indefinite	Possible literary recognition, rewards	—	Highly competitive at upper reaches
Mystery novel—I	1–3 years	Recognition, possible fans, book contract, awards	$500–$50,000 or more (advance against royalties)	Highly competitive; friends in local writing group discouraging; requires perseverance and tolerance for a speculative venture

E—Sandy already has experience
I—In progress
*Time is money
**Possible rewards, with hard work!

most rewards, along with the most challenges. As we worked, I named her page "Sandy's Way-to-the-Heart Chart: Deciding the Zona Rosa Way." Today it's one of our most popular exorcises.

But the bottom line, I told her, was her gut-level response when she looked over her notes. Too often I've seen women struggle with writing they consider salable, rather than writing what their burning desires dictated, because one too many people—a husband, mother, or father—have said, "You're not going to make any money at *that*!"

Reading someone's writing for the first time is among the

more exciting things in my life: no matter how raw it may still be in terms of technique, or how little the author yet knows about syntax and grammar, the content is almost always magical. Unlike an editor or agent, who must look for what's finished, salable, I have the privilege of watching the process. And in Zona Rosa, we are forever surprised and delighted by what comes out when we let the chaos flow.

6.

I'm the automatic weapon of poetry and I've got extra rounds in my pockets. Go ahead, mister, incite me to write.
—Kitt Haley Alexander, "AK 47"

Remember That the Personal Is the Universal, or Why Sharing Our Secrets Is Good. "Writing is not necessarily something to be ashamed of," science fiction writer Robert Heinlein said, "but do it in private and wash your hands afterwards." While I loved his quote, I didn't agree with it. I've never been much of a secret keeper; in fact, I've never seen much sense in them. When someone reads my books, they usually feel they know me inside out—possibly better than they'd ever want to. But on the other hand, I don't go around like a politician about to run for office, wondering what might tumble out of my closet before Election Day.

When I began writing *Fatal Flowers,* much of the material I was covering was painful; indeed at times it even made me sweat with anxiety. But I soon found a rule to write by while wrestling with my truths: if something was true to me, it was probably true to someone else, simply because we're not alone in the universe (also, I was only obligated to tell *my* truths as I experienced them—not someone else's).

And while I had many critics when the book was published, I also saw that I had been right in telling my darkest secrets when people came up to thank me and to say that they had had exactly the same experiences. Even more remarkably, they said this most often about the parts of the book I almost left out, thinking they were too wild and crazy.

It's a credo that has worked for me ever since, and one that other authors have expressed in one form or another. Erica Jong and poet James Dickey advised that one should always go to the edge with one's writing, even to the edge of the ludicrous—because that's where we begin to fly. Or, as one woman tells another over cocktails in a *New Yorker* cartoon, "Method works, dear, but madness takes all." Letting it rip until something sparks is the way to uncover that reluctant image, idea, or experience.

And after a while, from beneath the baby fat of our words, a silhouette—as the French charmingly refer to the figure—will emerge. Soon we'll find we have a lot of pages through which we can flip, underlining the hot spots and connecting the dots, checking and rechecking our story's silhouette for shapeliness along the way. Unless we aspire to be literary Picassos, we don't want an arm where a leg should be, or our story's neck to protrude from its belly.

Think of yourself as painting a picture with words—preferably with people in it, as a friend recommended of photographs. Then cut some of those words out, and add some others. Doing this over and over is how a book is made.

Jill Conner Browne, the adorable author of the adorable *Sweet Potato Queen* books, says she never revises, and she has a folksy style that suits her readers just fine. (And, as she told an interviewer, she had to get that first book proposal out so she could pay her electric bill!) On the other hand, Hemingway said, when asked why it had taken him so long to write a certain novel, "I couldn't get the words right." And most of us are like that, especially at first.

While some pieces of writing will work out, some won't. But none will be failures, and all will be worthwhile. Writing anything is writing practice, and it's invaluable. Even our "flops"—like failed pancakes—are delicious, and they become part of the compost heap that generates our next, more divine poem or story.

"Never trash, burn, or delete the words you have written," advised novelist Terry Kay, after he rewrote a novel begun in the '70s, to publish it in 2000. And if there's anything that drives me crazy, other than the excuse, "I can't find it" (haven't you developed a filing system yet, girl?!), it's a woman telling me that she destroyed her work in a fit of pique. "How do you know there wasn't something good in there?" I'll ask, then describe how I've often gone back over pages and pages of drivel to find that one perfect phrase I needed at the moment. "And what about later, when the universities want your papers?" I add, upping the ante as she looks at me in amazement at the idea that her work might actually be worth something someday.

"The first thing you have to do is be born with talent," a supercilious—male—agent said when I told him about the marvelous writers of Zona Rosa. I could have kicked him in the shins—or elsewhere, thinking of all the women I have seen persevere until talent was born, even if it had only been a twinkle in their eyes in the beginning. Nor did he know that when the Zona Rosans make up their minds, there is virtually nothing that can stop them. But still, he represented the kind of voice in our heads to which we must say a resounding NO!

Besides "Do I have talent?" newcomers often ask, "Am I a writer?" To which I reply, "A writer is someone who writes." And how do you write a book? By writing one sentence, then another, then another. "Write moments," prize-winning short-story writer Laura Durnell's teacher told her in what she considered the best piece of writing advice she had received. Or, as Anne Lamott's writer dad advised, write "bird by bird."

It's okay to write about the same thing over and over—most writers do, in one form or another, until the exorcism is complete, and you tire of that particular subject yourself. In fact, writing about the same thing over and over in different forms is good writing practice. I frequently write a poem about something that ends up in my prose. In her book *The Situation and the Story: The Art of Personal Narrative,* Vivian Gornick says that there's the situation and the story. The situation may not change. But the story can.

When I worked in Poetry in the Schools, I made a list on the blackboard during our first few minutes together: *Feelings, Fantasies, Dreams, Memories, Ideas, Experiences,* and *The World around Us.* I told the kids that since we all had all those raw materials inside us—we all knew how to talk, and we all had the five senses, unless we were like Helen Keller—there was nothing holding us back from writing poems. All we had to do was paint pictures with words, using concrete images—words that have to do with things we can see, hear, touch, taste, and smell—to talk about what was real. I also told them that while we could depend on one or more of these raw materials when we wrote, the more of them we put into a poem or piece of writing, the better it was likely to be. Kids from kindergarten through twelfth grade understood this immediately, and I later found that the same suggestion worked with Zona Rosans of all ages.

The great southern writer Flannery O'Connor said, "Everyone who has had a childhood has enough to write about for a lifetime," and memory trips ideas for many of us. Ruby, a vibrant Zona Rosan who died in her seventies, leaving us bereft, told us the story of being sent to the country as a child to stay with her grandmother on a farm in a house with no toys, and no other kids for miles. "I would go out into the dirt yard," she said, and call 'Doodle up! Doodle up!' to try to lure the doodle bugs out of their holes in the ground—that was my excitement for the day!" That Ruby could amuse herself in that way was of a piece with the incredible stories she wrote about her early life—and the memories she drew on to write them.

Part of the fun of writing is developing the means. Gibson, eighty-six, likes to sit down with her morning coffee and a pen and yellow legal pad whether or not she feels a poem coming on.

"You asked me yesterday why I printed my manuscript in such a large font," Maggie, eighty-five, wrote in an e-mail. "It was because before my cataract operations I barely saw those pinpricks of punctuation. . . . Oh, god, it's three A.M.!" I wondered whether I, too, will be up till dawn in my mid-eighties, passionately embracing my project of the moment.

Jill, once a National Guard expert riflist, and our reigning expert on things technological, introduced us to flash drives, Pendaflex files, and pen scanners. We also call on Jody, one of our favorite guys and technocrat extraordinaire, when we need further instruction. Though some new Zona Rosans try to pull the I-can't-do-the-tech-stuff cop-out, they soon learn it won't fly, as there are always people who can show us, or even do it for us. Not knowing how to get online is also a deficit when we need to do research or write another Zona Rosan for feedback.

As I remind them, I wrote three books on manual typewriters, along with all the cut and paste that it took to make a book happen, "and, believe me, computers are better!"

Or as Stephen Covey said, paraphrasing Einstein (isn't it amazing how great people always say the same things?), "The thinking that brought you where you are is not the thinking that will take you where you want to be."

7.

This is also the real secret of the arts—be a beginner.
—SHUNRYU SUZUKI

Allow Yourself to Fail, or Anything Worth Doing Is Worth Doing Badly. When I visited Marda in her summer house in Highlands, North Carolina, I immediately noticed the exquisite vase on her coffee table. It looked as though it was made of layers and layers of poured glass, with some of the thin layers cut away to create a beautiful flower design. "That's cameo glass," Marda explained, then went on to tell me she had purchased it from its creator, Kelsey Murphy, after writing an article about her for *Verandah* magazine. Kelsey was a young woman who had heard of this ancient method of glassmaking and determined to learn to do it herself, no matter how long it took. "She said she counted on ninety-five percent breakage during the first year," Marda went on. As I gazed at the beauty Kelsey had so painstakingly created, and thought about the process she had undertaken to learn how to make it, I thought about the women of Zona Rosa and our own commitment to creative writing.

For a long time I couldn't make piecrust—my crusts fell apart or burned at the bottom or edges. But just when I felt that pastry making was something I would never conquer, I tried one more time, and *voila!*—the perfect, flaky, succulent pastry, ready to hold my best butterscotch filling. I love to use sewing and cooking—something most of us know a little about—and the other things we all grew up seeing other women do as metaphors for writing, because when we break the process down, it really is that simple: one stitch or ingredient after another.

Life coach Martha Beck says that to overcome her tendency toward perfectionism, she writes *Shitty First Draft* at the top of the first page of her manuscript as she begins her monthly column for *O* magazine (as Anne Lamott recommended in her book *Bird by Bird*). Wise woman that she is, she knows that before she can come up with anything, she has to let the chaos—with all its craziness—flow.

Isn't this the way we learned to do all the simple skills we take for granted? For example, I'm typing on this laptop, yet when I took typing in high school, I was far from a natural, plodding along at walrus-flipper speed while the other girls tap-tap-tapped their way to becoming secretaries to rich CEOs. But simply by keeping on, I finally became an adequate typist, with a mastery of the skill I now find necessary for my true love, writing. Like learning enough French to get by, playing the piano, or putting on lipstick without a mirror, anything we try gets easier with practice. The freedom to fail is one of the best gifts we can give ourselves.

Giving ourselves the freedom to fail is also one of the best ways of demystifying the writing process, which otherwise could put us into brain freeze at the very thought of it. "I'm just a working mom," says prolific and successful writer Barbara Kingsolver, when we know she's really anything but; no one but a woman with a mission could have produced her socially conscious novels, such as *The Bean Trees* and *The Poisonwood Bible,* one after the other. Jane Smiley, author of *Thirteen Ways of Looking at the Novel,* for which she read a hundred novels in one year, says she can write while talking on the phone, and thinks we should be able to do so, too. By now you're aware of my fondness for *New Yorker* cartoons, and one of my recent favorites, embodying as it does a less than mystical approach to the act of writing, is one in which a little girl who is scribbling on the sidewalk explains to a little boy, "I try to write a little bit every day."

Female chauvinist that I am (the phrase actually appears in the title of one of my books), I prefer to quote a femme any day. But sometimes I just have to share a guy's wisdom. Since we were held down through the ages by the Bondage of the Pink, a lot of them got there first, and their experiences are worth noting.

Before he became famous, Stephen Spender told T. S. Eliot that he wanted "to be a poet." Eliot responded, "I can understand your wanting to write poems, but I don't quite know what you mean by 'being a poet.'" He was making clear that writing is an act, not a state of being—however many authors we see in their glory on *Oprah, The Today Show,* and C-Span 2.

8.

It's never too late, in fiction or in life, to revise.

—NANCY THAYER

Start Yesterday, or Deborah's Extreme Makeover. After hearing how Susan changed her life and moved to France, Deborah, blessed with electric energy as well as great confidence, stepped out in faith, and within the next year, she had changed her life by becoming debt-free for the first time since she can remember, all toward the end of becoming a writer. Indeed, some of us—despite our immersion in life-changing tactics—were shocked at the speed with which she went about it.

Deborah had been self-supporting since high school and through five marriages, supporting her hell-on-wheels mother, who had become pregnant with her out of wedlock at age sixteen, and now her college-age daughter as well. In addition, her love of clothes and the new—she always looks like a fashion plate—and fine things of every kind, plus her desire to prove that, yes, a girl from her deprived background could make it big-time, had added to her financial burdens.

But soon she had left behind the failing company she was loaning her own money to and declared bankruptcy, giving up what had once been her dream house—and writing about her angst along the way. She insisted that her mother and her daughter move out on their own, telling her mom that she could go to sports bars and pick up the much younger black men she preferred just as easily from a home for the elderly. She also encouraged her daughter, who was already working at a well-paying summer job, to order a copy of *Finance for Dummies* from Amazon.com. For Deborah, to think is to write is to act: we watched and read about her processes aloud in Zona Rosa like stories hot off the presses—from the pain of giving up her house, to standing for the first time in her life in an unemployment line, through fights with her mother, who threatened to take her to court for neglecting the elderly.

In typical Deborah style, an old boyfriend, now a retired airline pilot, popped up on the Internet to invite her to meet him "in Monaco—I'll be in a convertible big enough for all your luggage" (like most Stars, Deborah doesn't travel light!) during the week her stuff was being auctioned in an estate sale, thus saving her the pain of watching all those antiques, designer skirts, and garter belts go. "We didn't really hit it off, but it was good to be away just then."

And while she's the kind of woman men love to offer gifts to ("Yes, I've had a couple of offers. But I don't want to do that," she said when I asked whether any of her many beaux had offered to help her financially), she changed her lifestyle with her integrity intact, doing whatever it took, whether it was storing her remaining furniture and sharing a house for a while with another woman, or taking whatever job she could get when her money started running out. For a while she was even doing manual labor at a plant nursery; when the company recognized her smarts she was quickly promoted to manager. At the same time, winner that she is, she was moving toward her dream of writing full-time, and enjoying life more. Before we knew it, she had even more time to meet men on Match.com (eventually moving on to Lust.com), and she was hard at work on her book in progress, tentatively but appropriately titled *The Cook and Fuck Book*—crediting the Zona Rosans every step of the way:

My awakening began at the Zona Rosa writers' retreat at the beach last July. That was the first realization. I could actually be a writer . . . I should have known that things were going to be wild when our group of women consumed 9 bottles of wine on the first evening, with only Wendy, who was in A.A., abstaining. . . . That night Eden and I told the others about being Sacred Sexual Priestesses and how we had found one another's G-spots. . . . They learned that I live life maybe a little too fully and write poetry ridden with angst and sex . . . that as a recovering Baptist, I am prone to excess in all its varieties and men and sex were at the top of my list. . . . I was just fine with masking my mental illness and acting like I was normal before I went to this retreat and started exploring myself. [It was] those damn exorcises of Rosemary's where you have to go inside and get real with yourself and then write about it. . . . I started with her assignment to write about what I fear most. . . . Of course, mine was about my fear of going mad. . . . I knew that there was some big emotional breakthrough or breakdown bubbling up to the surface and I continued to numb it with alcohol and drugs. What if I didn't medicate myself and just let it all come bubbling out—how ugly would it look? I imagined Linda Blair in *The Exorcist* with her spinning head and projectile vomiting. If I totally unloosed this stuff, would there be an explosion out of my head or my butt or more likely . . . my vagina? . . . Would I crawl into a corner of the room and rock and cry like I did as a baby? . . . Would I start screaming and beating something until I fell into a heap? Would I be in the middle of fucking some faceless man . . . and start orgasming and not be able to stop? . . . So here I am, 8 months later sitting at my computer contemplating whether I can come up with anything anyone would be interested in reading . . . wondering where I will live in a month when I have to give up my house . . . wondering how I am going to pay the bills. . . . My whole world is being rocked and changed and I have never been happier or more peaceful. It amuses me that after making $250,000 in my best year, I can be content now with my $300 a week unemployment. . . . I look into the mirror and finally think I am enough. I tell myself I am a writer and I'm starting to believe it.

As Freud said, we can't have an insight until we are ready to use it—and once Deborah had hers, she wanted to act on it, not wasting a minute. It was the way I felt when, as an anxious young housewife, I heard a professor at Emory University read from modern poetry for the first time and saw my life as a writer unscroll before me, like Dorothy's yellow brick road.

Indeed, it's an epiphany many of us in Zona Rosa have had, leading us not only to begin writing, but to start yesterday. The fortunate among us need make only a few changes in order to begin. But some of us, like Deborah, find our selves changing from the inside out to make room for brand-new lives.

9.

Don't run faster than your guardian angel can fly.

—ANONYMOUS

Listen to Your Voice of No. In Gregg Levoy's book, *Callings,* he explains that behind every resistance there is a No, and "it will lodge itself in the middle of the road between our intentions and achievements." When Marsha had all but finished her exquisite novel, the one she had gotten up at four A.M. for four years in a row to write, suddenly the voice of her No sprang to life, making her resistant to doing the small revisions that were needed before sending it out into the world.

"Has this happened with other things?" I asked, and she acknowledged that yes, over the years, she had lost interest in what had once been a passion just as she was about to achieve success. This time, when her voice of No manifested itself, other things were going on in her life, and they had become an easy out. But once she was aware that her voice of No came from somewhere deep inside her, and that she needed to listen to it more closely, she was able to go on with her book with a renewed enthusiasm.

At first, almost all of us have to battle the voice of No. An anonymous Zona Rosan listed three full pages of her No's, from "Too much breaking news to follow" to "My apartment is too cluttered," to "I need to pay my bills," to "No boyfriend to encourage me," and "Nothing matters anyway." Beside the last one, she wrote, "I know this is a bad attitude," and she was right.

But if we don't listen to the voice of our No at least long enough to know what it says, and even treat it with respect, like an honored guest, it will keep coming back, like a repressed thought, to sabotage us. Have you noticed that when you tell yourself not to think about something, like that piece of chocolate in the kitchen that's calling to you right now, its voice becomes louder and louder?

Once we acknowledge the voice of our No, we can always remind ourselves of the alternative, such as the walk that would make us feel better than if we grabbed up that chocolate and ate the whole box.

For some of us, like Marsha, dealing with our voice of No indicates a need for exploration; for others, it's as simple as saying "NO!" or "STOP!" whenever it invades our territory. And if your voice is saying negative things about your writing itself, remember that while we need that sweetheart of a girl-friend, the Good Critic, her opposite, Cruella the Cruel, is as useless as she is ugly. (I think of my good critic as being spelled with a caring *C,* and my bad one, whom I banish at her first appearance, as starting with a knife-edged *K.*) This might be a good time, too, to make use of our stroke/gratitude/plea-sure book therapy from chapter 2, and to remind ourselves

288 of MARDA ROSA

that affirmations and visualizations are among our most important accessories.

10.

First say to yourself what you would be; and then do what you have to do.

—EPICTETUS

Hanging with Magical Marda, or How I Learned to Diverge. Back in the late '60s, in *The Medium Is the Massage*, Marshall McLuhan described "convergers" and "divergers." Convergers converge on their problems, creating further conflict for themselves; divergers move around them, continuing to travel forward.

Marda is like that, moving around obstacles with such grace that few are even aware she's doing it. Indeed, the life she's created for herself appears effortless, like sleight of hand. When I met her at a literary conference in New Orleans in the late '80s I saw only the glamorous blonde, the kind who looks right in a full-length mink, and who sounds natural with the words "Sugah" and "Honey" dripping from her lips as only a true southern belle can utter them. Because her disguise was so perfect, I didn't know that I was meeting the most adept diverger around.

I soon learned that Marda was also an international travel writer, voyaging abroad to write articles for magazines like *Travel & Leisure* (today, she's travel editor for *Verandah* magazine). She had chosen New Orleans, she said, because, after traveling the world, she had considered other places, such as Paris, but had decided that New Orleans had everything she loved, including the French (and Creole) influence—parties, the arts, and an easy bar life. "Plus, everyone speaks English!"

When we met again, she was ensconced in a beautiful apartment with a large living room filled with her grand piano and a balcony overhanging Royal Street in the French Quarter, where she held "salons" on Sunday afternoons to support local poets, writers, and musicians, and where all were invited to perform. (She also made good things happen for us in Highlands, North Carolina, where she spends the summer months, by planning our first week-long Zona Rosa retreat there.)

It was clear from the well-thumbed books that were stacked everywhere that she was a serious reader and writer, despite her incredible social life. As I got to know her better, I would learn that she read for a long time each night, wherever in the world she might be, and however late the hour. At her condo in Highlands, she reclines on a chaise, the nearby dining room table piled with books and more books. And I knew that there were weeks when she had to bite the bullet and meet deadlines—which, with typical effervescence, she labeled "marshmallows—a sweeter, softer word, don't you think?"

When she was writing a book with her close friend Kenneth—collaborating is a difficult process at best—Marda did whatever it took to find solutions to differences; as she said, she didn't want to "be a name on his black voodoo candle." When *Galatoire's: Biography of a Bistro,* the story of New Orleans' most famous restaurant, and a book full of juicy anecdotes, was published, they both enjoyed the limelight as the book sold out.

But was this divine, if hardworking, even obsessive lifestyle—one that would be the envy of many women— handed to Marda on a silver platter? Not at all. She was from

Laurel, Mississippi, current population 18,393, where she married young and had four children, two of them twins, leading a life a long way from that of the world traveler she is today. After a while, she began writing a column on the arts, worked in radio and TV, and eventually branched out into travel.

All this happened over a long period of time, during which her husband, she noticed, was becoming more reclusive, and content to remain in Laurel. But did she press for more attention, or cause a ruckus and break up her marriage? Not at all. She continued with what was working for her—her writing, travels, and making friends (she makes them wherever she goes), all the while gestating the idea of a move to New Orleans, 130 miles from Laurel, where "not far away waited the creative atmosphere I craved." When she proposed this to her husband, he agreed, happy to have more time to himself. (They are still married, and on good terms. Christmases and other holidays are often spent together with their kids in Laurel.)

Indeed, my favorite story of Marda's skill at diverging is about her and her husband: When she still lived in Laurel, they went out each Saturday night to one of the few local restaurants, their entertainment for the week. Like many wives, she planned their outings. But one night during their dinner out, he said, "Why do you always plan what we'll do? Next week, I'll plan where we'll go," to which she murmured assent. But then when the next Saturday night came, and the next, he said nothing about going out and—here's where her powers of diverging come in—neither did she. "Instead I just went to bed with a bowl of popcorn. And after a few weeks, I started planning our dinners out again." Like many southern women, Marda prefers simply going her own way, doing her own thing, to making a fuss.

Because of her warmth and charm, and since New Orleans is a place that almost *everyone* alights at one time or another (even after Katrina), anyone who hangs out with Marda is bound to meet fascinating people. Once she tugged me over to meet Jessica Lange and Sam Shepherd as they slouched in blue jeans at the bar at the Bombay Club. During a literary conference, we chatted with Gennifer Flowers about lip gloss and more intimate things. "Call me and let's have lunch," Gennifer was repeating as we left.

When we got back to the Carousel Bar at the Montelone Hotel, where we joined our pals from the conference, we both moaned when we learned that we had just missed seeing Jude Law and Sean Penn. But I'm sure if we had been there, Magical Marda would have found an effortless way to become acquainted.

11.

I'm in a state of continuous excitement and I hope that it lasts forever.
                                        —PARAPHRASE OF OSCAR WILDE

In Praise of Obsession, or Move into Process and Make It Permanent Address. Have you ever noticed how people are drawn to the activities, or at least to images of the activities, that require a great deal of their participants? We know that the ballerina *en pointe* practiced for years and years, and that the woman who makes it up Mount Everest has put in hours and hours of strength-training in preparing to trek at high altitudes. My niece Lia is Miss March, one of the skiers in a 2005 calendar featuring women athletes, and I love looking at the photo of the strong woman I once held as a baby, flashing down a mountain at top speed.

My personal favorite of the Zona Rosa credos is the directive to "Extend chi," used in tai chi to indicate pushing yourself beyond your original goal. Like the credo "Say yes to stress," it's the best thing we can do to jazz up our creativity, and also the most exciting. We all live with what I call the Myth of Perfect Mental Health, a.k.a. the balanced life, but it's obsession that takes us where we want to go.

"Though I realized that I could easily fall in my exhausted state, I felt a sense of liberation and strength, knowing that this was an effort worth trying with all my heart," wrote Lynn Hill of climbing the nose of El Capitan, after she had already had a major fall. In her book *Climbing Free,* she describes being totally engaged, living completely.

What's left out in too many accounts of the creative process is the *joy,* sheer joy—the exhilaration of creating something out of nothing (which I'm feeling at this moment as I write this sentence). Many writers have admitted to feeling turned on as they write. Like plunging our bare hands directly into the succulent foods we're preparing, like the sexy British cook Nigella Lawson does on TV, when we're writing we're plunging our hands directly into the sensual matter of life— and what could be headier? Indeed, if husbands, boyfriends, and lovers knew how much sexier we feel when we're living in a creative burst—my name for just such joyous obsession— they would not only encourage, but insist on it.

In *Letters to a Young Poet,* the great German poet Rainer Maria Rilke recommends that the aspiring writer ask (her)self, "Do I have to write to live?" In Zona Rosa, we ask this another way: "Do I write even when my sex life is great, the kids are all well, and I have money in the bank—or when I have none of these?"

As you may have noticed in chapter 1, "The Story of My Writing (and Other) Life," my life has not always been a perfectly balanced one populated by doting mentors, the mentally healthy, or rich men who paved the way. But I had the one thing that is the name of the game—obsession.

"She looks like she was rode hard and put up wet," people say in the South and the West about a horse that's been pushed to her limits. (It's also a phrase sometimes used about people, but we won't get into that.) It's a good way of describing the lengths to which we should go to uncover what lives in our brains beneath their top layers of cliché. To get to our best ideas, we need to write until we've completely "worn that thang out," another southern crudity.

Some thinkers recommend against too much introspection. Spiritual leader Eckhart Tolle, author of *The Power of Now,* says spiritual progress can be measured by how long we can sit without thinking. In *The Curse of the Self: Self-Awareness, Egotism, and the Quality of Human Life,* author Mark Leary says that we can be too self-aware, and that this can fill our minds with self-defeating cacophony. (Remember those negative messages from chapter 2?). But I prefer to put this another way: How can we become so involved in our creative projects, the excitement of our lives, that the trivial falls away?

As we've demonstrated in Zona Rosa over and over, you don't have to be flaky, unhappily married, or too serious to have fun to be a writer. You simply have to sit in a chair—or even stand up, as some writers have preferred—and write words on paper. Well, maybe you have to be a little bit flaky, or what the outside world calls flaky: creating art, like achieving anything that requires a focused vision, calls forth a certain degree of mania. But it's more the delicious kind described by

Kay Redfield Jamison in *Exuberance*. (In another, earlier book, *Touched by Fire*, Jamison describes the many artists and writers throughout history who have been afflicted with bipolar disorder—and achieved greatness anyway.)

"I've been spending so much time on family that I've almost forgotten the important things" read the caption beneath a *New Yorker* cartoon. The speaker was a businessman, briefcase in hand, but it could have been appropriately spoken by almost any woman I know. Because we are so used to seeing one another in our usual roles of caregiving or people pleasing, there is sometimes nothing more beautiful to us than seeing another woman totally immersed, at least for the moment, in a project that is hers alone.

I will never forget Jill, whom you met in chapter 6, on her hands and knees on the living room rug of our cottage in the South of France, her new pink beret atop her curls, and wearing the old pink ballet slippers she had brought to ground her, totally and happily absorbed in sorting the pages she had laid out from her book-in-progress.

At that moment, no one would have suspected how she had bravely and publicly read her account of having to choose whether to allow her maimed and brain-damaged son to live or die, or that her freedom in the moment came from having nothing left to lose—only that she was happy, and immersed in something that was hers and hers alone.

❀

I used to love to dance to disco: "It's Raining Men" by The Weather Girls and anything by The Village People were my favorites. While I was on the dance floor, I was never thinking about anything else (unless it was the sexy guy I was with). I even danced on the stage at Dr. Feelgood's, one of Savannah's more colorful discos, with my hairdresser, a.k.a. Miss Thunder Pussy, who was in drag. I didn't know how good I was, or whether I was making a fool of myself—though I must not have been, for one beau asked me to be his partner in a dance competition. At forty, newly arrived in the sensual city and recovering from my third divorce, there I was, lost in the moment—and *dancing*.

My joy and its immediacy was what I felt when I first began writing, an excitement that has never wavered, and which makes me willing to do the work that following my bliss entails. It's also an elation I've seen over and over in the Zona Rosans, as they give up judging themselves and commit to their writing and lives, whatever that requires—and find themselves dissolved into the happiness that comes with a passion, even an obsession, of one's own.

Knee-jerk Reaction #8: Imagining that great lives, great books, stories, poems—great *anything*!—come about without planning and, yes, hard if oft delicious work. That the process is less important than the rewards. And that they are not created by people like you and me.

PILATES ON PAPER

Honey, I Shrunk My Talent. Have I neglected that precious baby, my writing? Let me name the ways, you might say. And it's a good idea to confess to them now, in order to clear the decks for the exorcises to follow. Joyce Carol Oates, who is nothing if not a prolific novelist, said that she'd rather "eat ground glass than waste time"—a feeling I share, since time is the medium I need most in my life to manifest my destiny. Once I overheard a very smart woman, a professor of note and editor and coauthor of a book on how women find time to write, talking to her husband over the phone; she kept the call brief and obviously said what he wanted to hear. "I don't like to get into useless chitchat, especially arguments," she said after she hung up, revealing one of her secrets. When you make your list, include everything you do now that steals time, from those useless arguments with your significant other, to an over-the-top Office Max or Barnes & Noble habit, to failing to set boundaries with your adult children. For a long time, I kept a handwritten laminated poster in my study that read: "Poor Planning on Your Part Doesn't Mean a Crisis on My Part." Just looking at it when one of my kids called saved the day—and my writing hand. And when I stopped answering the phone at all during my "office hours," I found even more riches. "The only goal that means anything is the one you can do today," someone smart said. In addition to present-tense time wasters, you, like many of us, might want to look back at the eons you wasted in the past on Bad Love, friends who didn't work out, or a job you hated, not to speak of parents who weren't as perfect as we would have liked them to be. But, as others have said before me, nothing is ever lost on a writer, and we can write about that stuff without getting stuck there.

Am I a Hummingbird or a Woodpecker? Some of us like to flit from idea to idea, and we flit for a very long time indeed—even forever. I often ask the Zona Rosans when they'll be ready to stop darting from project to project, leaving a trail of perfectly good first drafts behind them, and begin hacking away, like a determined woodpecker, at a particularly promising piece of writing. A period of being a hummingbird is appropriate when we first begin to write—remember "Let the chaos flow"?—but after a while, if you want to go further, you'll have to focus in. When Carol O. sent me color photos of a ruby-throated hummingbird and a red-headed woodpecker, I pointed out to the group that while the woodpecker was taking time out to feed her young, she would soon be pecking away again! Indeed, this may be the time you need to make a decision-making chart, like "Sandy's Way-to-the-Heart Chart: Deciding the Zona Rosa Way."

Getting Ready to Play. Zona Rosan Jan shared an amusing account of how, as a child, she would spend hours inviting her playmates over, getting out her tea set, laying out the doll clothes, and getting out her dolls—after which she lost interest and convinced her friends to go bike riding instead, which led her mother to say, "You spend more time getting ready to play than you do playing!" It was hard to imagine Jan playing with dolls in the first place—she's a Nascar fan who's inclined to wear a Mr. Goodwrench cap. But when we read her piece in Zona Rosa, we all saw the metaphor for what some of us were doing with our writing—we were spending more time "getting ready to play" than actually playing. So ask yourself whether you do the same!

Where I Am Now in My Writing, Where I Would Like to Be a Year from Now. Or five or ten years from now. Here's where we make a time line, breaking our goals down into the smallest increments and actions, as suggested by time management expert Alan Lakein in his classic *How to Get Control of Your Time*

SUSAN'S TIME LINE: 2001

JANUARY	FEBRUARY	MARCH	APRIL	MAY	JUNE
WRITE EVERY DAY ───►					
Organize for move ──────────────────────────────┤					
Read for next project ─────────────────────────────►					
Await query replies ──────────────────────►					
Work on writers' retreats ────────────────────────►					
Travel business ──►					
			Taxes	Put house on market	Provence to find house?
First major shipment of furniture to family			Get hair cut—first good-hair day Renew driver's license!	Move to Big	Canoe
			Get house emptied	Work on next project ──────►	
			Second load of things to family		
			Organize for painting and carpeting		
			MAIL MANUSCRIPT TO STEPHANIE		
			Change health insurance		
			Final shipment of things		

and Your Life, and Barbara Sher in *Wishcraft* (or as another of her great titles says, *It's Only Too Late If You Don't Start Now*). I make my time lines for six months at a time; some of us make them for three months, some for a year. And they take different forms. *But the most important part of making a time line is giving yourself a line or two of credit at the top of your page for what you have already achieved,* even if it was simply going to Office

PAMELLA'S TIME LINE: 2002

	MONDAY	TUESDAY	WEDNESDAY	THURSDAY	FRIDAY
July	Novel 5–6am Swim 7–8am Work 11–4pm Teach 5–8:30pm	Aerobics 6–7am Teach 9am– 8:15pm	Novel 5–6am Swim 7–8am Work 11–7pm	Aerobics 6–7am Work 11–7pm (1st & 3rd til 9pm)	Finish the story for the novel. Increase working hours to compen- sate for teaching in- come.
August	Novel 5–6am Swim 7–8am Work 11–4pm Teach 5–8:30pm	Aerobics 6–7am Teach 9am– 8:15pm	Novel 5–6am Swim 7–8am Work 11–7pm	Aerobics 6–7am Work 11–7pm (1st & 3rd til 9pm)	Finish the story for the novel Kataoka/ Spivey.
September	Novel 5–6am Swim 7–8am Work 11–4pm Teach 5–8:30pm	Aerobics 6–7am Teach 9am– 8:15pm	Novel 5–6am Swim 7–8am Work 11–7pm	Aerobics 6–7am Work 11–7pm (1st & 3rd til 9pm)	Begin rewrite of novel. Write sample query for novel. Wine bar opens
October	Novel 5–6am Swim 7–8am Work 11–4pm Teach 5–8:30pm	Aerobics 6–7am Teach 9am– 8:15pm	Novel 5–6am Swim 7–8am Work 11–7pm	Aerobics 6–7am Work 11–7pm (1st & 3rd til 9pm)	Begin rewrite of novel. Write sample query for agent for novel. Rosemary's Work- shop in Italy
November	Novel 5–6am Swim 7–8am Work 11–4pm Teach 5–8:30pm	Aerobics 6–7am Teach 9am– 8:15pm	Novel 5–6am Swim 7–8am Work 11–7pm	Aerobics 6–7am Work 11–7pm (1st & 3rd til 9pm)	Begin rewrite of novel. Write sample query for agent for novel. Rosemary's Work- shop in Italy
December	Novel 5–6am Swim 7–8am Work 11–4pm Teach 5–8:30pm	Aerobics 6–7am Teach 9am– 8:15pm	Novel 5–6am Swim 7–8am Work 11–7pm	Aerobics 6–7am Work 11–7pm (1st & 3rd til 9pm)	Read a good book. Enjoy the family. Decorate and cook. Write time line for 2003.

Max for supplies or joining a writing group. And be sure to include the predictable obstacles and minutiae of life—such as
Susan's "get hair cut—first good hair day" and "renew driver's
license?" In my January-to-June time line, done across a page
with the months at the top heading columns, I always include

"Get income tax extension" and "Make appointment for mammogram." Otherwise, no matter how good a plan we've made, we'll be thrown off balance when these nonwriting activities inevitably come up. If your time line is a month-by-month plan, as mine is, you'll also need to plan your ideal day. (Please note: instead of trying to force yourself into an unnatural schedule—a sure formula for failure—assess your best biological times for writing, and, if you can, do it then, however weird your schedule may seem to anyone else.)

And now, just for the fun of it, fantasize the results of your efforts. At the Writers Colony in Dairy Hollow, a clock in the foyer is marked with *My Fifteen Minutes of Fame*. I liked it so much that I Xeroxed the clock face to use as a graphic for a new exorcise (see below). When you do this one, feel free to fly to the clouds, as did Audrey—the sky's the limit!

Your

Fifteen

Minutes

of Fame

Describe Below!

CHAPTER NINE

A BEVY OF PERFECT T.I.T.S

All the Writing How-to You Will Ever Need

1.

Let the beauty we love be what we do.

—RUMI

In his book *The Art of Loving,* psychologist Erich Fromm says that the primary problem facing all of us is our sense of separateness, of being alone in the universe. We use various means to overcome this feeling, among them orgiastic events, in which we temporarily break down barriers, share experiences with strangers, and get outside our daily lives, and in social conformity, in which we seek to become as like the other members of our tribe as possible.

But Fromm also writes that the best ways of feeling less alone are those that require more of us—making art and having loving relationships. In other words, going to Mardi Gras and being a good neighbor are fine. But developing deep friendships and creating something out of nothing are far better roads to happiness. Which is what makes Zona Rosa divine—in it, we share a heavenly playing field for both.

I've never heard anyone say they regretted the time they spent writing—and many have told me that it changed their lives. Every one of them, it appears, has been blessed by the process. And some of us come to love writing so much that we go on and on, meeting ever greater writing challenges, until we suddenly wake up one day and find that yes, *I am a writer!*

Eyelash Curlers for the Brain, or the Smart-Girl Reminders, are our credos or quick takes on the writing process and the ways we've found to make it easier. We use them to remind ourselves of what's important when we come up against blocks, and we always start with our original credo, "Ac-cent-tchu-ate the positive, e-lim-i-nate the negative," from the song by Johnny Mercer. And now we have a passel of them, a few of which you've already met, including the following:

Say Yes to Stress

Slow Down to Go Faster

No Guts, No Story

Let the Chaos Flow

The Personal Is the Universal

There Are No Writing Blocks, Only Feeling Blocks

Use the F-word—Focus

Extend Chi

Move Out and Draw Fire

Sentimentality Is the Death of Art

Revision Revises Us

Everything Drives to the Good of the Work (Not Our Egos)

In this chapter, you will also be introduced to some of our other favorite tools, like the Self-Talk Notebook; "A Bevy of Perfect Tits," or the acronyms we use in discussing our work; "The Zona Rosa Crash Course on POV," or point of view, as it's called by the pros; and the list I made to make it easier on myself as I read manuscripts, "The Thirteen (Possible) Boo-Boos." And for those who are serious about becoming published authors, there's "The Emotional Tai Chi of Getting Your Work Out There."

2.

It is looking at things for a long time that ripens you and gives you a deeper understanding.

—VINCENT VAN GOGH

Slow Down to Go Faster. By choosing writing, you've already opted for lasting, rather than instant, success. At the same time, it's a joy so flighty, so hummingbird-like, that we often need to ground ourselves in order to demystify it. "Pleasure, enlightenment, and consolation are what a poem should give us," I heard at a high-toned academic conference. And that's what good writing of any kind gives us. (I call poetry, my first love, the needlepoint of literature, or the "useless" art, because one is unlikely to have a huge readership or make much money off it. And therein lies its beauty.)

You've taken a step toward slowness and against multitasking, because if there's one thing writing requires, it's that old-fashioned virtue, patience. "The noise of urgency creates the illusion of importance," says Stephen Covey, going on to explain that when we give in to it, we're actually prioritizing the trivial. "[Urgency] is not about survival—it's about deterioration." The easiest way to do something is rarely the best way.

As Julie Morgenstern points out in *Organizing from the Inside Out,* "Everything always takes more time than we think it will." Julie cited a big breakthrough in her own writing goals when she developed the concept of "Julie's Sandbox"—the hours of time that she had to "play"—after she realized that the time slot she had allotted to write her book wasn't working.

Her new idea sounds like much more fun, you may be thinking, and it is. The ecstasy is in the obsession, in allowing ourselves to practically leave our own bodies, fly away from the everyday in order to immerse ourselves in a vision of our own creation. As I worked and reworked a poem for three years, my pleasure increased exponentially with the time spent.

When Claire B. first came to Zona Rosa, tremulous with her desire to write, she told us about her diaries: red, leather-bound books that she fills year by year, with no year overlapping into the next. She is passionately addicted to these volumes, she said, and what she writes has to be contained within the book for that particular year. Thus when she decided in an initial journal to catch up to where she is now by writing her whole life story, she wrote in a tiny script—then as she approached her present-tense experience, her handwriting expanded. As she held up the book, showing us samples of both kinds of pages, everyone laughed, knowing what I always say when people bring in writing tools that limit their output—and suggested that Claire B. should simply buy a second book for each year (or a bigger notebook). At the same time, I admired her obsessiveness. "You may be our next Proust," I told her when she described the novel she wanted to write. Then I suggested that she bring in an outline in order to keep the book from becoming a catalog of her whole life.

3.

Even God lends a hand to honest boldness.

—MENANDER

No Guts, No Story. Living around Zane, I've heard a lot about the military, and at times, I've even co-opted some of his training mottoes to apply to creative writing. Just as he would sometimes sleep on the ground in the rain beside his Bradley in order to inspire his platoon, I seek to inspire the Zona Rosans to stretch themselves. Indeed, "No guts, no story," from "No guts, no glory," has become one of our more important credos. But you may have wondered how "Move out and draw fire" could relate to writing. Both are terms used to instruct soldiers to put themselves at risk in order to zero in on the enemy— which in our case as writers is our tendency to fudge.

Some of us have been so schooled in self-effacement that we cringe at our first mention of ourselves, much less at letting it all hang out. Anne D., mother of seven and one of the more talented humorists in Zona Rosa, wrote that "one of my excuses for not writing . . . was there was too much of me in [it]. . . . I am peeping around the corner all the time. . . . I am the main character and I am trying to be loved."

"I want to hear more of you, not less," I told her, reassuring her that yes, we loved hearing about her foibles and mishaps.

Sometimes, when the going gets tough, and the truth looms too large, we hide behind sentimentality and the values with which we've been brought up. When such impulses arise, it's good to think of them as a white picket fence that's pretty in a tacky, Norman Rockwell sort of way, but which is also electrified to keep the truth out. It's also when we remind ourselves of our credo, "Sentimentality is the death of art."

It's only when we begin going deeper that we realize how much more there is to say. Lisa Kron, author and one-woman performer of *Facing Life's Problems* and *101 Humiliating Stories,* thought she had faced her demons on the stage. But she told the *New York Times,* "I'd thought I was so frank and funny, but really I was totally protective." In her next play, *Well,* she wrote about the really hard stuff, such as her mother Ann's illnesses, and whether or not she believed they were a figment of her mother's imagination—and whether her own illnesses during college had been equally unreal.

As I often tell the Zona Rosans, "In anything we write, something has to happen, preferably from within." Others have said that fiction (or any literary work) is a process of placing characters in a situation in which something is learned or discovered.

4.

Finally, one has to just sit down and write.

—NATALIE GOLDBERG

There Are No Writing Blocks, Only Feeling Blocks. Now that you're about to take the Big Risk, a good way to jump-start your writing is by plunging in to one of our most life-changing (and difficult) exorcises, "Write About the Thing You Most Don't Want to Write About." And if you're not quite ready for that one, try "Why I Can't Write About the Thing I Most Don't Want to Write About."

Cynthia, a talented writer, felt blocked for months, never finishing any of the promising short stories she started, until one night she asked to read the letter she had written to her parents over Christmas, expressing her anger at them. About what? We didn't know, for though the letter was long, it was also abstract, and I questioned my wisdom at allowing her to take up so much of the group's time by reading it. I was also a little surprised to hear that at her age—forty—she was still harboring such resentments.

But the next month, the way paved by our acceptance of her foggy letter, Cynthia had her breakthrough. Her real truths poured out in a piece so vivid that we were all mesmerized. In it, she described the very real ways her parents had kept her from expressing herself, from the time she had been molested by a neighbor, to when she had fallen in love during high school with Mike, a boy her age. When her mother found out they'd had sex, she had taken Cynthia to the health department for a pelvic examination, and then invited their pastor to hear her "confession." These humiliations were followed by her two

brothers' arrests for beating Mike up—"This is your fault"—
and her parents' insistence, after deciding to counter-sue, that
she go to court and testify that Mike had raped her:

"I looked at my parents. There was murder in Mom's eyes. I
hadn't meant to mess up . . . I just couldn't remember the story
the lawyer had told me to say. And besides, I'd taken an oath.
The judge asked me, 'Why did you have sex with this boy?' 'Because I love him.' Her stern face stared at me for a moment, then
she told me to leave the room. The next thing I knew . . . she
had thrown out both cases." From then on, until she had written
her Christmas declaration of independence, Cynthia had been
submissive—and depressed. "That was enough life for me," she
wrote. "I stepped back into line right away."

As I finished reading her piece to the group, Cynthia's face
was glowing in a way we had never seen before, and I had little
doubt that I would be seeing finished stories from then on.
Sometimes our windshields get fogged, but Truth gets our
juices flowing as little else can.

Once we've written out our past traumas, we're back in present tense, like Claire with her red leather journals. We're in the
flow, energized and free to use what's of the moment, such as
how the River Seine looks when you walk beside it, or that nig-
gling unresolved issue right beneath the surface of consciousness.

5.

Genius is simply attention to detail.

—THOMAS CARLYLE

The Feng Shui of Grammar, or Why Syntax Matters. "I feel silly asking
this," asked Sue, who has a master's in music therapy, during the

break at a two-day Zona Rosa workshop in North Carolina. "But what is syntax?"

"Just the way the words are put together in a sentence," I said, suddenly back in my little furnished apartment in Savannah, pounding away on a manual typewriter, piling up the yellow second sheets that would become *Fatal Flowers*. I realized that I had written two books, maybe more, without ever once thinking of the word *syntax,* much less diagramming a sentence. Though I may have known what it meant, it was definitely not something I thought much about in the abstract.

Instead, I was struggling to put sentences together in a way that I hoped would engage, rivet, and mesmerize my reader, a goal that was facilitated by the fact that for the first twelve years of my writing life, I had written virtually nothing but poetry. I had been obsessed with an art form that demands full attention to every syllable, phrase, and line, an obsession that resulted in my first book, a collection of poems.

I also knew what jumped out at me on the page, like a little bump in the road. When I was reading someone else's manuscript, I felt confident in liberally marking it up with purple ink.

But when Sue asked her question, I knew I needed to simplify. To do so, I turned to Zona Rosans who were experts at the rules of grammar. When a question arose about, say, a comma (yes, we do talk about commas and such in Zona Rosa; recently we argued over whether the word *whose* could be used instead of *which* to apply to the fabric of the pants a character in Barbara's story was wearing), we called on our resident grammarians, among them Barbara, Anne, and Cleo.

Before she retired, Cleo taught English and grammar at a classy prep school for forty years, and she's still in touch with many of her students, some of whom have become successful writers. For years Anne taught a class on Business Writing via mail. Susan J. had taught English and composition for decades at a local junior college. And Danielle spent much of her time copyediting books I could barely understand.

I made a list of "Cleo's Ways to Make Things Right," but after reading the handout she had used with her former students, I realized that it could be titled "Cleo's Ways to Make Things Hard to Understand." She had little truck with the new and was a stickler for the usages of the past, despite the fact that language is being used in new ways every day, and that *The New York Times Magazine* has long devoted a regular column by William Safire to the subject.

I realized I needed to make a little guide for the Zona Rosans—a handout that I hoped would also make things easier for me. This became "The Thirteen (Possible) Boo-Boos" list, on which I listed numerically the things that caused those bumps on the manuscripts, from the least serious to the most imperative. Then, when I wrote the number beside a sentence or phrase, they could refer to the list:

The Thirteen (Possible) Boo-Boos

1. Punctuation, spelling
2. Syntax, grammar
3. Redundancy
4. Abstraction
5. Overwriting, underwriting
6. Transitions, segues; wrong placement of flash forwards, flashbacks
7. Wrong words

8. Clichéd or inaccurate imagery; image anorexia; mixed metaphors/similes
9. Shallow characterization; false dialogue
10. Underdeveloped subtext
11. False or shallow emotional content
12. Inappropriate voice, tone, POV
13. Ineffective or unsatisfying overall structure (shape, form, unity)

After a while, they all knew it by heart, and to their credit, most of their numbers were 1's, 2's, and 5's—spelling and punctuation; syntax and grammar; and over- or underwriting. They became so adept, in fact, that I created "The Thirteen (Possible) Boo-Boos Redux" list.

Then came the stroke of genius that turned things around. I asked them to list my suggested changes, and, if they wished, comment on them. Those who did this—like Jossie, who graded herself as though she were in grammar school— immediately leaped ahead in the quality of their writing:

Jossie's Report Card	Current Grade
I do not use italics.	A
I do not use useless words.	B+
I only use one point of view per section or chapter.	A
I study the rules of punctuation and get better at it weekly.	B
I work on sentence structure and get better at it every day.	B

What I'm Good At in My Writing
I do not overuse ellipses.
I develop a good story line.

I provide sufficient detail.

I do good research and provide accurate/real descriptions.

I have a clear style.

I write good dialogue.

I appreciate the need for others to review and give feedback on my writing.

I appreciate the need to cut and revise and I do it.

I appreciate the need to edit and cut even more and I do it.

To further refine our thinking on such matters, and because so many of us were confused about point of view, or "whose mind are we in anyway?" I created a handout called:

A Zona Rosa Crash Course on Point of View

Point of View, or POV, means the point of view of the character in a piece of writing. This is usually illustrated by that character's thoughts or perceptions.

First Person POV uses the first-person "I," and this POV is more intimate. We are inside that person. This is usually consistent throughout the piece of writing, though some writers use variations of this, such as all characters in first-person POV—a difficult style, as each voice must be distinct; or one character in first person, the other(s) in third person; this, too, is tricky to carry off.

Second-Person POV (which is used less often) uses the word *you* and can be the POV of a narrative observer, or of the character. This POV is difficult to use successfully; for a good book with this POV, see *Winter Birds* by Jim Grimsley; also *Bright Lights, Big City* by Jay MacInerney.

Third Person is the most commonly used POV. In third-person, limited POV, we are in one person's mind. In third-person omniscient observer, the writer/narrator can tell us not only what each character is doing and saying, but what is in every character's mind.

Aside from exceptions to the first-person POV, the most difficult form of POV is third-person omniscient observer, with the reader seeing into the minds and perceptions of more than one character in the same section or chapter. For this reason, a popular way of using third person is to switch between character POVs from section to section or chapter to chapter. Readers generally find this style to be more readable.

Remember, the most important thing is that the POV be invisible to the reader. Or to paraphrase Marcel Proust, "A work in which there are still theories is like an object which still has the price tag."

Next, I gave out "A Bevy of Perfect Tits" or a list of the ever-evolving acronyms we use when we talk about our writing:

A Bevy of Perfect Tits

TIT: Talk It Through—to yourself or with someone else
PET: Paraphrase Every Time—in order to know what you really want to say
BID: Break It Down—a good thing to do when you get stuck
KISS: Keep It Simple, Sweetheart
CLOD: Clumps of Description—avoid them!
LOPP: Lop Off Prepositional Phrases
DEA: Death to (Excess) Adverbs (with thanks to Mark Twain)

UDA:	Useless Diction Alert, or "useless" words, e.g., *even, just, quite, sometimes*
OED:	Out-of-control Ellipses—Delete (Some of us seem to consider those little dots to be an all-purpose punctuation mark. They're *not*—indeed, they're only to be used for omissions from the text, and an occasional pause.)
PHOTO OP:	Create an image for your reader
NUANCE OP:	Layer in subtext
SIB:	Subtext Is Basic—character is everything
CUTESY ALERT/ ANTI-FRILL DEVICE:	Cut that stuff—especially the angels and fairies!
SUCKS:	Sentimentality's relationship to art!
COAGULATE:	Gather all like materials, then choose the best way to say it.
TTQ:	Twins, Triplets, Quadruplets, and other multiple births, a.k.a. redundancies. Sorry, but you'll have to kill off some of your darlings, honey.
JUST:	Just You Start Typing
LDL:	Learn Don't Lean

I thought I had all the bases covered until a newcomer asked, "What is a manuscript?" "Just some pages of writing," I said, determined this time to keep it simple.

6.

If I had ten hours to chop down a tree, I would spend eight hours
sharpening the ax.

—ABRAHAM LINCOLN

Your Self-Talk Notebook, in which you talk to yourself about your
writing, may be your best tool for developing writing criteria.
When I first began writing, I referred to *Writing Made Simple,*
an oversized paperback Mother bought at Davison's department store for one dollar. She had kept it through the years and
I inherited it. The chapters gave simple directions on how to
write a story, a novel, a play, or an article, and when I got my
first article assignment from the magazine *Atlanta,* I followed
its directions, and surprise—out came a well-written essay.
That was when I first realized that yes, writing could be made
simple.

Later, as I struggled to learn to write poetry, I started a
notebook in which I copied poems and passages from writing
that I loved; I did this in longhand, which, I later realized,
helped me feel how the author had constructed it. I also made
lists of the things I liked in a piece of writing, and the qualities
I wanted to avoid. With my left brain, I watched myself in the
right-brain activity of writing, and wrote down what I saw—
then listed ways to improve my process. I also wrote mini-
reviews of almost everything I read, which also helped in
defining my criteria. I described the qualities that I wanted my
writing to have, such as "energy," "verve," "elegance," "ambiguity" (as in "to bridge the gap between immediacy and
depth," which to this day is one of my writing credos), and, always, "emotional honesty." Since truth was always a part of my

criteria, I hung Keats's lines "Beauty is truth, truth beauty, that is all ye know on earth, and all ye need to know" above my desk, along with other sources of inspiration.

I also learned that irony, or saying the exact opposite of what I meant, was a good—and often a more palatable—way to tell my truths, and added it to my list. After a while, I was able to describe the exact steps I took to write a poem, and exactly what I wanted that poem to be like. I also learned to scrape beneath the surface of an idea to see what the poem was really about.

Soon I was using any means I could to hasten the process. I audiotaped my poems in progress and played them back to myself, then talked to myself in my notebook about the strengths I wanted to heighten and what I still needed to work on. I pasted stanzas or paragraphs in various sequences in long sheets and laid them out on the bed so I could look at them whole, with interchangeable pieces that I could lay on top of a section to see which I liked it better. And I recorded everything in the Self-Talk Notebook. When I was doing this, Zona Rosa had not yet been born; little did I know that the Self-Talk Notebook was to become one of our most useful tools.

If you're willing to do the work of keeping such a notebook, you, too, will find that your writing skills will soar beyond your wildest dreams. You'll quickly move ahead of those who depend on a sudden flash of inspiration, or the muse, however much of a stud he may be.

A good place to begin is by becoming more analytical about the books you read. Think, and write, about the books that were so scrumptious that reading the last word was like a little death. What mesmerizes you until the end? What makes a book seem to come to life in your hands—lots of colorful images? intriguing dialogue? well-written sentences? a heroine you can believe in? (And no, we're not tamping down our originality when we look at how others have done it; whatever qualities you seek to integrate into your own writing will quickly become yours alone, like a fingerprint.)

Look, too, at the books you start and leave unread, and why. Anne always creates a special category for these in her annual review list. Trust that over time you will learn what sets a piece of writing on fire for you. Soon you'll be able to answer the essential question, "What Do I Like in a Piece of Writing?" Along the way, "List Some Words or Write a Sentence Describing What You Want Your Writing to Be Like." ("I want my book to be so delicious you'd eat it off a sore leg," Zona Rosan Courtney wrote, using an image that was nothing if not memorable.) And over time, those criteria will become part of your own personal style.

7.

All styles are good except for the tiresome sort.

—VOLTAIRE

The Perfect Black Dress, and How Style Develops. Long before I wrote books, I wrote book reviews and magazine articles, and since at first I didn't know what I was doing, I just typed up a lot of stuff on my manual typewriter, then cut the paragraphs apart and stacked them on the living room rug according to subject. Then I chose the best ones from each stack, put them into order, glued them together, added some stuff that seemed to be missing, wrote some nice transitions, and—voila! I had a finished product.

To a new writer, considerations like whether to use a semicolon or a period, or whether a phrase is better at the beginning or the end of a sentence, can feel overwhelming. "Can't I just tell my story and let it go at that?" she might ask.

Yes, that's a good start, I say, but if you're writing for others, some cleanup will have to take place. As Anne Lamott says, "A frustrated reader is a hostile reader."

It's easier to see the big stuff—the large cuts that may need to be made, the problems with structure, the anorexic parts of the manuscript—if you have written well, line by line, paragraph by paragraph. And while this may seem wasteful, it gives us a clear vision of the whole, not to speak of being good writing practice.

Sometimes it's just a matter of cutting and pasting, and stitching up the sagging spots—too bad Estée Lauder doesn't make a cream for this. Think plastic surgery—painless, of course—and the fantasy of having all your worst spots miraculously zapped.

Often it's a matter of putting something where it belongs, rather than where it is. Or it just means finding all the places where we've said the same thing, over and over again—we all do it—and deciding how and where we've said it best, then assigning the rest to an outtakes file.

A harder question, once we've gotten rid of our redundancies, is what to take out and what to leave in. A good motto is "Tell the reader everything she needs to know, but never tell her more than she needs to know." Or as fashionista Diana Vreeland said, "Elegance is refusal."

Think of your house or apartment: what if you couldn't find anything—your shoes were in the tub, your new sequined skirt was in the trash, your favorite bracelet hanging from the ceiling.

Think of the guest on *Oprah* whose habit of clutter, not to speak of filth, was so over the top that the audience gasped in unison.

A good rule of thumb is that you can redecorate after—but not before—you de-clutter. Once you've cleaned up syntax, grammar, and the inevitable redundancies, and are left with a manuscript like an all-white room with perhaps one white leather chair, check to see if what you've created suffers from "image anorexia." If so, add some color, like that perfect cushion or throw—or better yet, something more unique. A metaphor for my writing, my own living room contains, in addition to Lily's bold paintings, one real (but dead) lizard that hangs from the crown molding by its little feet, immortalized there. As Ms. Vreeland also advised, "Be vulgar if you must. But never be boring."

Simplicity and clarity, like that perfect black dress with those perfect black pumps, are good goals, and the ones I adhere to in marking up the Zona Rosans' manuscripts. Simplicity of style can be stunning, knocking everybody else out of the room. At the same time, there may be nothing in the world harder to achieve. Just as our style in clothing evolves through our choices, a personal style in writing begins when we start using our own work as a precedent.

Indeed, this pursuit of elegance has led to a Zona Rosa questionnaire in which I point out that you can safely leave the flourishes, the long Faulknerian twists and turns to others who feel they are inevitable.

Take Off That Extra Piece of Jewelry, or How to Get Your Work into Shape

Remember what your mother used to tell you about that one bracelet too many (not to speak of that extra ten pounds!)

Some questions to ask yourself:

1. What is this about?
2. What is this *really* about? In other words, ferret out subtext. What you're writing may be about something altogether different from what you thought or even intended.
3. What is this line/paragraph/section about?
4. Is this line/paragraph/section redundant when read among other lines/paragraphs/sections? If so, coagulate into clumps, and choose the best versions.
5. Divide and conquer: can some sections be divided in order to serve as foreshadowing and/or conclusions?
6. Can the plot line be tightened to further clarify? Toward this end, and re: 6, 7, and 8, a brief, strong-verb outline is useful.
7. Where is my beginning, middle, and end? How does the arc of the entire work feel?
8. Is my writing scrupulously clear and simple throughout?
9. Do the fripperies, diversions, et al. that I've added drive to the good of the work? If not, remove.

Oh, and as Doris reminded us and even explained it for us dummies, don't depend on a deus ex machina, or "god out of a machine," while writing your stories. At the end of some Greek dramas, the plot is resolved when the stage manager lowers a box (the machine) and hauls bad characters away. So don't take the easy way out—you or your character's truth is held in a lot higher regard these days, even if it leads to a less than happy ending.

8.

Does not art begin with aberration?

—JEAN-MICHEL DUBUFFET

Flaws, Fatal Flaws, and Fabulous Flaws. The flaw in a work of art is often what gives it its special style, its panache. Flaws can be fixed, but Fatal Flaws, if allowed to run rampant, can ruin a piece of writing. But a Fabulous Flaw can bring it to life in a way nothing else can. Sometimes when writers take a risk, do something that's over the top, it works to their writing's advantage. I remember when someone said to me that I couldn't subtitle *Fatal Flowers* "On Sin, Sex, and Suicide in the Deep South," or use the graphic imagery that became the trademark of my early poems—but I did it anyway. And my readers understood.

Consider photographer Sally Mann's admonition: "If it doesn't have ambiguity, don't bother." If you don't know what the word means, look it up. But simply put, Ms. Mann was referring to the inconsistencies of our thoughts and feelings, and how we need to make art in a way that takes that into account. Indeed, the ability to express ambiguity is often one of those Fabulous Flaws. Southerners have a reputation for creating literature—and one of the hallmarks of the southern mind, it's said, is our ability to believe two or more opposing things at the same time. Or as poet W. H. Auden put it, "Great art is clear thinking about mixed feelings."

That ethereal, abstract language you love so much, those big words that send others to the dictionary—are they an asset that adds to your writing, or a Fatal Flaw? In Nuala O'Faolain's *My Dream of You,* the adverbs—"ly" words—hanging at the ends of the otherwise wonderful sentences, drove me crazy, yet I adored her Irish voice. In *A Million Little Pieces,* James Frey describes his descent into and rise from drug addiction in a text without real paragraphs, and with capital letters in the middle of sentences— but I was riveted by his relentless voice, despite learning that not all that he claimed was true. In Rick Moody's *Purple America,* the whole first chapter is one long sentence about a man and his relationship with his crippled mother, yet it grabbed me in a way that something more prosaic might not have. John Updike's sentences go on and on, with one appendage clause after another— yet every one of them is masterful. Flaws can be fixed, but a Fatal Flaw, if not attended to, can ruin your work.

A Fabulous Flaw, on the other hand, is often something that, in a fit of inspiration, we deliberately carry to an extreme. The trick is to know the difference, and that depends on how well we've developed our own personal criteria, as described above in the Self-Talk Notebook. Here are my own personal lists, plus a couple of my favorite quotes:

Flaws	*Fatal Flaws*
Spelling errors & typos	Lack of originality
Syntax in need of fixing	Inauthenticity:
Low gasoline:	*of voice*
low on verbs	*of content*
low on imagery	Sentimentality
passive sentence construction	Lack of empathy for characters
Redundancy:	*projecting or judgmental*
of language	Doesn't add up:
of content	*A doesn't lead to B*
Confusion, lack of clarity	
Lumpy or disorganized shape:	
absence of form & structure	

FABULOUS FLAWS!!!

anything so over the top that it works!

I consider one of my own Fabulous Flaws to be my ability to cut loose and follow through on quirky ideas that seemingly come out of the blue—amazingly, they more often than not work. Which reinforces my faith in the unconscious and its wisdom, and my belief that if an idea, however unrelated, comes to us while we're writing, it probably has a reason for being there.

Now that we're zeroing in on the writing process, make your own lists. And while this is an ambitious exorcise for those of us who are just beginning, it's good to realize that rules are also made to be broken.

9.

In the beginning technique may overcome joy, but in the end technique becomes our joy.

—DARCY DANIELL, PAINTER

Secrets of the Pros, or Revision Revises Us. One secret is that we don't wait until we feel inspired to write.

When Zane, seeing what an ordinary activity writing is, began writing his own book, I would ask him occasionally whether he'd worked on it recently. He often answered, "I didn't feel like it."

"What does that have to do with it?!" I asked less than tactfully. Zane is one of those resistant ones, given me as a gift, a target for teaching practice. An insistent pessimist, when asked about his goals for his life, he says, "To get from here to the grave as painlessly as possible." I reply, ever the teacher, "Don't you mean, be in good health, get enough rest, enjoy your life—and maybe move to Mexico?"

When I'm in the midst of a major writing project, I adjust what I do after hours to match my moods. If I'm writing dark, I read light and watch sitcoms, finding that even they make me cry; but when I'm writing light, I can read the heaviest of tomes. Whatever my choices, they're based on my need to keep the best parts of myself ready to do the work, like an athlete lifting weights. The Zona Rosans like to hear about how I've had to lose twenty pounds and become a bombshell all over again every time I finish a book in order to promote it, because by that point, I'm so wrecked.

One of our exorcises in Zona Rosa is to describe "The Defects of My Virtues, the Virtues of My Defects." This one can apply to either writing or life. And we who've been writing for a while are usually aware of our tendencies, whether they're flights of lyrical language, getting so carried away in a metaphor that we lose sense of its underlying meaning, or assuming that the reader can read our minds no matter how abstractly we present our message. Sometimes a quality at which we excel is the very one we need to rein in, and at the same time, with work and awareness we often develop excellence in an area that we at one time considered a weakness. When I first heard about meter, I felt crazed, that I would never be able to conquer it, despite my passion for poetry; today I consider it one of the strengths of my poetry. And I learned to do it my way; that is, using an organic meter that evolved naturally from my first drafts.

"Damn the trees!" I said to the group, defending my habit of making many, many drafts until I get it right. And in truth, I consider this book, or any other, to be worth whole forests. We expect to use a lot of paper and do a lot of drafts. We've learned to love some words you may at first consider ugly ducklings, like the three P's: Patience, Plodding, and Paper.

We also try every possible way of doing something, whether it's writing a paragraph, a chapter, or a section. For us, the *mot juste*, or just the right word, is not a casual affair—we explore every option. (" 'Don't ever say anything the way you've heard it said before,' " Janet Fitch, author of *White Oleander*, said on *Oprah*, quoting her writing teacher.)

To illustrate this, I bring my own manuscripts in progress, like this book, to our meetings, so the Zona Rosans can see firsthand the many drafts—and boo-boos—even an experienced writer makes.

I explain that, as with every other book I've written, I don't really know what I'm doing, only that I'm doing it—that, like Christopher Columbus, I'm starting on a journey toward an unknown. And like Chris, I'll keep on until I reach that shore, or the last page is finished. I'll undoubtedly be afflicted along the way—as we all are during a long writing project—with storms of "bad writing days," which in Zona Rosa no more hold us back than "bad-hair days."

Because *everything drives to the good of the work* rather than our egos, we appreciate good feedback. By now, our criteria for what we like in a piece of writing are usually pretty highly developed. So when someone makes a suggestion, we're likely to know in an instant whether or not we agree, and if we do, we're willing to do whatever it takes to implement it. It's only then that we become eligible to compete for the Real Writer award.

I told the Zona Rosans what my friend Carol Polsgrove, author of two well-received books and my former editor at *Mother Jones,* said after reading what I considered to be the finished manuscript of the first Zona Rosa book: "This is wonderful!" Then she added that she thought the book should be structured differently, that she was cutting up the pages with scissors, pasting them together in a new way, and sending them back to me via FedEx. For days—every time I walked by the package—I resisted opening it. But when I did, I saw in a split second that Carol was right, and I sat down to spend the next three months following through on her suggestions.

Most of the Zona Rosans, too, adopt this attitude. "This is like a box of candy!" Ellen wrote me after receiving her purple-marked manuscript after a workshop in New Orleans. "I'm just dying to get home and get into it!" (Over twenty-four years, only three people have seemed put off by our loving suggestions.)

As writers, we trust that some of our ideas will be divine, others less so. Like Kelsey Murphy, the glass sculptor, we expect a lot of breakage—we're in love not only with process, but the beauty of our visions.

10.

An author is a writer who never quits.

—ZONA ROSAN JILL ANGEL DAVIS

The Emotional Tai Chi of Getting Your Work Out There. Remember Ruth, from chapter 4, and how mad she got when, after only a few submissions, an agent made a suggestion that could have bettered her manuscript but she felt it was an insult?

As we discussed, too many people get bent out of shape at the very idea of putting their work out there, even though— and perhaps especially because—it has been their intention from the beginning. I also realize from the Zona Rosans' questions that they sometimes don't know when a piece of writing is finished, and that the two situations are related: if we don't know when something is finished, how can we possibly consider sharing it with the world, or even the tiny audience of our favorite literary magazine?

There *is* a solution to this, which is to make putting our babies out into the world, once we have perfected them and set them aside to cry alone awhile, a left-brain activity that we can follow with dispatch, giving it about the same attention and emotion we might give to updating our address book or doing our income tax (no, doing our income tax isn't altogether painless, and no, we don't want to go to jail, but it's not necessarily gut-wrenching, either). Indeed, sometimes after the excitement of writing, such tedium can be downright relaxing. And while you may actually enjoy writing the log line, query letter, and synopsis, and even researching the right agents, it's really just something that has to be done in order to meet a goal.

This is the place where being a mistress of risk taking and having a tough skin gives us a definite edge. "Leave your ego behind. . . . Think like an avalanche," advised high-risk skier Andrew McLean in the coverage of his wedding in "Vows" in the *New York Times*. Toward that end, I made a chart, complete with our lip print logo, designed by Zona Rosan Jenny H., from my actual lips, my favorite deep-red lipstick, to serve as a solid guide to getting your work out there—and maybe even published!

PROCESS #1: THE PRODUCT

1. Finish work*
2. Create log line
3. Write synopsis/query

* a) Revise; b) Revise; c)Revise

HOW DO I KNOW WHEN THE BOOK IS FINISHED?

- When I, as the reader, have a sense of closure
- When words, images, voice, and tone are the best possible
- When nothing needs to be added, nothing taken away
- When there are no redundancies except for deliberate ones, e.g., codas
- When spelling, syntax, grammar are correct

When, to the best of my ability, MY VISION IS REALIZED

Now that you've done all this, have a chocolate bar, a cup of tea, or a bottle of champagne. Then sit down to work on your . . . NEXT BOOK!

PROCESS #2: GETTING IT OUT THERE

1. Answer these questions:
   - What books are like mine?
   - How is mine different?
   - Who is my reader?
   - How can I help promote it?

2. Brainstorm contacts—acquaintances from lit conferences, writing groups et al.

3. Research agents:
   - Read acknowledgments of similar books.
   - Research, e.g., *The Literary Marketplace* (at the library), any of numerous books sold at bookstores.
   - Ask colleagues.
   - And Google, Google, Google!

4. Contact agents:
   - Through e-mail if okay with agent in question.
   - Send exactly what agent requests.
   - Keep query letter and synopsis short, succinct, and accurate (no bragging, please, and nothing cutesy).
   - Enclose a SASE.
   - Write to thank agents when they've taken the time to consider your work.
   - Offer an exclusive period of time to consider your book if they show interest, e.g., six weeks (during which you agree not to market it elsewhere).
   - Consider a Postal Blitz, in which you mail out copies to many agents at once, as per directions above.

5. Create Plan B:
   - Research independent and university presses—are any of them right for you?
   - Consider co-publishing with a reputable press—but only after you have taken all the other steps.

11.

The point is not to cross the desert, but to be in it.

—Robyn Davidson, *Tracks*

We Can't Say It Too Many Times—Use the F-Word—Focus. Have you ever noticed that even when a cat is stalking its prey, it's still relaxed, supremely centered, like a cool babe playing pool without a doubt of her skills?

Marda and I stopped on the sidewalk in New Orleans to watch a cat standing beneath a newly decorated Christmas tree on busy Royal Street. Apparently mesmerized by a certain round ornament and its slight sway, she sat immobile, her gaze unwavering despite the crowds walking by. She looked as though she would sit there all day if necessary to find the right moment to pounce on her glitter-covered prey, and for a moment, we were equally magnetized. Then we looked at each other—of course! She reminded us of the way we writers keep our eyes on our prize for as long as it takes.

A cartoon in the *New Yorker* captioned "The Cat's Diary" described the cat's life in three frames representing three days. On days one, two, and three, the cat did the same things— ate, slept, and played with yarn but in a different order. (And please note that she always included napping, one of my big favorite ways of re-creating myself. Indeed, an ability to nap on demand may be one of the best assets for a writer who's been pushing her brain.) Isn't this the perfect plan for us as writers to, as Stephen Covey advises, "put the big rocks"—the important things—"in first"? I loved this concept so much that I created a handout for the Zona Rosans, using the cat's diary as inspiration for the writer's ideal day.

And don't we have a lot to learn from cats? Have you ever met one who is not serene, composed, and dead certain of what she wants out of life?

A Writer's Diary

Be bourgeois in your life so you can be flamboyant in your art.

—GUSTAVE FLAUBERT

wrote, slept, ate, walked	walked, wrote, slept, ate	ate, slept, wrote, walked

12.

I will try not to panic, to keep my standard of living modest, and to work steadily, even shyly, in the spirit of those medieval carvers who so fondly sculpted the undersides of choir seats.

—JOHN UPDIKE

Little Oases Everywhere, or One-Hour Brain Repair. List the ways you refresh your writing brain, whether it's a nap (my habit, from which I awake thirty minutes later, feeling like it's a new day), reruns of *Sex and the City,* or a twenty-minute walk. Knowing how to shake the cumulative excitement of riding your horse as fast as she can go is a skill every writer needs, just as there need to be times each day when you're completely off-duty and doing something totally unrelated.

Mitzi, who owns *Mitzy and Romano*, an upscale Atlanta dress shop an hour from her home in the picture-perfect town of Madison, Georgia, has a commute, a teenage son and stepson, and a sexy sculptor husband, but she also makes time to write. At our retreat in North Carolina, she told us about her Eight O'Clock Rule: nothing, no matter what—a crisis at the shop, a call from a needy friend—was allowed to mar her evenings after eight P.M. Like Scarlett O'Hara, Mitzi has mastered the invaluable art of putting off until tomorrow what she doesn't want to deal with today, and is able to enjoy her life despite its complexity.

This week in the evenings I'm flipping through the delicious stack of magazines by my bed and reading a biography of the twentieth-century courtesan Pamela Harriman. It has absolutely nothing to do with this book, on which I'm slaving during the daytime hours.

13.

The material for this book was collected directly from nature at great personal risk to the author.

—HELEN ROWLAND

Detours and Dislocations, or More about Moving around Obstacles. A perfect day is one in which I drink coffee in bed, writing in my journal, harvesting the riches of the unconscious, the dream world from the night before. Afterward, I go for a walk listening to an inspiring tape, enjoy a beautiful breakfast, then sit at my desk, lost in my writing for hours, almost forgetting to get up to go to the bathroom. Next I have lunch, along with a little reading or TV, followed by a perfect nap, from which I rise refreshed to take a cup of tea back to my desk, ending the day with what I like least—e-mail—then giving myself a lift by talking on the phone to a girlfriend. Later I have a bath by candlelight, dinner on a tray in bed, eaten while I catch up on my reading, or just watch a tape of *Desperate Housewives*. And during this perfect day, I've barely had to think at all, as in think about myself. I've simply been doing my thing.

But are all my days like this? Of course not. There are the doctor's appointments, the trips to the supermarket, the endless errands. There's filling the needs of various family members. There's reading the mail and paying the bills. And then there are those days when it's impossible for me to live this way even in part—days when I'm racing through the airport, trying to find that other terminal, or driving from one city to another—though even then I always have parts of my work with me. And those are good days, too, for as dancer choreographer Mark Morris said in the *New York Times*, "They are all perfect days. There is no such thing as the other kind."

Sometimes detours come from outside us. Once I thought I had left bad weather behind by going to Anne's house for our Zona Rosa meeting, only to find heavy rain and a blackout. The storm was even worse than the one in Savannah, and for the first time in years, we had to cancel Zona Rosa.

But it turned out to be a delicious time, as Anne and I read and perused manuscripts by candlelight and the little book lights we have for just such emergencies (since for us a blackout on reading is impossible). I recalled with pleasure Robert Louis Stevenson's line from a children's poem about going to bed by day. (By the way, I've learned from many smart women that going to bed early is a strategy they adopt to give themselves an edge. For those of us with big plans, the eleven o'clock news just isn't worth it.)

But more often the obstacles come from within. While writing *Fatal Flowers,* I developed a little trick to keep myself going. As I walked down the sidewalk in Savannah, staring at the moss growing between the bricks while wondering what had made me think that I could write a full-length book, I suddenly said to myself, "I don't have to do this—I can get a nine-to-five job like everyone else." When my mind screamed back, "Oh, no, then I'd have to write the book at night," I realized how committed I was, and that I would finish the book, no matter what.

Throughout the years, whenever my mind threw up roadblocks and I found myself slogging through my own personal Sahara, I learned to say to myself, I'll do this one more year, and if it's not working out, I'll do something else. Of course, I'd forgotten my doubts within days, and was once more filled with passion for my project.

It's interesting to note that other writers, such as Edith Wharton, have also regarded the middle of a writing project as a desert: "What is writing a novel like? 1. The beginning: A ride through a spring wood. 2. The middle: The Gobi Desert. 3. The end: A night with a lover. I am in the Gobi Desert," she wrote in the last lines of her last diary.

Or you might find your own personal image. Amanda and I laughed, agreeing that it's like "slogging through sorghum syrup," and she's written enough at this point to know that the sticky stuff eventually washes away.

The point is, something *will* happen, so it's good to have a plan in place—like notebooks or drafts of manuscripts you take with you everywhere. You will still be able to go forward, even with sandstorms brewing in your own personal desert. As choreographer Twyla Tharp says in her book *The Creative Habit: Learn It and Use It for Life*, self-discipline is everything (yes, she goes to bed at nine, so she can get to the gym by five A.M.). So set your goal and establish your process; once it's held in place by habit, you'll find that you can roll with the rest. Wayne Dyer writes in *The Power of Intention* that from the moment of conception, we contain the seed of what the universe intends for us. But that doesn't mean we don't have to cooperate.

Before I began writing this book, I knew I needed to tighten up my daily schedule in order to get the work done, and I needed to include some downtime and fun stuff. I also needed to prepare. Before I began writing I spent three days going through the notes I had accumulated over the years for this project, putting them into labeled folders (I was late in coming to labels—for years I kept journals that I had to look inside to find the year, but since the light dawned, I've never let *anything* go unlabeled!).

Next, I placed the folders in a pretty basket with handles that made it easier to carry around the house or to put into the car to take with me on trips. When I got the flip-down files recommended by Jill, a bunch went into that, too, but it soon popped its seams because I had put so much in it.

By the way, baskets and suitcases of all sizes are good means for organizing our stuff. Beside the endless shoes and books, my bedroom is filled with suitcases stuffed with notes and drafts of other books in progress, and one always sits out, ready to be repacked for my next trip—which I often make before I've unpacked from the last one.

But, as the popular bumper sticker says, "Shit Happens." Just last week I wrote in my journal about a period when I was working hard to get part of this book to my agent, Gail:

How People, Places, and Pets Helped Me Write My Book
Or Why Women Go to Writers' Colonies

1. My son Dwayne, who lives five minutes away: "I've met a girl—can I bring her over? I'm de-cluttering my apartment—can I store my weights at your house? And don't you want to buy these two TVs? I have too many. Can you help me shop for a bed? Can't we do it **now**?"

2. My daughter Lily is moving from across the street and into another apartment across town. "I don't want to bother you," she says, "but can I just leave all this stuff at your house, especially my paintings? Can I do this laundry there before I go? Can I put some boxes in your car for you to take to Goodwill? And can I have some of this stuff from your refrigerator?"

3. I've been nicer to Zane than usual lately in order to avoid time-consuming arguments. Now, lonely on the road, he calls to chat—and chat and chat, about politics, people he's meeting, TV shows, books, whatever—but mainly, sex. "What? You're not in the mood?" he says. Then when I want to hang up: "I wasn't finished yet. You're no fun anymore!" I'm thinking about the book *How to Change Your Life and Everyone in It*—it's beside my bed right now, but I don't have time to read it.

4. Amber, my cat, wakes me during the night, in one of two ways: walking across my collection of high heels, bumping them down one by one, or jumping onto my dresser top, where she scatters my jewelry. Interestingly, she only does these things when I'm already under pressure, my mind

churning with thoughts—like this week, when I'm determined to get the manuscript off to Gail.

5. My lovely assistant Annie works fifteen hours, reading and correcting at the computer. At hour thirteen, we see that half the corrections and most of the formatting we've done hasn't saved. All the numbers have been jumbled and rearranged as by some hand from on high. "And why didn't you use those little symbols?" she says of the foreign words. "Because I don't know how, sweetie," I say as we try to figure out what to do next. "It must be your software," Annie says of the other stuff. I'm sure my son coming over with the new girlfriend, bringing the two TVs, bringing in other pals, and stomping through the dining room, where we're working, had nothing to do with it. . . .

6. I spend nine hours correcting the boo-boos. I wanted to get the manuscript off today, but around seven o'clock, I realize that's not going to happen.

7. Office Max, where the guy told me last week that no, I didn't need all the color cartridges to be filled in order to print in black, is too far from my house. But I have to go there anyway, only to talk twice, when I'm back home, to the Epson guy about why said cartridges aren't working. (I put my head down on the steering wheel in the parking lot, hysterical—why wasn't the car key connecting?)

8. Then, I'm at the post office, fifteen minutes before closing time, the manuscript like a baby in my arms, smiling and happy as I chat with a writer friend who just happens to be in line, too. No, she hasn't gotten anything done on her new book, she says—I see the envy in her eyes that I'm getting work off. As I walk back to my car—this time, the key works perfectly—I'm walking on air, all the craziness of the past week drained away.

But even as I read my words to the Zona Rosans, who laughed in recognition, I knew that it wouldn't be the last detour in my writing life.

Knee-jerk Reaction #9: Not keeping our eyes on the big picture while trusting in the small steps. Imagining that taking the path of least resistance will take us where we want to go. Thinking that giving up our dreams is easier than living them out.

THE LAST BOOK THERAPY: WHEN YOU READ ABOUT WRITING, ONLY READ THE FUN STUFF

There was something about the solitude of writing that appealed to me from an early age. The image it conjured was that of being in touch with my deeper self, without distractions. In my favorite children's book, *Mehitable*, the heroine wandered the moors, coming upon fairies, and I was right there alongside her. And to me writing is not unlike that. Too, there was the Carnegie library downtown in Atlanta, the first place Mother let me go alone by bus at ten. I imagined reading every book in the library, from *A* through *Z,* as if by osmosis. Sometimes they would seem to jump into my hands, as though the gods were choosing for me. ("When a book falls off the shelf, it's pulled down by Hermes, the trickster god," explained Zona Rosan Barbara, a mythology scholar.) Indeed, they called to me until I was finally imagining my own books among them, though I never dreamed that some of them would be about the writing process itself.

Nowadays when I read books about the writing life (as opposed to just plain writing), I like the ones that, less technical, sound as though they were written by real people, and have stories in them—like Anne Lamott's *Bird by Bird* (in which she is her ever-quotable self), Nancy Mairs's *Voice Lessons: On Becoming a (Woman) Writer* (among the more honest accounts of the writer's life), Stephen King's *On Writing* (he explores the effects of a devastating accident on his writing and life), Natalie Goldberg's *Long Quiet Highway* (she parallels her paths toward writing and Zen Buddhism), *If You Want to Write: A Book about Art, Independence, and Spirit* by Brenda Ueland (published when she was in her nineties), and if you're a yoga buff, or want to be, Jeff Davis's *The Journey from the Center to the Page,* an engaging account of the yoga practices he prescribes to center us while we're writing.

To my mind it's good to get at it obliquely, and one of my favorites is *The Devil at Large*, Erica Jong's rich account of her writing friendship with Henry Miller, in which she quotes Miller: "There is only one thing that interests me vitally now, and that is the recording of all that which is omitted in books." (I, like many writers, love dish about other writers.) In addition, I find nothing is more delicious than looking at another author's marked-up drafts, as we can sometimes find in the pages of old *Paris Review*s or, better yet, at a nearby university library.

Then there are the books that address our creativity in a freewheeling way, without being related to a specific art form, such as Robert Fritz's two books *Creating* and *The Path of Least Resistance;* both advise us on how to live in a continual creative burst.

But remember that reading books about writing is a lot like reading books about sex—no substitute for the real thing. (Also, some books about writing are notoriously ill written, which just goes to show how hard it is to capture its mystery on paper.)

Right now, I'd rather see you dive in and start writing—after stocking your desk with a few good, even hilarious books on grammar, like *Woe Is I* and *Words Fail Me* by Patricia O'Conner, and *Eats, Shoots & Leaves* by Lynne Truss. And, of course, a good dictionary.

FIREWORKS, OR THE BIG ZONA ROSA PARTY IN THE SKY

As the years went by, it seemed that we were celebrating more and more. As the Zona Rosans healed themselves, changed their lives, and finished and published books, the champagne flowed over and over. The literary heavens became so populated by Zona Rosans that we could barely look up from our desks without seeing them at any time of day or night.

So many new people were visiting, calling, or joining us—each beautiful in her own way, carrying her own story, with her own tasks ahead of her—that they were like meteors, or sparkling fireworks on the horizon. Each month brought news of our successes; at one point I counted thirty published books—albeit some of them self-published—by Zona Rosans. Joy, as least as far as we were concerned, had become our steady diet.

When life was difficult, we were there to share our challenges. Nor were we afflicted with what Ann Patchett called "friendship envy" in a piece in the *New York Times* on why women bonded over *Sex and the City*. "It's always wonderful when you find your tribe," a smiling stranger said to me at a writers' conference when I commented that every time I ran into him, he looked happy. And we were like that in Zona Rosa.

When I learned that Janice G., who had come to speak to us on neurolinguistic programming, had died of breast cancer, I also heard of her request that her ashes be mixed with glitter and divided into two hundred tiny containers for her best friends. I thought her last statement was just about perfect, and worthy of one who had been touched by Zona Rosa.

In fact, to a woman (and occasional man), we were exhibiting the "Ten Warning Signs of Good Health," as described by Comprehensive Psychiatric Resources:

1. Persistent presence of support network
2. Chronic positive expectation; tendency to form events in a constructive light
3. Episodic outbreaks of joyful, happy experiences
4. Sense of spiritual involvement
5. Tendency to adapt to changing conditions
6. Rapid response and recovery of stress response system to repeated challenges
7. Increased appetite for physical activity
8. Tendency to identify and communicate feelings
9. Repeated episodes of gratitude and generosity
10. Persistent sense of humor

In *French Women Don't Get Fat,* Mireille Guiliano writes that for a rebellious generation in France in 1968, the motto was *Il est interdit d'interdire*—It is forbidden to forbid. And in Zona Rosa, too, we never forbid one another anything. I sometimes wave my musical pink scepter over the heads of the Zona Rosans, inducting them into the Sisterhood of Non-Saints.

Indeed, at times Zona Rosa seems like one big indulgence, one that parallels and spills over onto our every endeavor as we give one another permission to enjoy just about everything. Though our original intent was serious—to express our truths in writing, and to heal ourselves along the way—the pleasure is built in.

"It's the one time of the month I let myself eat fried chicken," says Claudia G., whose gorgeous voluptuousness I wouldn't have wanted to see diminished by an inch. The day she brought what she called "My Third Brother's Third Wife's Strawberry Cream Cake"—strawberry layers, put together with more strawberries and cream cheese, and the perfect rosy tint—I declared it the official Zona Rosa dessert (for the recipe for this divine concoction, see Appendix A).

Like my cat Amber, we have learned to live by the pleasure principle, stretching in the sun and eating when we feel like it. Yet beneath our laughter and purrs of contentment lies our seriousness of intent. And at many moments along the way I've realized afresh the importance of Zona Rosa, and why it exists.

In France, our Zona Rosa group visited Saint-Remy's, the hospital where Vincent Van Gogh had last been hospitalized. Now it is a mental hospital for women who are artists, and whose paintings line the walls. As I walked the corridor, I felt stunned by the creativity of women, even or especially women under duress.

When we got back to our house in La Cadière d'Azur, Jill said, as though reading my mind, "I wonder if we could do some kind of outreach . . . ?" Lynn had already begun an annual Zona Rosa workshop in Atlanta for people learning English as a second language, and using our creativity to help others was becoming important to us. A small spark was flaring inside my brain, and I knew that's the way all good things begin.

Or was it really Mother, driving my dreams again—her spirit descending to fill my mind, push me forward as she had so long before? I had often thought that she might have been saved had she had a Zona Rosa of her own. Indeed, one of my more painful realizations has been that because of Mother's Bondage to the Pink, she never had the kind of girlfriends who might have embraced and supported her.

I thought of Mother again at our annual Zona Rosa party on the last night of our beach retreat. Attended by a number of our husbands and skeptical significant others, Sissy did stand-up, using her best Junior League persona; Deborah read from her racier poems; and belly dancer Esther danced in a sequined chiffon costume. Then Kathleen, a former bass player for an Athens, Georgia, rock band, sang the Zona Rosa song she had composed, with thanks to the song "I Left My Heart in San Francisco," made famous by Tony Bennett in 1962, as the Zonettes, a.k.a. Anne, Jill, and Pamella, swayed behind her like the Andrews Sisters:

I got my start in Zona Rosa—
I first found there, the book in me.
That magic sisterhood
fosters everything that's good—
the mental fog has cleared—
the air out here is rare.
I found my heart in Zona Rosa
beside the gray and windy sea.
When I come here again to Savannah
I'll thank my stars—
I learned to parse
with Rose-ma-ree . . .

As they swayed and sang, I looked up at the sky, seeing more Stars in the Zona Rosa than I ever would have dreamed. And for a moment, I imagined Mother, looking down and sharing just a little of our happiness.

This book, which my mother inspired, is an invitation to you to join us in Zona Rosa, in spirit and practice, and in person. Perhaps by now you've done all the exorcises and are well on your way to becoming the writer and woman you were meant to be. I hope you have found both inspiration and practical advice. And last but not least, I suggest that you consider:

- joining us at a Zona Rosa workshop or retreat
- arranging a Zona Rosa workshop in your area (with the help of me or my lovely assistants)
- starting your own Sub Rosa peer group (see Appendix C)
- attending a workshop to become a certified Sub Rosa facilitator, and if qualified, a trained Zona Rosa leader

There are many ways to become a permanent part of our vast network of smart, high-achieving women (and sometimes men)—not to speak of enjoying the fun and the foods of the goddesses!—and we welcome you to contact us.

To join the Zona Rosa network, arrange a Zona Rosa workshop in your area, attend a Zona Rosa workshop or retreat, or learn about workshops through which you can become a certified Sub Rosa or Zona Rosa leader, write us at info@myzonarosa.com. Members receive access to "Ask Rosemary," in which your questions are answered, monthly exorcises and other materials, early notification of upcoming Zona Rosa events, and news of yours or other Zona Rosa and Sub Rosa groups, including writing by members, and more. Or check our web page at www .myzonarosa.com for general information and news of the many achievements, awards, and publications of our members, plus the latest postings on our Zona Rosa Book Club, Zona Rosa products created just for you, and news of our Zona Rosa Books imprint.

MY THIRD BROTHER'S THIRD WIFE'S
STRAWBERRY CREAM CAKE,
OR THE OFFICIAL ZONA ROSA DESSERT

Contributed by Zona Rosan Claudia Graham, who once famously remarked, "The first time I had great sex, I almost went home and told my husband."

1. Combine one box two-layer Duncan Hines white cake mix and 1 3-ounce package strawberry gelatin. Sift. Add 1 cup Wesson oil and 4 eggs, one at a time, beating well. Stir in 2 cups sliced fresh strawberries. Pour into three greased and floured cake pans, and bake in a preheated 350-degree oven for 18–20 minutes. DO NOT OVERCOOK.

2. Beat together 4 3-ounce packages of softened cream cheese, 2 sticks of butter, and 4 tsps. vanilla. Gradually add 10 cups sifted powdered sugar, mixing to spreading consistency, then

use food coloring to tint to a rosy hue. Use to frost cooled cake layers.

3. *Carbs and calories in each slice? Don't even ask!*

APPENDIX B

A SLEW OF WRITING FEARS—DO ANY OF THEM HIT HOME?

Recent additions to our list of fears that might hold us back in our writing include Fear of Poverty (or the bag-lady syndrome—even Oprah is said to have had it, at one time burying $50,000 in her backyard), Fear of Significance (isn't it easier to stay in that gray, tamped-down area where no one notices us?), Fear of Stardom (or other people's envy), Fear of Phoniness (who are *we* to pretend to be writers!?), Fear of Recoil (as on the part of other people), Fear of Retribution (what we know will come down on us if we do or write those things), Fear of Husband (that he'll up and leave us, or just of conflicts with him), Fear of Exposure (like the Fear of Shame), Fear of Badness (because if we break the rules, we'll be, by definition, bad), Fear of Flakiness (after all, aren't all artists crazy?), Fear of Dirt ("If you're a writer and your house is too clean, something is wrong!" says novelist Jim Grimsley), Fear of Subtext (as per Martin, the Sea Island attorney who vehemently denied the sexism in his autobiographical novel), Fear of Sobriety (as per Benny, who couldn't deal with talking about his writing without a few stiff drinks first), and Fear of Work (yes, writing—like self-love—is work, even if it is fun!).

Then there's Fear of Empowerment—a biggie for us women, because if we become empowered: (a) the people around us may call us a bitch, slut, or worse; and (b) we won't have any more excuses or reasons to claim victimization. (Though there's an upside: "I've noticed that bitches get more credit when they're halfway nice than martyrs do for being that way all the time!" said Jill, who despite multiple life challenges, any of which would have laid out many of us, was determined to claim the power that was hers.)

TAP INTO THE POWER OF THE PINK—
START YOUR OWN SUB ROSA GROUP!

As I travel around the country leading Zona Rosa groups, I find I'm often frustrated at leaving just as the good stuff is beginning to happen. When I began suggesting that the groups keep meeting in my absence, I quickly found that the vibrations continued to resonate, and soon I was hearing great things about the Zona Rosans' writing and lives, and the great connections and support systems they generated, similar to the AOL (Ass on the Line) group in Atlanta. Soon, they were happening all over the place, and all of them had their own resident experts on practically everything, from grammar to revising to publishing.

We decided to call the groups Sub Rosa, after the phrase that means "under the rose, an ancient symbol of secrecy," a perfect symbol of what we share in Zona Rosa.

You can start your own Sub Rosa group by following the

principles in this book, which is also full of the acronyms, credos, and jump starts we've come to depend on in Zona Rosa. Please feel free to share them through the use of this book—every Sub Rosan should have a copy—but please do not photocopy and disseminate the copyrighted materials here.

In the meantime, here are some suggestions, designed to keep your experience as close to ours in the official Zona Rosa groups as possible.

YOUR SUB ROSA GROUP: SOME SUGGESTIONS FOR TONE AND STRUCTURE

The Basics: Each Sub Rosa session will need a leader. Since this is a peer group, I suggest that the participants lead the sessions on a rotating basis.

Create a Policy. In Zona Rosa, our only criterion for admission is the desire to take part. Writers can range from total beginners to those working on a third or fourth book, and all genres—poetry, fiction, and creative nonfiction—are honored. *Important: within the group we are all "beginners," sharing our experiences from wherever we are, but none of us reign as "expert."*

Also a Schedule: Our ongoing Zona Rosa groups meet once a month for four or more hours, which gives plenty of time for participants to write between meetings. The once-a-month schedule also makes it easier for participants to attend each meeting. You may or may not want to adhere to such a schedule. Someone also needs to be in charge of a phone and e-mail list, and meeting reminders.

Structure: At the beginning of each meeting, read "The Zona Rosa Promises" (in the very beginning of this book). Next, go around the room, giving each woman a chance to speak for a limited time if she wishes. This is also a good time to introduce newcomers. I ask each of them to talk for a few minutes about where they are with their writing and where they would like to be, as well as to tell us anything personal they're willing to share. At this time, to further ensure your sisters' comfort, you may want to discuss a policy of anonymity about what goes on in the group, saying that later sharing of their truths and secrets with the world at large will be up to them.

Leader Suggests a Topic of General Discussion: Perhaps use readings from this or other books. Everyone should have one or both Zona Rosa books as references. Subjects that are good jump starts are sources of inspiration (e.g., quotations or special experiences); reports of progress and writing successes (it's always nice to applaud here!); obstacles to writing and discoveries about how to deal with them (for women, whose lives tend to be fragmented by caretaking and the fulfillment of other goals, this topic is particularly important); or something as specific as means and standards for revising. Indeed, since these subjects are ongoing, it's appropriate for members to discuss them on an ongoing basis. *And just as in grammar school, raising our hands is sometimes the best way to share.*

Next, Ask Who Wishes to Read from the Exorcises Suggested the Previous Month: Since these short pieces are designed to help writers tap in to new material and to break through blocks, they are not to be treated as writings-in-progress, though members might respond to the strengths of a particular piece. Indeed, a number of Zona Rosans have ended up publishing pieces that began as exorcises.

The Leader, along with the Group, Throws Out Exorcises for the Coming Month: This book includes many exorcises, as does *The Woman Who Spilled Words All Over Herself.* But they can also come from other sources, including the members themselves. In fact, we usually brainstorm new exorcises at every meeting, creating them out of our burning issues of the moment. *This is a good time for a break, and for sampling the Foods of the Goddesses that the Sub Rosans are already competing to bring!*

Call and Response is what a reading and the participants' voiced response is called in some churches. And *response* is our preferred word for what we give in Zona Rosa when we hear others' manuscripts. Members can read from their own work, or ask someone else in the group to read for them. Set a time limit, and if there are too many manuscripts for a given meeting, rotate them on a meeting-by-meeting basis. Members may or may not supply copies of their work for the rest of the group. This can be either an individual or a group decision, as doing so is time-consuming for women who may already be very busy. And as we've learned in Zona Rosa, hearing the work read aloud without copies before us helps us develop our ability to listen. The reader should introduce her material if necessary. She should also read loud enough to be heard, and slowly enough for understanding. This is good practice for reading in public later.

IMPORTANT: Useful Responses to Manuscripts Are: (1) Emphasize portions of the work to which you respond positively, and other strengths—this can't be overdone, so don't stint on praise—it's the world's greatest motivator! (2) Next, mention areas of possible confusion; this will give the writer an idea of where she might need to clarify and simplify. (3) Last, give concrete and/or useful suggestions of a positive nature, e.g., "It might be interesting if you moved that scene forward," or "Did you realize that you repeated the image of the mountain man in the pink ruffled skirt three times?"

Keep in Mind: Discernment, perceptiveness, and kindness are always welcome. On the other hand, we are not here to judge content on moral grounds, to share biases about experiences or materials, or to respond out of cultural, racial, or class prejudices. Nor are we here to judge among various writing styles and genres, whether mainstream or literary; whether poetry, memoir, creative nonfiction, or fiction. We are here only to support writing strengths and to make suggestions that drive to the good of the work. *Remember, when negativity comes into the room, creativity flies out the window—thus we leave competitiveness, judgment, envy, and social expectations at the door.*

In Conclusion, the leader might ask for further questions or suggestions, and whether anyone has a burning issue she needs to discuss before leaving. **Each Sub Rosan should leave the meeting feeling supported in her vision. While we may be at different levels in our writing, remember that the Sub Rosa groups are meant to be a win-win situation for each of us!**

Write to us with news and questions about your Sub Rosa group! Contact us at info@myzonarosa.com. Or see our Web page at www.myzonarosa.com.

ACKNOWLEDGMENTS

To mention my gratitude (that glorious emotion!) to every Zona Rosan who contributed to *Secrets of the Zona Rosa* would be like seeking to thank the hundreds of Zona Rosans who, like small silver fish flitting through the sea, dart in and out of my mind every day. Indeed, this book could almost be said to be a group effort: while I did the writing and came up with the ideas, they provided the inspiration. As Dan Baker writes in his book *What Happy People Know,* love is appreciation, and Zona Rosa is, above all, an appreciation society.

I would like especially to thank my sisters (and sometimes brothers) in Zona Rosa who facilitated the writing of this book while I also basked in their company. Thank you, Lynn and Katherine, for providing me with beautiful places beside the South Carolina sea and in the North Carolina mountains to write, and, of course, thank you for your general inspiration.

Thank you, Marda, for visiting me at the mountain house every few days to say, "Yes, you can do it," as well as giving me the benefit of your writing experience while I crunched the revisions of this book into time between Zona Rosa commitments and retreats.

Special thanks go to Jill, who besides inspiring me with her beautiful spirit, read the entire manuscript during our beach retreat instead of working on her own writing, who also sat beside me hour after hour in Italy, poring over quotes to find just the right ones to enrich this book, and who, last but not least, turned my screen saver a rosy Zona Rosa pink. I would also like to thank Connie, whose insights, brilliance, and professionalism, even at the beginning of her writing career, inspired me while writing this book. And, always, my endless thanks to my darling sister Anne, who was on call to provide answers to my hurried questions from her store of knowledge of grammar and syntax, not to speak of her on-target interpretations of emotional content.

Without Susan S., the Queen of Planning, our Zona Rosa retreats abroad wouldn't exist! As well, she was the brain behind our first week-long retreats in the United States. (She also inspired us by researching her historical novel for eleven years and reading all of Proust within four and a half years.) Pamella, fluent in cooking both French and Italian, as well as her sous chef Judith, have kept us well fed while our minds and computers clicked. At the same time, Pamella impressed us with her own writing, and Judith with her award-winning outreach programs for mothers in Texas prisons.

A confetti of hurrahs to the Zona Rosa "brains"—read marketing geniuses—Charlotte, Lynn, Pamella, Jill, Gray, Anne, Nancy, Brandi, Sandy W., Marianne L., Jenny W., and others. They are putting their heads together to make sure that Zona Rosa grows and expands and becomes even more accessible to future Zona Rosans. Thanks to Jenny H. and Susan J., artists extraordinaire, for their creative output. And thanks, too, to my tireless and ever-helpful assistants, Annie, Caitlin, Donna, Marianne, Jody, and Amanda, some of them good writers in their own right.

Thanks without end to the many women (and men) who gave me permission to tell their stories and to quote from their writings—Isabel, Honor, Celeste, Karen, Ronnie, Claire, Temple, Linda, Deborah, Cynthia, Carol O., Jan E., Nikki, Charlotte, Janice, Christina, Mary Catherine, Dianna, Ann, Kathleen, Carolyn, Jane, Jalaine, Tracy, and Audrey, to name but a few (and apologies to those who gave permission but whose stories couldn't be included in this book because of editorial considerations). *Secrets of the Zona Rosa* couldn't have existed without them and their willingness to share. I would also like to thank those who have otherwise inspired me—even the ones who did so by providing just the right grains of sand to heighten my sensitivity to the needs of others.

Then there are my numerous writer friends, especially the old ones—among them, Joyce Maynard, Erica Jong, Dorothy Allison, Honor Moore, Carol Polsgrove, John Berendt, Nick Taylor, Bruce Feiler, and Pat Conroy—who have inspired me through the years, as well as the many newer author pals who keep me on my literary toes.

Many thanks to my agent, Gail Ross, who is nothing short of a dynamo, as well as the world's best cheerleader; her former assistant Jenna, who saw this book through the proposal stage; the rest of Gail's warm and loving staff; and Lisa Considine, the first editor to work with me on these ideas.

I especially thank Flora Esterly, editor for this book, who has been a wonder at extracting whatever was necessary from me during the hurried last months of its completion. And thank you to all the lovely, hardworking people at Henry Holt and Company who have helped bring this book into the world.

Last but not least, I thank my family for their input, and even their interference, which taught me lessons in staying on track: my daughter Laura, a.k.a. Lulu, for her highly educated responses (she put the smart in "smart"); my daughter Darcy, a.k.a. Lily, for her instant, intuitive, and always accurate artistic feedback; my son Laurens, a.k.a. Dwayne, just for being his lovable, if distracting, self; and my husband, Zane, for setting aside watching car races on TV in order to read my pages, as well as give me the insights provided by his built-in nonsense detector.

ROSEMARY DANIELL is the founder and leader of Zona Rosa, a series of life-changing writing workshops attended by thousands of women (and the occasional man) over the past twenty-five years, with events in Atlanta, Savannah, and other cities, as well as in Europe, as described in *People* and *Southern Living*. She is the author of *The Woman Who Spilled Words All Over Herself*, *Fatal Flowers*, *Sleeping with Soldiers*, and four other books of poetry and prose. Her articles and reviews have been publised in *Self*, *Harper's Bazaar*, *Mademoiselle*, *Mother Jones*, *Travel and Leisure*, *Men's Fitness*, *The New York Times Book Review*, *Los Angeles Times Book Review*, *Newsday*, and *The Philadelphia Inquirer*. She has appeared on many national television and radio shows, and speaks at writers' conferences around the country. Her awards include the 1999 Palimpsest Prize and two National Endowment for the Arts fellowships. She lives in Savannah, Georgia.